The Challenges of a Secular Quebec

The Challenges of a Secular Quebec

BILL 21 IN PERSPECTIVE

Edited by
LUCIA FERRETTI and FRANÇOIS ROCHER,
translated by George Tombs

UBCPress · Vancouver · Toronto

32 31 30 29 28 27 26 25 24 23   5 4 3 2 1

Printed in Canada on FSC-certified ancient-forest-free paper (100% post-consumer recycled) that is processed chlorine- and acid-free.

Library and Archives Canada Cataloguing in Publication

Title: The challenges of a secular Quebec: Bill 21 in perspective / edited by Lucia Ferretti and François Rocher; translated by George Tombs.

Other titles: Enjeux d'un Québec laïque. English

Names: Ferretti, Lucia, editor. | Rocher, François, editor. | Tombs, George, translator.

Description: Translation of: Les enjeux d'un Québec laïque. | Includes bibliographical references and index.

Identifiers: Canadiana (print) 20230441513 | Canadiana (ebook) 20230441947 | ISBN 9780774868426 (hardcover) | ISBN 9780774868457 (EPUB) | ISBN 9780774868440 (PDF)

Subjects: LCSH: Secularism – Québec (Province) | LCSH: Religion and state – Québec (Province) | LCSH: Religious law and legislation – Québec (Province) | LCSH: Québec (Province). Loi sur la laïcité de l'État.

Classification: LCC BL2765.C3 E5513 2023 | DDC 322/.109714 – dc23

UBC Press gratefully acknowledges the financial support for our publishing program of the Government of Canada and the British Columbia Arts Council.

UBC Press and the editors would also like to thank the Secrétariat du Québec aux relations canadiennes for their financial support for this publication.

Originally published as: *Les enjeux d'un Québec laïque. La loi 21 en perspective* © Del Busso Éditeur, 2020.

UBC Press
The University of British Columbia
2029 West Mall
Vancouver, BC V6T 1Z2
www.ubcpress.ca

Contents

Foreword

ROBERTO PERIN

Two solitudes: this image characterizes well the reaction in English Canada to the Act Respecting the Laicity of the State (Bill 21) adopted by the Quebec government in 2019. Since Lucia Ferretti perceptively analyzes that response in the pages that follow, my aim here is to ask: What are the solitudes at play? The expression refers, of course, to the title of Hugh MacLennan's novel, which was first published in 1945. Shaken by the hostility stirred up between Canada's two major linguistic communities by the issue of conscription during the Second World War, the author bemoans the virtual lack of contact and communication historically marking this relationship, a situation persisting to this day. MacLennan evokes the prospect of encounter and dialogue through the character of Paul Taillard, the son of a French Canadian father and an Irish Protestant mother, who is more open to modernity than his compatriots. We cannot fault MacLennan for depicting Quebec as a backward, Catholic Church–dominated, agrarian society suspicious of change and defiantly proud of its large families. Such a view, now discredited by historians in the wake of the Quiet Revolution, was common currency at the time, even in academic circles, as US sociologist E.C. Hughes's study *French Canada in Transition*, published just three years earlier, well illustrates. We can criticize, however, the author's failure to engage with the character of Marius, Paul's older and "pure laine" half-brother, dismissed as a nationalist and, as a result, left in the shadows in the novel. Such a failure is symptomatic of English-speaking Canada's recurring inability to come to terms with, let alone understand, Quebec nationalism. I would therefore contend that one of the solitudes is not French Canada or Quebec per se. In fact, Athanase Taillard, Paul's father, is well connected to English Canadians through politics, business, and landownership. Instead, the elephant in the room is French Canadian or Quebec nationalism.

It is remarkable, given contemporary Quebec's evolution, how few English speakers have seriously studied this topic. At most, there are a handful of individuals, who are rarely cited and easily forgotten. What do abound, though, are labels and easy judgments over the past eighty years. During the Second World War, the party opposed to conscription was termed, at best, insular and, at worst, fascist. Yet this was the grouping that laid the foundations for the mass-based democratic party in Canada. Meanwhile Premier Maurice Duplessis (1936–39, 1944–59) was often depicted as an authoritarian reactionary in the same league as Spain's Francisco Franco, Portugal's Antonio Salazar, or Argentina's Juan Peron. In contrast, most historians now see Duplessis as an economic liberal convinced that the province's development depended on foreign investment, who was no different really than most other Canadian political leaders. While the Quiet Revolution gave commentators a brief respite as they commended what they perceived as Quebec's efforts to catch up to the rest of North America, another villain soon occupied centre stage. René Lévesque was demonized as a bigot and a separatist whose extremist views would turn the province into a Third World state. Admittedly, there was a moment in the 1960s, which was all too brief, when he was invited to speak to audiences in English-speaking Canada on the tedious topic of "what does Quebec want?" But as the Parti Québécois's star rose, doors started to slam shut.

When, much to everyone's surprise, the party came to power in 1976, the English-language media turned Lévesque into the incarnation of Mr. Hyde, Dr. Jekyll's nemesis. The Charter of the French Language (Bill 101), adopted the following year, was universally anathematized in that media as dictatorial, fascistic, and racist, despite the solemn promises of the Parti Québécois leaders to protect minority language rights for English speakers and First Nations in Quebec. The referendum on sovereignty held in 1980 further deepened English-speaking Canada's sense of alienation from Quebec nationalism and, one might argue, from Quebec itself. Scenarios of military intervention, partition, ethnic cleansing, and economic catastrophe were evoked. In this context, it was easy to forget that René Lévesque spoke almost unaccented English, having grown up in New Carlisle; that he had travelled the world as a war correspondent, notably in Europe and Korea; and that he had electrified French-speaking audiences through his acclaimed, prize-winning broadcasts on international affairs aired on Radio-Canada in the 1950s. Responding to the wartime claim that Britain would have its neck wrung like a chicken by the end of 1941, Winston Churchill quipped: some chicken, some neck. Paraphrasing his words with regard to the slurs against René Lévesque, we could retort: some bigot, some narrow mind.

Commentators today acknowledge that the Charter of the French Language put an end to the decade-long linguistic wars and brought about the harmonious integration of immigrants into the French public school system. As for Lévesque's dictatorial tendencies, who remembers that his government adopted the most rigorous and effective legislation on the financing of elections and political parties in North America where the contributions of big business continue to exercise undue influence in public life?

It was around this time that I began my career as an academic. My first position was at the University of Edinburgh where events in Quebec generated quite a bit of excitement because of the rise of Scottish nationalism. I soon left to take up an appointment at York University. To my surprise, there was no such interest. My courses on Quebec history and nationalism were undersubscribed. In response, I developed a specialization in the history of migration, which, because of Toronto's place as the country's prime immigrant reception area, elicited greater enthusiasm. When I began teaching in graduate school, I discovered how abysmal was advanced students' knowledge of Quebec's history. Most of them did not engage with the assigned readings on this topic and were quite content to skim works available in translation. I doubt that all but a small minority can read a scholarly article in French in their field of interest. If an academic elite is unable to absorb a key component of their past, what hope is there for the future? The trench separating the solitudes is getting deeper. Very few are those who are willing or able to build bridges.

Some would argue that the picture painted here is too bleak, proudly pointing to the growth of bilingualism and the popularity of French immersion programs. According to Statistics Canada, however, Quebec accounts for almost two-thirds of the recent rise in French-English bilinguals, a majority of whom, it must be stressed, have French as their mother tongue. In fact, English-speaking Canada saw a decline in the number of bilingual youngsters aged ten to twenty within a decade. As for French immersion schools, increased enrolments have little to do with Francophilia or some aspiration to promote dialogue but are largely driven by ambitious middle-class parents' determination to provide elite education to their children at public expense. Once again, Quebec, together with New Brunswick, post the highest percentages of students in such establishments, whereas, in most other provinces, the figure stands at less than 15 percent. In any event, studies have consistently shown that immersion does not yield in and of itself proficiency in French: many students are either unwilling or unable to express themselves in that language in other than formal school settings, even during recreation. Nor do such programs produce a cohort that is more disposed to, or curious about, Quebec culture. At times, quite the opposite is the case.

With the second referendum on sovereignty held in 1995, English-speaking Canada's antagonism towards Quebec nationalism became even more pronounced. The constitutional reforms put forward by the Meech Lake and Charlottetown Accords, concluded in 1987 and 1992 and leading to the failed Canadian referendum of that year, generated heated public discussions. Figures such as novelist Mordecai Richler and historian Esther Delisle branded Quebec nationalism as anti-Semitic and racist in a largely successful campaign to delegitimate it in the eyes of English speakers. The extempore remarks by Premier Jacques Parizeau (1994–96) on the evening of the sovereignty referendum, attributing its failure to money and ethnics, seemed to confirm their allegations. Few in English-speaking Canada know that Parizeau's wife of thirty-four years was author Alicja Poznanska, who fought in the Polish resistance, took part in the Warsaw uprisings of 1944, and was imprisoned in the Bergen-Belsen concentration camp. Or that the second wife of Lucien Bouchard, Parizeau's successor as premier (1996–2001) was Audrey Best. Born in France of a US father and a French mother, she was raised in California and still had US citizenship at the time of the referendum. Although the Parti Québécois held office in its aftermath, the failure to rally the Quebec electorate broke the party's hegemony of the nationalist movement. There soon emerged two new political groups: Québec solidaire on the left, a democratic socialist alternative to the Parti Québécois, and Coalition Avenir Québec on the right, dubbed by many as soft nationalist, whose founder, François Legault, was a former minister of the Parti Québécois.

In the early years of the millennium, the whole political class was confronted by the issue of how to balance its commitment to secularism with the demands of groups that felt that the strict observance of their faith required some form of public expression. This happened after the Quebec government secularized the educational system reorganized along linguistic, rather than religious, lines. Liberal Premier Jean Charest (2003–12) set up a special commission headed by authoritative academics Gérard Bouchard and Charles Taylor to study the matter. Following their 2008 report and in light of a series of significant decisions by the Supreme Court of Canada, successive Liberal and Parti Québécois governments tried unsuccessfully to deal with this thorny question, a failure that further polarized opinion both in Quebec and in the rest of Canada. Given this context, the authors of the present book argue convincingly that government action was needed. Newly elected Premier François Legault promised to cut the Gordian knot. In 2019, the National Assembly adopted Bill 21, thus triggering several legal challenges. It is therefore desirable in the lead up to Supreme Court rulings that the discussion of the legislation be informed and reasoned. This edited work, translated from the French, aims to achieve that objective.

The contributors are all respected scholars coming from a variety of disciplines including philosophy, sociology, history, political science, law, and education. The book's multidisciplinary character commends it as a noteworthy and thought-provoking contribution to the debate.

A few of the authors are known to me as we have collaborated in the past on projects such as conferences, publications, and media interviews. While I do not share their belief in the need to prohibit teachers from wearing religious symbols in the classroom, the case in favour of such a ban originates not from racist or authoritarian thought but, rather, as François Rocher argues, from the Enlightenment and efforts since the nineteenth century to separate the tangled and complex union existing between church and state.

Be that as it may, if there is one key point that I would wish the reader to glean from this book, it is that church and state relations in Canada are not, nor have they ever been, homogeneous. As Marc Chevrier maintains in his chapter and as I myself have argued elsewhere, the Catholic Church came very close to being a state church in Quebec. For obvious demographic reasons, nowhere else in Canada was this the case. As well, because no single Protestant denomination became dominant in the country, no church could claim privileged status with the state. While Great Britain established the Church of England after the Conquest of 1759, this policy produced conflict in the colonies in the face of the demographic weakness of the Anglicans. In fact, church establishment was a key grievance leading up to the insurrections of 1837, with the reformers in Lower and Upper Canada advocating distinct solutions: secularism in the former and disestablishment in the latter. As political agitation mounted, Great Britain began to follow separate paths in dealing with this vexed question, even after the Act of Union of 1840 created a unitary government. In Quebec, the Catholic Church was awarded a position of privilege for its role as an agent of social and political stability in times of internal and external turmoil, whereas, in Ontario, the policy of disestablishment was gradually accepted and finally achieved in the 1850s. As a result, a non-denominational Protestantism, which later developed into an "evangelical consensus," became culturally and institutionally dominant in English-speaking Canada.

Today, this picture remains a highly disparate and complicated one. Only in Quebec has there been public discussion of secularism, thanks largely to the Bouchard-Taylor Commission and legislative efforts to react to it. Nevertheless, despite Bill 21, the government continues to provide public funds to private schools, fifty of which have a clear denominational character. Meanwhile, the public school curriculum at the primary and secondary level mandates courses on ethics and religious culture from a secular point of view (called *Culture et citoyenneté québécoises*). Some parents, however, find such courses wanting because they are not sufficiently critical of the role of religion in society. Of the other provinces, Newfoundland and Labrador is the only one whose situation somewhat approximates that of Quebec. A referendum held there in 1997 approved a proposal to make the school system non-denominational. As in Quebec, curricular changes followed: religion was to be presented in a non-confessional, though largely Christian, perspective in line with the composition of the province's population. The difference in the approaches of the two provinces to the teaching of religion makes clear that secularism and non-denominationalism are not, and have never been, the same thing.

Elsewhere in English-speaking Canada there has been no public discussion of state funding of denominational schools. At present, the education systems of Nova Scotia, New Brunswick, Prince Edward Island, Manitoba, and British Columbia are officially non-confessional, although the latter two provinces, like Quebec, provide subsidies for independent schools, including Catholic ones. By contrast, Ontario, Saskatchewan, and Alberta, as well as the Yukon, Nunavut, and Northwest Territories, fully finance Catholic schools. Even though isolated groups have tried to stir up a debate on this question, politicians are anxious to avoid what they see as a highly divisive issue threatening to undermine their electoral support. Because of this great diversity, the Supreme Court of Canada would be well advised to show sensitivity to Quebec's unique position and not attempt a one-size-fits-all approach in its examination of Bill 21.

The UBC Press is to be commended for making this work available in English, thus contributing to what might become a dialogue on the question of the Catholic Church and religion's role in public life. It is also my hope that other academic presses will follow UBC Press's example in stimulating communication between the solitudes. Neighbours, after all, should be talking to, not ignoring, each other.

The Challenges of a Secular Quebec

Introduction

LUCIA FERRETTI AND FRANÇOIS ROCHER

On June 16, 2019, the Quebec National Assembly adopted the Act Respecting the Laicity of the State (Bill 21).[1] The enactment of this legislation did not put a stop to the debate over the legality, and even the legitimacy, of the government's initiative. To some extent, the act provides a framework for how Quebec parliamentary, governmental, and judicial institutions should uphold the principles of secularism in fulfilling their mission. Basically, the law proposes prohibiting the wearing of religious symbols by people in defined categories of employment within the public or para-public service and in positions of authority (for example, justices of the peace, jurists, peace officers, public sector teachers, and principals). Moreover, it requires public employees to perform their duties with their faces uncovered and requires people receiving a public service in person to do the same.

Bill 21 is part of a shared conversation in Quebec that has been going on for some time now and has often been marked by bitter interventions, invectives of all kinds, accusations of racism and xenophobia, and ad hominem condemnations. This shared conversation began in the lead-up to the Bouchard-Taylor Commission in February 2007, following which the Liberal government led by Jean Charest tabled Bill 94 in 2010, which died on the order paper.[2] The Parti Québécois government introduced the Charter of Values in 2013, which also died on the order paper,[3] and the Liberal government led by Philippe Couillard tabled Bill 62 in 2015.[4] On each of these occasions, the principles of secularism were discussed and debated at length by citizens, academics, representatives of different religious denominations, jurists, and activists defending the rights of ethnocultural and religious minorities. The principle of laicity is widely supported by a majority of Quebeckers. However, in practice, support for this principle varies depending on the nature of the religious symbols worn by public officials in positions of authority or by public schoolteachers. A majority of Quebeckers support the following bans, even for teachers: the banning of the burqa, the niqab (that hides the face), the hijab (that covers the head and hair), the kirpan, a conspicuous cross, and the *dastar* (Sikh turban). Nevertheless, there is still opposition to Bill 21 in Quebec and the rest of Canada – opposition that is to be expected in a democratic society – and this opposition has now been taken to the courts. The Manitoba government has even invited Quebec civil servants who feel threatened by Bill 21 to move to that province, although the invitation does not seem to have generated much of a response.

At this point, it may be tempting to assume that the arguments and preferences of the various parties have crystallized and that there is nothing further to add to the debate. However, we need to avoid making too many assumptions because a judicial saga over Quebec laicity is looming on the horizon. Despite all the discussions that have taken place on this issue, we believe the principles underlying secularism still deserve to be explored in greater depth, if only to shed new light on the way in which people in Quebec understand the principles of the separation of state and religion as well as the religious neutrality of the state. At the same time, it is important to consider Quebec's specific context, given its unique history in North America. This context justifies government intervention in the area of secularism, just as it justifies the character of government interventions put forward in Bill 21. We also believe it is important to respond strongly to the arguments put forward by the critics of Quebec's model of secularism. Similarly, at a time when the courts are being called on to rule on the legality and constitutionality of the Act Respecting the Laicity of the State, there is an urgent need to recall the legal grounds of interpretations of Canadian legal norms that respect Quebec's difference. In addition, some people may argue that the very act of invoking the notwithstanding clause in the Canadian Charter of Rights and Freedoms (Canadian Charter) explicitly acknowledges the supposedly discriminatory nature of a Quebec law with respect to religious minorities.[5] The reality of the situation is far more complex and nuanced than that. Finally, considerations of how religious symbols worn by teachers are perceived by students should consider the scope and meaning of communication in the pedagogical context, which goes beyond the individual rights of those directly concerned. These are the particular issues that we explore in the different chapters of this book.

This book is divided into four sections. The first section puts into perspective the issues arising from the secular nature of the state in the Quebec context. The second section provides a historical and sociological overview of debates in Quebec on this issue, taking into consideration the voices of Muslim women. The third section looks at the legal challenges associated with Bill 21. The last section of the book addresses the meaning of religious symbols in the school environment.

Putting Things in Perspective

In the first chapter, François Rocher considers the concept of secularism and the different meanings associated with this concept. He reminds us that defining secularism takes place in a particular social context. Choosing how to define secularism implies taking a stand on the field of struggle between different understandings of the political community and of the conditions required to share a common space. In this regard, citizens, analysts, commentators, and intellectuals speaking out on the way in which secularism operates in practice do so based on a particular vision of the principles that should govern society; they do so implicitly or explicitly, which indelibly shapes what they say. Therefore, we are seeing a profusion of labels aimed at discrediting the positions of people on different sides of the debate, all with the intention of showing the moral superiority of one position over another. The author argues that the four principles of laicity are clearly stated in Bill 21. What creates a problem is the way in which these principles are ordered in a hierarchy. Opponents of Bill 21 hold that the principle of freedom of conscience and religion, emphasizing respect for individual convictions, should hold precedence over other principles. For supporters of the approach taken in Bill 21, the principle of state neutrality, and the obligation for people in different categories of public sector employment to respect this principle, should be paramount. The approach taken in Bill 21 is not incompatible with democratic liberalism. However, it is based on a vision of democratic liberalism that diverges from the one most commonly found in Canada outside Quebec and in certain circles within Quebec – a vision of democratic liberalism that is also widely shared by the courts.

Lucia Ferretti begins by outlining what she considers to be the limited scope of Bill 21. She recalls that it meets all the criteria according to which a law is considered to have strong democratic legitimacy. She considers opposition to this law to be more political than legal, given the means being deployed to strike down the law: indeed, the drive to invalidate the law aims to delegitimize any attempt by the state and citizens of Quebec to make their own choices in regulating the relationship between public authorities and religious organizations. The author then proceeds to analyze legal texts, from which she draws several conclusions. Freedom of religion is defined and defended so broadly in Canada that it ends up running counter to the spirit of the most important international covenants. Freedom of religion is not understood as forming a part of freedom of conscience. Instead, freedom of conscience is understood as forming a part of freedom of religion. The Canadian model of regulating religion is maximalist, very liberal, and multiculturalist, and it has widespread effects. This model favours the penetration of religious normativities within the state, and it encourages fundamentalist interpretations. The model has serious consequences, particularly for First Nations and women. Finally, by giving precedence to the "government of judges" over "parliamentary sovereignty," this model undermines Quebec's ability to develop its own model for regulating religion. The model also fuels social tensions. How can we speak of the rule of law when its application to Quebec has so little concern for democracy within Quebec?

Historical and Sociological Perspectives

The evolution of the relationship over time between the church (whether Catholic or Protestant) and the state sheds light on the secularism debate. Indeed, Marc Chevrier considers the church to have been a political institution in Quebec from the era of New France until the 1960s. The Catholic Church embodied a Catholic city, which was grafted onto civil and political institutions in a relationship of dependence, competition, and collaboration. This implicit union or alliance binding the church and political power together originated in large part from British imperial policy. It was secured by the dictatorship of the Special Council in 1838–41. It then pursued its growth, thanks in part to jurists who orchestrated the dual membership of Catholics in two cities of public law – the one religious and the other civil. Once Quebec succeeded to the imperial legislator and United Canada, it built up this unique dual system of public law in North America. By enacting legislation, Quebec extended the system to encompass powerful Protestant denominations and other religions. However, questions have been raised about provincial jurisdiction in matters of religion, a jurisdiction that some would like to deny or reduce, based on the opinions of several Supreme Court of Canada justices. These opinions, Marc Chevrier observes, go back to the legal texts resulting from the British Conquest of 1759–63 and are used to support the supposedly exclusive right of the Federal Parliament to regulate religious freedom and observance. In other words, this thesis links state violence to the sovereign right to allocate religious rights and is also reminiscent of the philosopher Thomas Hobbes, for whom the state comprised two cities – the one spiritual and the other political.

This "Westphalian" thesis was weakened, however, by the constitutional amendment of 1997, which unconditionally deconfessionalized the Quebec public school system. Newfoundland moved to create a non-denominational public school system as well but was obliged by the Constitution to maintain some religious presence in its schools. Beyond the legal aspects involved, the real issue is whether Quebec will have to adhere to a pan-Canadian civil religion that enables religion to permeate into the political realm or whether Quebec will be able to live under a single-city system, free of religious influence, while respecting freedom of religion and conscience.

Micheline Labelle analyzes the various and sometimes bitter debates around Bill 21 from a critical point of view. She reminds us that this act is rooted in the history of Quebec, which has seen a progressive move to secularize public institutions, a move that has occasionally been accompanied by conflict. Moreover, she finds the arguments used to support or oppose the act are reminiscent of arguments in early 2010 between the signatories of the Manifesto for a Pluralist Quebec (Manifeste pour un Québec pluraliste; see Bosset et al. 2010) and the Declaration of Intellectuals for Secularism (Déclaration des intellectuels pour la laïcité; see Baril et al. 2010). The author shows how the attacks on the Act Respecting the Laicity of the State are inspired by the vision of Canadian multiculturalism, which is based on refusing to recognize the Quebec national question and the collective rights that go with it. Moreover, some opponents of Bill 21 have resorted to radical theories denouncing the "whiteness" of relations of domination and neocolonialism and postulating that power relations are ever-present in the production and maintenance of inequalities in social institutions. However, the most virulent accusations have come from religious circles supported by that part of the Left upholding the virtues of pluralism, inclusion, and openness. It is in this context that the court challenge to Bill 21 – led by a student, Ichark Nourel Hak, and supported by the National Council of Canadian Muslims and the Canadian Civil Liberties Association – is analyzed. Labelle points out, in conclusion, that these debates are not unique to Quebec: they are part of communitarian struggles and political currents that actually reach beyond national borders.

As a political scientist and feminist, Yasmina Chouakri has been meeting immigrant women of all nationalities and religious faiths for several years. In her chapter in this book, she speaks for women whose voices are not often heard: women from countries with a Muslim majority. Islam in Quebec is not limited to the conservative currents that are most forcefully expressed in the public sphere. There is also a modern and emancipating Islam in Quebec. Most so-called Muslim women are not merely women assigned to a religion or even compelled to wear a veil.

Conservative Islam seeks to impose a vision of religion that stigmatizes and essentializes Muslim women. The author regrets that this vision is now taken up not only by the Liberal parties and governments in Quebec and Canada but also by feminists, who comprise the associative movement that practises intersectional analysis, as well as by the multiculturalist Left. In reality, Bill 21 is not a problem for the majority of so-called Muslim women, for whom religious issues are far from the focus of their concerns. What they want most of all is the removal of structural barriers that compromise their access to meaningful employment and prevent them from attaining the financial autonomy that they want. These barriers include the representation of Muslim women created by conservative Islam and its allies.

Legal Perspectives

Julie Latour brings together everything there is to know about secularism in general and the Act Respecting the Laicity of the State in particular. She shows that Quebec laicity is, above all, a generator of rights: indeed, secularism is the primary condition of freedom – particularly, freedom of religion – of which it forms an intrinsic part. Laicity has come to be recognized as one of the founding principles of Quebec. It has become a cornerstone of the architecture of fundamental rights. Laicity has a structural value and is a fundamental right, which means that the state is therefore required to offer secular institutions and public services.

Laicity also promotes the full exercise of freedom of thought and opinion and increases the protection of existing civil rights. The act is thus destined to form a legal triptych of fundamental importance along with the Quebec Charter of Human Rights and Freedoms (Quebec Charter) and the Quebec Civil Code.[6] While the act is in keeping with the continuity of the law, it is also a source of innovation. It fulfills an important and real purpose, in line with Quebec's historic legal traditions and unique character. It serves as the foundation of a pluralist society, strengthening democracy, the essence of which, in the words of jurist Aharon Barak (2002), is characterized by a dialogue between individual rights and the needs of the community. Finally, the act is consistent with the most recent trends in Canadian constitutional law that have signalled the end of "open" secularism. It pursues a legitimate objective by allowing for the deployment of the citizen who is at once free, open to being with others, and aware of belonging to a larger political community based on the principle of equality in diversity.

Several cases have been brought before the courts asking that either the entire Act Respecting the Laicity of the State or almost half of its provisions be declared unconstitutional. Daniel Turp maintains that this is a massive constitutional challenge of unprecedented scope. In his "massive rebuttal," he examines each of the arguments put forward by opponents of Bill 21, relating to the use of notwithstanding provisions, the infringement of rights guaranteed by the Quebec Charter and the Canadian Charter, and the division of legislative powers enshrined in the British North America Act of 1867.[7] He shows how these arguments rest on shaky grounds and why the courts should reject them. He concludes by pointing out that the Quebec government adopted this legislation bearing in mind both the interpretation favoured by the Supreme Court of Canada on limits to the wearing of religious symbols and the role of the idea of multiculturalism in its interpretations. Quebec, meanwhile, has chosen a different path by making laicity an essential condition for the protection of freedom of conscience and the equality of all Quebeckers.

Section 28 of the Canadian Charter affirms the equal guarantee of rights for both men and women. Can it be used to circumvent section 33 ("the notwithstanding clause") in such a way that the Act Respecting the Laicity of the State loses one of its protections from legal challenges? This question is now being debated in English Canada. Some legal experts are working on it, while others do not believe it is possible. Guillaume Rousseau introduces us to the leading participants in this debate and weighs the value of their arguments. He maintains that there is no basis for such a claim. Then he takes part himself in the debate from a Quebec perspective. In discussing the history of section 28 of the Canadian Charter, he shows that English Canadian feminists did not succeed in having women's rights and freedoms enshrined as a specific chapter in the charter that was beyond the reach of the notwithstanding clauses; all that Pierre Elliott Trudeau's government granted was to shelter women's rights from section 27 (interpreting the charter based on the objective of promoting multiculturalism). On the other hand, he shows that several English-speaking provinces made their adoption of the Canadian Charter conditional on the inclusion of section 33. Quebec also wanted to protect the sovereignty of its legislature from judicial review of the constitutionality of its laws. In fact, since 1982, Quebec has frequently invoked this section, particularly to defend laws that for historical reasons benefit women. Rousseau concludes that it is a good thing that section 28 is only an interpretative provision and not an autonomous substantive right: what a paradox it would be if, in the name of equality between men and women, we were to invalidate laws that favoured women!

We may ask to what extent Quebec can assert a specific model of relations between the state and religion that is not invalidated by Canadian courts. Patrick Taillon answers that the use of the "dialogue theory," as advocated by the Supreme Court of Canada itself, opens the door to the possibility that the courts may be sensitive to the intentions of political authorities in weighing and balancing rights. He shows that, over the past decade, the Supreme Court has changed its interpretation of the scope and limits of freedom to express religious beliefs. It has progressively moved from a maximalist reading, which cultivates the impression that the individual right to express religious beliefs is unlimited, to a reading that recognizes the importance of balancing this right and seeking to recalibrate it in light of the legitimate interests pursued by legislators. For its part, Quebec has used all the legal instruments at its disposal – first, to assert an approach that differs from the one shared by the rest of Canada and, second, to attempt to correct the Supreme Court's maximalist interpretation, in particular, by granting secularism a quasi-constitutional status in the hierarchy of norms. Canadian law, within the framework of a federal state that recognizes the provinces' variety of preferences, could be sensitive to Quebec's difference by drawing on the European experience, which offers examples of systems for the protection of fundamental rights that allow for the coexistence of a variety of approaches to the relationship between federated entities and religions. In other words, respect for the spirit of federalism should allow for a diversity of interpretations of religious freedom and state neutrality. In a federal state, there should be no uniform, standardized, or universal norm since each society within that state must find a reasonable balance that is appropriate to its own context and historical experience.

Educational Perspectives

"The medium is the message." Marshall McLuhan's ([1964] 2013, 10) famous formulation is as true as ever. In the classroom, a teacher not only transmits a message, but he or she is also a message. Moreover, a symbol is a symbol: a symbol is not "insignificant" since that would contradict its very nature. A teacher who wears a religious symbol in class is therefore actively sending a dual message: on the one hand, a symbol identifying religious faith and, on the other hand, a symbol that is the subject matter of the course. Based on theorists of the functions of language including Roman Jakobson, Charles-Étienne Gill maintains that any symbol not relevant to communicating the subject matter, or to the conditions promoting it, constitutes interference – noise – both in terms of communication and of the teaching relationship. This argument leads to the question: should the right of some teachers to generate noise prevail over the right of students – a captive audience subject to authority – to receive knowledge without interference? Communications theory clearly shows that it is impossible not to interpret a symbol when the situation requires it to be observed. Respect for the freedom of conscience of students and their parents therefore militates in favour of prohibiting religious symbols for teachers and other school personnel in positions of authority.

How can we explain the "ideological inversions" that show up in the virulent debate on secularism: a pluralist Left that dissociates itself from the secularist Left's age-old struggle in favour of secularism and a nationalist current – frequently conservative – that instead makes secularism its hobby horse? To understand this, Normand Baillargeon takes us back to Ferdinand Buisson, an important figure in the fight for secularism in France. Secularism was indeed born on the Left and even on the radical Left. Buisson was a Protestant who was close to the First International in the late nineteenth century, close to anarchist circles all his life, and one of the cofounders of the Ligue des droits de l'Homme (French League of Human Rights). At the beginning of the 1880s, he was recruited by Jules Ferry, the prime minister of France, to implement the law of the Third Republic creating a public, secular, and compulsory elementary school system. For this thinker of secularism, the school was the central institution of the republic, and it had to give students the tools to emancipate themselves, if they so desired, from their social milieu, cultural background, and dominant ideologies. It had to ensure they were free beings, committed to building human solidarity beyond cultural and community ties. Baillargeon shows how this freedom and universalism have become suspect, especially among thinkers of the communitarian Left, who bitterly defend "open" secularism. This latter form of secularism aims to anchor each person in their social milieu and culture of origin and to fold them into a fixed identity without any possibility of evolution. This fixed identity is deemed to be under attack by the project of republican secularism. "Open" secularism thus appears as the offshoot of postmodernism and theories of identity.

There is an ongoing debate on the prohibition of the wearing of religious symbols in the school setting by teachers and other personnel in authority. Paul Sabourin brings to the debate findings from the sociology of knowledge. First, the meaning or absence of meaning given to religious objects cannot be reduced to a purely personal, subjective, or psychological dimension. Indeed, the meaning of religious objects is a product elaborated and shared for so long that these objects are still very generally perceived for what they are – namely, religious objects. Second, the role of the school is not to transmit beliefs or experiential knowledge, particularly religious ones. Rather, it is to transmit immanent knowledge and, above all, to help students develop the all-important skill of critical thinking.

* * *

The different perspectives presented in this book help shed nuanced light on the merits of the Quebec government's initiative to regulate the relationship between religion and the state in the Quebec context. The authors do not assess the scope of the law in the same way; their angles of analysis and their sensitivities are not all the same; their evaluation of the place and value of the Catholic Church in the history of Quebec may vary; and, finally, their relationship to faith and religion is very personal. But the authors present a range of arguments in support of Bill 21 from several disciplines: law, history, sociology, communications, philosophy, and political science. The authors take seriously their role as academics, practitioners, analysts, and teachers in contributing to the public debate and in fulfilling their duty to think critically.

We believe in the need to establish a fruitful dialogue with the critics of the Act Respecting the Laicity of the State. In order to do this, we would like these critics to see the act as something other than the sum of all evil. Some of these critics maintain that the act could complete the process of oppression of minorities that supposedly defines contemporary Quebec, as embodied by François Legault and the Coalition Avenir Quebec. Our intention is intellectual and civic: we seek to understand the meaning of Bill 21 in the particular context of Quebec. In light of the contributions brought together in this book, it is hard to see how this legislation can be at one and the same time a kind of societal slippage, a whiff of populism redolent of exclusive nationalism seeking to reproduce colonial relationships, "the affirmation of the civilizational superiority of the white Catholic francophone community" (Celis et al. 2020, 5), a racialization of religious groups illustrating "white ignorance and colonial innocence" (5), a deepening of economic inequalities particularly affecting racialized women in the labour market confirmed by "a decolonizing feminist analysis," the expression – both in the debates and in the law itself – of discursive practices with "supremacist overtones" (7), and the result of work eroding nothing less than the "foundations of Quebec democracy" (9). In striking at the legitimacy of Bill 21, this demonization of the act makes discussion difficult. All the authors contributing to this volume defend Quebec's right to make its own choices. We also maintain the general principle that this law is legitimate and will ultimately promote the harmonious development of Quebec as a society and nation.

Notes

1 Act Respecting the Laicity of the State, SQ 2019, c. 12.

2 Bill 94, An Act to Establish Guidelines for Requests for Accommodation within the Administration and Certain Institutions, 2010, which was introduced in a detailed study during the 39th Legislature, 1st Session and was reinstated during

the 39th Legislature, 2nd Session on February 24, 2011 (Kathleen Weil, Minister of Justice).

3 Bill 60, Charter Affirming the Values of State Secularism and Religious Neutrality and of Equality between Women and Men, and Providing a Framework for Accommodation Requests, November 7, 2013, which was introduced during the 40th Legislature, 1st Session (Bernard Drainville, Minister responsible for Democratic Institutions and Active Citizenship).

4 Bill 62, An Act to Promote Respect for the Religious Neutrality of the State and Aimed in Particular at Regulating Requests for Accommodation for Religious Reasons in Certain Organizations, SQ 2017, c. 19.

5 Canadian Charter of Rights and Freedoms, Part 1 of the Constitution Act, 1982, being Schedule B to the Canada Act 1982 (UK), 1982, c. 11.

6 Charter of Human Rights and Freedoms, RSQ 1977, c. C-12; Civil Code of Quebec, SQ 1991, c. 64.

7 British North America Act (UK), 1867, 30–31 Vict., c. 3.

References

Barak, Aharon. 2002. "A Judge on Judging: The Role of a Supreme Court in a Democracy." *Harvard Law Review* 116: 19–161.

Baril, Daniel, Marie-France Bazzo, Jacques Beauchemin, Paul Bégin, Henri Brun, Christian Dufour, Jacques Godbout, Jean-Claude Hébert, Yvan Lamonde, Bernard Landry, Julie Latour, Christiane Pelchat, and Guy Rocher. 2010. "Déclaration des Intellectuels pour la laïcité: Pour un Québec laïque et pluraliste." *Le Devoir*, 16 March. https://www.ledevoir.com/opinion/idees/285021/declaration-des-intellectuels-pour-la-laicite-pour-un-quebec-laique-et-pluraliste.

Bosset, Pierre, Dominique Leydet, Jocelyn Maclure, Micheline Milot, and Daniel Weinstock. 2010. "Manifeste pour un Québec pluraliste," *Le Devoir*, February 3. https://www.ledevoir.com/opinion/idees/282309/manifeste-pour-un-quebec-pluraliste.

Celis, Leila, Dia Dabby, Dominique Leydet, and Vincent Romani. 2020. *Modération ou extrémisme? Regards critiques sur la loi 21*. Quebec City: Presses de l'Université Laval.

McLuhan, Marshall. (1964) 2013. *Understanding Media: The Extensions of a Man*. Berkeley, CA: Gingko Press.

Part 1

Things in Perspective

Putting Things in Perspective
The Many Varieties of Secularism

1

FRANÇOIS ROCHER

Quebec society has been engaged in a debate on secularism for almost two decades now. Even so, citizens, social, and political actors in Quebec still do not agree on the meaning of secularism. In fact, exchanges back and forth on the subject tend to take the form of formal denunciations, with each side claiming to make a fair, well thought out, well documented, and relevant interpretation to meet the challenges facing Quebec. Secularism (officially referred to as "laicity" in the Quebec context) is often presented as a "value" and is used to defend certain ideas about the way in which the state should manage its relationships with diverse religions. For example, the web portal of the Ministry of Immigration, Francisation and Integration presents laicity as one of Quebec's key values, along with the French language, democracy, gender equality, and rights and responsibilities (Quebec, n.d.). Laicity is therefore a general, relatively abstract idea referring to the way in which the state seeks to distance itself from any influence that religious beliefs might have on the governance of the people. If at first this seems straightforward, why is secularism still being debated?

Part of the answer lies in the fact that secularism can also be seen as an ideology, a certain vision of the world that partly determines how other aspects of life in society should be organized. In the words of the sociologist of religion José Casanova (2009, 1051), secularism should be understood as a statecraft principle – that is, a principle establishing the separation between political and religious authority, so that the state remains neutral towards all religions, protects the freedom of conscience of each individual and facilitates the equal access of all citizens to democratic participation. In this respect, the state cannot promote a substantive vision of religions – it cannot make a value judgment about religions, whether that value judgment is positive or negative. On the contrary, Casanova goes on to say, once the state takes a particular view of religion – of what it is and what it does – we enter the realm of ideology. In this sense, being secular does not mean leaving religion behind or even emancipating oneself from it. Nor does it mean that secularism is based on a distinction between secular people who are assumed to think and act on their own as rational autonomous free agents, while religious people are somehow unfree, non-rational, or even intolerant and subservient to the dictates of religious authorities. In presenting secularism by removing any reference to religion, this point of view is in line with an ontology of the person and should not be confused with the principle of state organization that claims to be based on the principle of secularism.

There is another reason for the ongoing debate on secularism, however. Beyond the ideological meaning of secularism, fed by an aversion to the religious phenomenon, is the fact that it identifies organizational principles that are intertwined. These principles are generally of three or four orders. The sociologist of religion Jean-Paul Willaime (2009, 26; 2017, 145) bases what he calls "principle-driven secularism" on three elements: 1) freedom of conscience, thought, and religion (which includes the freedom to have and practise a religion or not to adhere to a religion); 2) equality of citizens (in terms of their rights and duties) regardless of their religious or philosophical preferences so that they are not discriminated against on the basis of their religious or philosophical affiliation; and 3) the respective autonomy of the state and religions – namely, the separation of the state and religions with a view to guaranteeing the freedom of the state from religions and the freedom of religions from the state (see also Baubérot 2007, 20). An additional principle can be added to the three just outlined – namely, the neutrality of the state to which Casanova refers such that the state does not maintain any particular position, whether negative or positive, on religion. In so doing, it does not seek to contain the expression of religious beliefs and preferences in the "private" sphere alone, reserving the "public" sphere (and, even more so, the "civic" sphere – that of relations between citizens, groups, and the state) for exchanges, democratic deliberations, and interactions free of religion.

Clearly, the question is knowing how these general principles are fleshed out in practice. If there seems to be a consensus in the literature on these four principles, how can we explain the virulence of the debates over the last few years? Why have we seen such a proliferation of labels opposing different visions of secularism, as if there was only one correct definition? In our opinion, the real question at issue lies elsewhere.

Secularism as a Field of Struggle

First, secularism is not easy to define and to put into practice. It is a field of struggle where each party seeks to promote its own cause by putting forward its own interpretation. Moreover, the discursive field perfectly illustrates the scale of this conflict. Not to be outdone, academics have developed many more or less flattering labels. The terms they use are not "neutral." In particular, open secularism is contrasted with conservative (as opposed to progressive) secularism or with strict secularism; inclusive secularism is contrasted with exclusive secularism; liberal thinkers confront republican (civic or conservative) thinkers; and so on.[1] In other words, stating one's case goes hand in hand with demonstrating the moral superiority of one's position. For example, political philosopher Jocelyn Maclure (2014, 17) presents liberal-pluralist secularism in the following terms:

> Liberal secularism sees the separation of State and religion and the religious neutrality of the State as primarily serving the protection of fundamental individual rights such as the right to equality and non-discrimination, and freedom of conscience and religion. I add the attribute "pluralistic" to qualify liberal secularist regimes that are

> sensitive to the recomposition and diversification of their populations and the plight of members of minority religious groups.

It would be hard to find a more caring and open-minded approach to the inclusion of individuals from a minority group. This model is contrasted with conservative secularism, which "considers special forms of recognition for the majority or historically dominant religion to be compatible with secularism ... When a public institution displays a religious symbol or incorporates a religious practice, it is thereby offering privileged support to a particular religion, thereby violating the principle of equal respect that the state owes to all citizens" (Maclure 2014, 18). According to this way of thinking, "conservative secularism" runs counter to the protection of freedom of conscience and religion and fails to show respect for all: it is therefore disqualified from the outset. The other ideal is that of republican secularism, which seeks to emancipate individuals and develop a common civic identity, which accordingly requires religious affiliations to be confined to the private sphere. This model aims to protect freedom of conscience and religion by prohibiting any infringement of these rights (it is therefore a negative freedom), but it refuses to make adjustments (or accommodations) on the basis of religious differences and preferences. The question arises whether this republican secularism would not be liberal, even if it were based on the same fundamental principles?

Once again, the construction of these ideal types is not neutral. Not everyone shares this understanding of liberalism, of its presumed openness to diversity of conviction and belief, and of republicanism (privileging negative freedoms). Legal scholar Jaclyn Neo and her colleagues (2019, 942–43) maintain, on the contrary, that the liberal approach is committed to religious freedom as a negative freedom and that the secular state simply does not seek to arbitrate between different "religious truths." Instead, the secular state seeks to provide a framework for peaceful coexistence and to guarantee the necessary conditions for religious freedom, which is a matter of private concern and personal choice.

Let us make an exception for those people who want to eliminate all reference to religious beliefs and affiliations, confining them to the private sphere alone. They deem religious beliefs and affiliations to be irrational, and they maintain that all religions are fundamentally oppressive, especially for women and non-heteronormative people. In our view, positions like this are outside of secularism since they challenge the principle of freedom of religion and essentialize it. On the other hand, insofar as the four constitutive principles listed earlier are respected within the limits imposed by respect for human rights and democracy, there are no good or bad forms of secularism, which is a "societal choice" made by means of political and legal institutions. However, this societal choice is not made in the abstract. It is made in a particular context and at a given moment, conveyed by actors engaged in public debate as citizens or elected representatives.

As historian Samuel Dalpé and legal scholar David Koussens (2016, 470) demonstrate, the media's treatment of secularism in recent years has focused on principles relating to "modalities for regulating the individual expression of beliefs" and the prohibition on wearing religious symbols. The debates on this issue are therefore essentially articulated around the question of religious symbols. For this reason, like all decisions of a political nature, the adoption of arrangements enshrining secularism at an institutional and practical level are decisions of a political nature; as such, they are the result of a societal debate, often fuelled by the political class. These arrangements are not free of calculations of all kinds (Côté and Mathieu 2016, 414–18; Lavoie 2016, 338–39). This issue nevertheless highlights conflicts that are polarized around divergent visions of the "common good." The explicit inclusion of secularism in law – through legislation and not just through the courts' interpretation of its constitutive principles – changes the way in which institutions operate. This process is not without its problems (Milot 2004, 30).

In this chapter, we maintain that the source of tensions and conflicts of interpretation lies less in the organizing principles of secularism themselves than in the way they are implicitly or explicitly ordered in the hierarchy of principles. In other words, some observers consider that the overarching principle – the one that should come first and determine all the others – is recognition and respect for freedom of religion, followed by equality of citizens. Other observers, meanwhile, give precedence to the principle of separation of religious and public powers and the principle of the neutrality of the state. In our view, both models are defensible. They are based on different normative visions of the role that the state should play in the organization of society. These visions, in themselves, are neither better nor worse. They are different. As sociologist Micheline Milot (2005, 14–15) reminds us, secularism must be understood as a regulatory idea rather than as an empirical reality. Indeed, secularism can take many forms depending on the contexts in which it is formulated and adopted and the conflicts experienced by these societies at different times. It therefore exists in several forms and can be the subject of several interpretations.

The drafters of the Act Respecting the Laicity of the State (Bill 21) have apparently preferred one model of secularism over another.[2] This model is favoured by the Quebec National Assembly and a significant proportion of Quebec citizens, judging by opinion polls. It conflicts with another model that orders the principles of secularism by giving precedence to the protection of individual rights. Opponents of Bill 21 take an approach to secularism that is also admittedly defensible. This approach has the advantage of being in continuity particularly with a legal tradition that has taken hold in Canada. As scholar in religious studies Solange Lefebvre (2008, 173) suggests, this may stem from the difference between the Latin and Anglo-Saxon models, the former having a more territorial identity, while Protestant cultures subscribe to a more internalized identity.

The Principles of Laicity Articulated in Bill 21

The Act Respecting the Laicity of the State, adopted by the National Assembly on June 16, 2019, aims to enshrine laicity as the leading characteristic of the state in Quebec's legal order. Among the reasons given in the preamble, the legislation emphasizes the importance of ensuring "a balance between the collective rights of the Quebec nation and human rights and freedoms," and it predetermines the order in which the principles of laicity are presented in section 2 of the act:

> The laicity of the State is based on the following principles:
>
> 1 the separation of State and religions
> 2 the religious neutrality of the State

3 the equality of all citizens
4 freedom of conscience and freedom of religion.

In the Blue Room of the National Assembly, Simon Jolin-Barrette, the minister responsible for Bill 21, recalled its three main measures on the day of its adoption: "The introduction into our law of the principle of laicity, the prohibition on wearing religious symbols for state employees in positions of authority, and the obligation to provide a public service with an uncovered face and to receive a public service with an uncovered face when necessary for reasons of identification and security" (Quebec 2019). Bill 21 incorporates the provisions of the Act to Foster Adherence to State Religious Neutrality (Bill 62), which was adopted in October 2017 when the Quebec Liberal Party was in power and concerns the obligation of public employees to perform their duties with their faces uncovered as well as the obligation of a person presenting themselves to receive a service.[3] In addition, the act contains two sections that specify that its provisions apply notwithstanding the sections relating to the protection of fundamental freedoms in the Quebec Charter of Human Rights and Freedoms (Quebec Charter) and the Canadian Charter of Rights and Freedoms (Canadian Charter).[4] The minister defended the prohibition of wearing religious symbols by certain categories of employees (including police officers, justices of the peace, correctional officers, prosecutors, principals and vice-principals, and teachers in the public school system) on the grounds that they need to demonstrate neutrality and reserve in both fact and appearance.

The application of the principles of laicity is circumscribed and essentially concerns the prohibition of the wearing of religious symbols by certain employees and the obligation to give and receive public services with an uncovered face. It leaves out entire areas of secularism that could also have been the subject of a legislative framework. Examples include the public funding of private denominational schools, the presence of chaplains in Quebec prisons, financial assistance for the protection of Quebec's religious heritage, tax benefits granted to religious organizations in the form of tax deductions for donations, refunds of municipal, school, and sales taxes, and so on. In short, the act merely affirms the principles of the separation and neutrality of the state insofar as it concerns certain employees of the state. The act was drafted and adopted following tensions over reasonable accommodation on religious grounds as well as social demands for limitations on certain forms of religious expression in the civic sphere. In other words, it addresses the relationship that individuals have with public bodies. The act does not seek to challenge manifestations of religious affiliation in the public sphere: individuals, whether or not they profess a religion, still have the right to display their preferences in whatever way that suits them.

The use of notwithstanding clauses in the Quebec and Canadian Charters raises the question of respect for the principle of equality of citizens and the absence of discrimination based on religious affiliation and beliefs. Minister Simon Jolin-Barrette justifies the notwithstanding provisions by appealing, in the name of accountability, to the principle of parliamentary sovereignty over the courts in determining the relationship between the state and religions. In other words, Bill 21 seeks to ensure the operative principles of separation and neutrality with respect to a single issue – that of religious symbols worn by certain government employees. It seeks to ensure that some public representatives in positions of authority who act on behalf of the state express and symbolize that neutrality. It should be noted that the ordering of the principles of laicity in Quebec gives precedence to the principle of the neutrality of the state, while also recognizing the principles of equality of citizens and freedom of conscience and religion.

The Precedence of the Neutrality of the State

The principle of neutrality is based on the precedence of political power over religious power. Thus, legal norms – the ability to participate in public affairs and democratic life – apply to all citizens, regardless of their beliefs and convictions. For Milot (2002, 34), "secularism is not an opinion about religion, but an opinion about the State," in the sense that the state is required to treat all religions equally. Secularism is thus based on the principle of neutrality since it is an indispensable condition for the exercise of freedom of conscience and religion. The state may therefore neither favour nor hinder any particular religion, which is why, as the jurist Catherine Haguenau-Moizard (2000, 57–58) reminds us, most of the legal norms concerning secularism concern the neutrality of the state, which itself is made up of several complementary elements. First, secularism recognizes the independence of the churches by granting them legal status, which allows them to organize themselves freely, to have autonomous financial resources, and to be free from interference by public authorities, provided that the churches respect the law. Second, it grants them a certain protection in the form of measures allowing individuals and religious groups, churches, and denominations to follow their own convictions. In other words, the state protects religions by sanctioning infringements of freedom or by offering services to religious organizations. As a result, the neutrality of the state entails a duty to ensure that religious and non-religious people have the freedom to exercise their religion or to enjoy freedom of conscience, despite the preferences of the majority (Milot 2002, 35).

Neutrality also entails the obligation of the state to remain impartial with respect to beliefs that cannot be deemed, *a priori*, good or bad as well as with respect to the type of life that people may choose to lead (Joppke 2007, 313). In other words, the state should take the position that it is not in a position to determine the intrinsic value of a belief, whether religious or secular. Nevertheless, it has "the duty to ensure that public order and the freedom of each individual are preserved, which could be compromised by the manifestation of certain religious convictions" (Milot 2009, 33). Neutrality is therefore not an abstract concept: instead, it refers to a social, cultural, legal, and political sphere in which norms, described by some people as dominant, have been established and are, by the same token, subject to challenge.

That said, is it possible, as philosophers Jocelyn Maclure and Charles Taylor (2010, 21) argue, that "in a society where there is no consensus on core beliefs, the state should avoid prioritizing the visions of the world and the good life that motivate the adherence of citizens to the basic principles of their political association"? In other words, the state does not have to choose, let alone favour, a particular world-view. This position is taken in the name of justice for those who do not share the beliefs of the majority and who would be marginalized for that reason. The state must ensure equal treatment of the personal values of individuals in the name of fairness and respect for diversity of belief and conviction. Maclure and Taylor therefore oppose the state's adherence, in the name of neutrality, to a secular moral philosophy that would have the disadvantage of being just as totalizing as religions are, turning citizens who adhere to religious faith into second-class citizens. However, this way of seeing things overlooks the existence in any society (in this respect, Quebec is no exception) of civic principles that frame life in society. Indeed, the interventions of the state are all inspired, in one way or another, by a particular vision of the common good and the good life, whether it is in relation to gender (for example, Quebec has adopted a law on pay equity), to the protection of personal information, to participation in democratic life, to social solidarity, to the sharing of wealth, to the protection of life, and so on. It is somewhat illusory to imagine that a state sharing the principles of democratic liberalism does not promote a particular vision of life in society and the obligations that flow from it for the individuals and groups that constitute it, whether implicitly or explicitly.

Neutrality cannot therefore be defined as the refusal to choose, to take sides, or to not intervene. The religious neutrality of the state, on the other hand, requires not acting for or against religions or personal convictions insofar as religions and convictions respect public order and fundamental freedoms (including freedom of conscience and religion). Sociologist Christian Joppke (2007, 314) points out that even when the state tries to be neutral, it nevertheless still favours a language, makes decisions about public holidays, defines the content of public education, and organizes ceremonies, all of which reflect the "societal culture" of the majority group to the detriment of those of minorities, including religious minorities.

These general considerations are of little help when it comes to translating the principle of neutrality into concrete actions taken by the state in accommodating religious beliefs and convictions. Beyond the universal principle of "neutrality," a question arises: what attitude should public authorities adopt, in practice, regarding the convictions of others and, more specifically, the obligations imposed on government employees? In this respect, Joppke (2007) points out that neutrality is something like the Roman god Janus, facing in two directions at the same time. It can be seen as an instrument of inclusion or of exclusion, depending on the preferences of the analysts and the actors. Neutrality is inclusive for those minorities who interpret it as conferring on them the right to pursue their way of life as they see fit. For others, the right to be different is interpreted as a factor of self-exclusion: in this respect, certain fundamentalist or orthodox practices, treated under the angle of state neutrality, instrumentalize religion for political purposes and allow faith communities to call for the segregation of the sexes in public places and for places of prayer in workplaces and public institutions as well as to refuse a public service from a person of the opposite sex.

The neutrality of the state can therefore be invoked, first, by those who want to limit the wearing of religious symbols by state employees and, second, by those who oppose any such prohibition. For people holding the first of these views, this principle requires not only that the service be provided in an impartial manner but also that those who receive the service perceive it as being delivered impartially. In other words, if the state has a duty to be neutral with respect to religions, government representatives and employees must display this neutrality. The state is not an abstract entity: instead, it is personified in men and women who convey a message through the way in which they behave and present themselves. For people holding the second of these views, such restrictions ignore the fact that services can be delivered impartially despite the appearance of the providers and that such measures are de facto discriminatory for those who do not display the symbolic attributes, or modes of representation, of the majority. To use Maclure and Taylor's (2010, 52) expression, "the requirement of neutrality is directed at institutions, not individuals." Another formulation, and one just as legitimate, would be to say that neutrality is an obligation of the state, which is itself not an abstract institution. One of the components of the state is the people who serve it.

As a result, questions about the meaning of "the neutrality of the state" seek to justify the acceptance or rejection of prohibitions that the state may impose on the providers or beneficiaries of public services, particularly with respect to the wearing of religious symbols. Yet a basic definition of neutrality would have the state simply seek to maintain distance from religions and to refrain from promoting a particular vision based on religious truth(s). Therefore, in the name of neutrality, the state itself – notably, in the person of its representatives – should refrain from displaying religious symbols.

In section 2, the Act Respecting the Laicity of the State affirms the separation of state and religions, before affirming the principle of religious neutrality. As mentioned earlier, the scope of the law is limited to the prohibition of wearing a religious symbol. However, in section 3, Bill 21 affirms the duty of religious neutrality – a duty previously provided for in Bill 62. Although Bill 21 does not explicitly refer to Bill 62, it nonetheless draws on the precedent of this previous Act, which defines the principle of neutrality in section 4:

> Adherence to the principle of State religious neutrality includes, in particular, the duty for personnel of public bodies to act, in the exercise of their functions, so as neither to favour nor to hinder a person because of the person's religious affiliation or non-affiliation or because of their own religious convictions or beliefs or those of a person in authority.

Bill 21 does not change this definition. Actually, the two pieces of legislation complement each other. Section 4 of Bill 62 meets all the characteristics of neutrality discussed earlier. In addition, the Quebec legislator has chosen to narrow the scope of the law to the prohibition on wearing a religious symbol and providing services with uncovered face for employees of public organizations. The provision to keep one's face uncovered also applies to persons receiving a public service in person, and this provision goes back to the adoption of Bill 62.

In sum, Bill 21, like its predecessor Bill 62, upholds a model of secularism whose cornerstone is the principle of the neutrality of the state. Indeed, this neutrality stems from the principle of separation. This approach is consistent with an active model of impartiality. According to this conception, the state and its representatives should not only be impartial in providing services: they should also appear to be impartial at all times. This active model is a departure from a passive model of impartiality, according to which government officials should act neutrally, fairly, and with integrity, should abide by their duty of confidentiality, and should not seek to proselytize others. However, the former conception of impartiality does not violate the principle of religious freedom insofar as individuals can belong to the religion of their choice and follow its precepts (Haguenau-Moizard 2000, 46). The core principle of Bill 21 differs from the passive conception of secularism that emphasizes the precedence of the principle of freedom of conscience and religion of individuals.

On the Precedence of Freedom of Conscience and Religion

There is another perspective that reverses the hierarchy of principles underlying secularism, which can be seen as an arrangement that defends the principle of freedom of conscience and religion of both individuals and groups. According to this perspective, neutrality towards the different conceptions of life in society involves recognizing and accepting differences and the multiplicity of preferences. It also means that the state not only refrains from passing judgment on these different conceptions but does not seek to contain or frame them. In other words, freedom of conscience and religion can only be guaranteed by the neutrality of the state. The philosophers Maclure and Taylor (2010) develop their reasoning further by proposing a hierarchy of principles, with institutional principles serving as moral principles. Thus, they write that "equal respect and freedom of conscience and religion are moral principles whose function is to regulate our action (or, in this case, the action of the state), whereas neutrality, separation, and accommodation are what might be called 'institutional principles' derived from the principles of equal respect and freedom of conscience" (33–34). Moral principles are in the order of ends, whereas institutional principles are in the order of means (Maclure 2014, 11). From this perspective, it is easy to understand that the means (that is, the principles of separation and neutrality) cannot be considered superior to the moral ideal pursued by secularism, which is to preserve equal respect for individuals, whatever their beliefs, in the name of justice and inclusion. This position disqualifies, from the outset, any restriction on the wearing of religious symbols unless such a limitation is compatible "with the principle of respect due to all or [to] protect the freedom of conscience and religion of others" (12).

The interpretation made by Maclure and Taylor (2010) is the one that has taken hold in Canada. Since the 1970s, the policy of multiculturalism, one of the objectives set out in the preamble to the Canadian Multiculturalism Act, is based on the recognition that "the diversity of Canadians as regards race, national or ethnic origin, colour and religion is a fundamental characteristic of Canadian society."[5] In this spirit, public institutions have a duty to take into account the multicultural character of society, and institutional practices must apply equally to all persons, regardless of their origin. As the jurist Léopold Vanbellingen (2015) points out, neutrality stems from the right to the free exercise of religion (based on the need not to favour one belief over others) and of each person to freely exercise his or her religion. This interpretation of secularism is present in the public debate in Quebec and widely shared in the rest of Canada. It maintains that individuals are allowed to display their religious affiliation even within the public service.

Invoking the value of societal pluralism necessarily implies respecting the individual practices of believers, both in their individual lives and in the context of social interactions. Such practices are clearly not limited to the wearing of religious symbols, but include, for example, dietary preferences, the right to prayer, and respect for religious holidays outside of the civic calendar (which, as we know, is derived from the Christian tradition). The Canadian legal framework upholds this interpretation of secularism. The Canadian Charter gives constitutional status, even pre-eminence, to the principle of freedom of religion, whereas the notion of secularism is never mentioned. In fact, freedom of religion is the first of the fundamental freedoms enumerated in section 2(a) of the charter, followed by the freedoms of thought, belief and opinion, and peaceful assembly and association. And this legal framework applies to all laws enacted by the provinces. Legal scholars have concluded that the scope of religious freedom is broad and can only be limited if it meets the criteria set out by the Supreme Court of Canada – namely, that the objective identified by the law must be real and pressing and that there is a sufficient degree of proportionality between the objective and the means used to achieve it.

This last aspect has three components: the restriction must be rationally connected to the objective; the restriction must not limit freedom in a way that is unreasonable to achieve the objective; and there must be proportionality between the effects of the measure limiting a right and the objective of the legislation. The guidelines for interpreting the law, which are based on an assessment of the urgency and proportionality between the objectives and the means with which the effects of a limit are imposed on a fundamental freedom, thus crystallize a certain conception of individual freedoms. In other words, a measure limiting a freedom – in this case, the freedom of religion – could not be based on the need to create a civic environment free of religious symbols on a preventive basis – for example, in order to avoid the multiplication of religious symbols. As sociologist Valérie Amiraux and legal scholar Jean-François Gaudreault-Desbiens (2016, 371) argue, "if the state alleges that a religious symbol poses a threat or harm, it will have to support this allegation with facts."

Moreover, Canadian law links freedom of religion with a specific vision of the right to equality and non-discrimination. This latter right concerns the idea of reasonable accommodation, which seeks to avoid all forms of indirect discrimination, particularly that which could be based on religious grounds. Political scientist Alma Mancilla (2011, 792) provides a cogent summary of this conception:

> The scope of religious freedom has been defined quite broadly in a number of Supreme Court of Canada decisions, some of which are well-known for their effect on the treatment of different religious denominations, particularly minority ones. In *R. v Big M. Drug Mart*, for example, the Supreme Court defined freedom of conscience and religion as including both freedom from coercion and restraint and the right to display one's beliefs and practices, establishing as the only limitations those that are necessary to preserve public order, health or morals, and the fundamental rights and freedoms of others. The same judgment also rules on the equality that must accompany this freedom, as well as on the pluralistic nature of Canada in matters of religion. Finally, in the domain of religious freedom, the Court gives precedence to the subjective criterion of the sincerity of one's personal belief over the objective criterion of the de facto existence of a precept recognized by all members or authorities of a religious denomination.

The vision that has emerged in the courts is compatible with, and even stems directly from, recognition of the pluralism of affiliations and preferences enshrined in the policy of Canadian multiculturalism. According to this conception, the state has a duty to protect religious beliefs. It must safeguard the freedom of conscience and religion of all citizens, regardless of their convictions. It cannot exclude anyone from the public service on this basis as long as public order and safety are guaranteed. The Canadian state has never explicitly articulated its secular character. For this reason, guidelines relevant to this secular character are defined through law. These guidelines ensure that practices concerning reasonable accommodation prevail since they are framed legally and are incompatible with any prohibition on the wearing of religious symbols in the absence of real and urgent objectives (Lavoie 2016, 338). The Canadian state, both federally and provincially, seems de facto to be secular insofar as it has never been dominated by the church, and has been able to preserve its autonomy with respect to religions (Milot 2004, 34–42). The separation of church and state, and the independence of the state from religions, are well established, which explains why the emphasis is placed on the preservation of freedom of conscience and religion, given that one of the defining characteristics of Canadian society is recognition of its pluralistic nature.

In sum, when we consider the four general principles that make up secularism, freedom of conscience and religion and the substantive equality of citizens are at the top of the hierarchy (as opposed to the principle of formal equality, according to which the law applies to all citizens consistently and in the same manner). This interpretation holds that the state cannot force anyone within the public service to renounce his or her deepest beliefs. These beliefs may be displayed in the practices, behaviours, dress, food preferences, and so on that flow from these convictions. From this principle stems the obligation of reasonable accommodation, which is the view embraced by classical liberal and pluralist thinkers, by multiculturalism, by the courts, by a majority of Canadian citizens, and by many people concerned with the preservation of individual rights. It is on these grounds that opposition has arisen to Bill 21's provisions on prohibiting religious symbols, in the same way that opposition arose to Bill 62 and its requirement to provide and receive public service with the face uncovered (Iavarone-Turcotte 2017).

Conclusion

Where Bill 21 is concerned, we suggest it is problematic to present secularism in Manichean either/or terms, drawing a line between correct and incorrect conceptions of secularism. We note that political and social actors, as well as many intellectuals and academics, tend to frame the debate in these terms. They position themselves and enter the field of struggle that secularism has become. The weapons they deploy on this battlefield include praising their own position and seeking to disqualify the position of their adversaries in one way or another. The clash of views on secularism has led to such vehement outbursts that people supporting Bill 21 are sometimes assumed to support discrimination and, by association, racism. Accusations along these lines are sometimes made by reasonable people in positions of authority. For example, Prime Minister Justin Trudeau's reputation was affected by the blackface episode during the October 2019 federal election campaign. Jack Jedwab (2019), the president of the Association for Canadian Studies and the Metropolis Institute, observed at the time: "Both Scheer's and Singh's criticisms of Trudeau and the related concerns about the spread of racism would be more credible if they denounced the discriminatory aspects of Bill 21 rather than bowing to the Quebec premier's demands and looking the other way on what Legault insists is a strictly provincial matter." The former leader of the New Democratic Party Tom Mulcair (2020) made a similar conflation in the pages of *Maclean's*. *Calgary Herald* columnist Catherine Ford (2019) claimed that Bill 21 "stands as an offence to the very decency of Canada, and boots minority rights and freedom of religion back into the dark ages."

Nevertheless, as long as religious beliefs are not presented from the outset in terms of a struggle for personal emancipation from what is seen as obscurantism, secularism can be understood in different ways. Secularism has different meanings and is therefore a complex idea. Moreover, the constitutive principles from which the practical applications of secularism are derived vary from one state to the next (Kuru

2009; Cady and Hurd 2010). We maintain that Quebec laicity is made up of four main principles that are clearly stated in the Act Respecting the Laicity of the State. However, the Quebec state endorses a vision of secularism that gives precedence to the principle of the neutrality of the state. The prohibition on the wearing of religious symbols by public sector employees in certain categories of employment is justified by the need to ensure that this neutrality is not only effective but is also perceived as such by the people coming into contact with these symbols. This approach is legitimate, coherent, and compatible with the other principles of secularism.

The opponents of Bill 21 adhere, for the most part, to a vision of secularism that gives precedence to the principle of freedom of conscience and religion of individuals. This perspective actually reverses the hierarchy of principles enshrined in Bill 21 in a way that is compatible with the self-image of Canadian society and that has culminated in the adoption of multiculturalism and its inclusion in the Canadian Charter. This vision is shared by many activists working in the field of human rights protection. It is also a legitimate approach, consistent with the general principles of secularism. Similarly, we are witnessing a debate that refers to different conceptualizations of political liberalism and its relationship to fundamental rights. In a study of the attitudes of Canadians and Quebeckers towards religious symbols displayed by religious minorities, the authors conclude that, in Quebec, upholding liberal values is associated with greater support for restrictions on the wearing of religious symbols by minority groups, whereas, in the rest of Canada, upholding liberal values is accompanied with opposition to such restrictions. Thus, "the difference between Quebec and the rest of Canada in the relationship between liberal values and support for restrictions appears to be more of a fundamental cultural difference – a history of two liberalisms" (Turgeon et al. 2019, 261). Canada's history is full of such misunderstandings and mutual incomprehension.

The courts will have an opportunity to rule on the validity of certain provisions of the Act Respecting the Laicity of the State. We can always hope that judges will show some sensitivity to another kind of diversity found within Canada – namely, the presence of Quebec, a distinct society. Indeed, Quebec, as a society, shares a different reading of the principles of liberalism, and the practical arrangements through which the state affirms its neutrality are derived from this reading. These arrangements may diverge from the multicultural doxa that informs Canadian minds and law.

Notes

1 These latter categories were stated by the philosopher Georges Leroux in his interview with Mathieu Bélisle (2018).

2 Act Respecting the Laicity of the State, SQ 2019, c. 12.

3 Act to Foster Adherence to State Religious Neutrality and, in Particular, to Provide a Framework for Requests for Accommodations on Religious Grounds in Certain Bodies, SQ 2017, c. 19.

4 Charter of Human Rights and Freedoms, RSQ 1977, c. C-12; Canadian Charter of Rights and Freedoms, Part 1 of the Constitution Act, 1982, being Schedule B to the Canada Act 1982 (UK), 1982, c. 11.

5 Canadian Multiculturalism Act, RSC 1985, c. 24 (4th Supp.).

References

Amiraux, Valérie, and Jean-François Gaudreault-Desbiens. 2016. "Libertés fondamentales et visibilité des signes religieux en France et au Québec: entre logiques nationales et non nationales du droit?" *Recherches sociographiques* 57 (2–3): 351–78.

Baubérot, Jean. 2007. *Les laïcités dans le monde*. Paris: Presses universitaires de France.

Bélisle, Mathieu. 2018. "Laïcité en question. Entretiens avec Georges Leroux, Yolande Geadah et Jacques Beauchemin." *L'Inconvénient* 72 (Spring): 15–27.

Cady, Linell E., and Elizabeth Shakman Hurd, eds. 2010. *Comparative Secularisms in a Global Age*. New York: Palgrave Macmillan.

Casanova, José. 2009. "The Secular and Secularisms." *Social Research* 76 (4): 1049–66.

Côté, Pauline, and Félix Mathieu. 2016. "Laïcité et valeurs dans l'économie du projet de loi no 60 Charte des valeurs." *Recherches sociographiques* 57 (2–3): 379–425.

Dalpé, Samuel, and David Koussens. 2016. "Le discours sur la laïcité pendant le débat sur la 'Charte des valeurs de la laïcité': Une analyse lexicométrique de la presse francophone québécoise." *Recherches sociographiques* 57 (2–3): 455–74.

Ford, Catherine. 2019. "Ford: Shame on Us for Keeping Quiet About Quebec's Bill 21." *Calgary Herald*, October 7. https://calgaryherald.com/opinion/columnists/ford-shame-on-us-for-keeping-quiet-about-quebecs-bill-21.

Haguenau-Moizard, Catherine. 2000. États et religions en Europe. Grenoble: Presses de l'Université de Grenoble.

Iavarone-Turcotte, Anne. 2017. "La Loi 62 et l'arbitraire: mythes et limites du droit dans la gestion des accommodements religieux." *Les ateliers de l'éthique / The Ethics Forum* 12 (2–3): 4–36.

Jedwab, Jack. 2019. "The Conservative and NDP Leaders Were Swift in Their Condemnation of Justin Trudeau's Use of Blackface: Where Is Their Fervor around Quebec's Bill 21?" *Policy Options Politiques*, October 2. https://policyoptions.irpp.org/fr/magazines/october-2019/quebecs-bill-21-should-also-stir-anti-racist-outrage-among-party-leaders/.

Joppke, Christian. 2007. "State Neutrality and Islamic Headscarf Laws in France and Germany." *Theory and Society* 36 (4): 313–42.

Kuru, Ahmet T. 2009. *Secularism and State Policies toward Religion: The United States, France, and Turkey*. Cambridge, UK: Cambridge University Press.

Lavoie, Bertrand. 2016. "La tension socio-juridique entre laïcité et multiculturalisme: le bijuridisme comme clé de compréhension des débats québécois sur le rapport entre le droit et la religion." *Recherches sociographiques* 57 (2–3): 333–49.

Lefebvre, Solange. 2008. "Le Canada et le Québec confrontés à la diversité ethnoreligieuse." *Hermès, La Revue* 2 (51): 171–76.

Lévesque, Sébastien, ed. *Penser la laïcité québécoise: fondements et défense d'une laïcité ouverte au Québec*. Quebec City: Presses de l'Université Laval.

Maclure, Jocelyn. 2014. "Comprendre la laïcité. Une proposition théorique." In Lévesque, 9–19.

Maclure, Jocelyn, and Charles Taylor. 2010. *Laïcité et liberté de conscience*. Montreal: Éditions du Boréal.

Mancilla, Alma. 2011. "Religion dans l'espace public et régulation politique: le parcours de la notion de laïcité dans le discours étatique québécois." *Recherches sociographiques* 52 (3): 789–810.

Milot, Micheline. 2002. *Laïcité dans le Nouveau Monde. Le cas du Québec*. Turnhout, Belgium: Brepols.

–. 2004. "Laïcisation au Canada et au Québec: un processus tranquille." *Studies in Religion / Sciences Religieuses* 33 (1): 27–49.

–. 2005. "Les principes de laïcité politique au Québec et au Canada." *Bulletin d'histoire politique* 13 (3): 13–27.

–. 2009. "L'émergence de la notion de laïcité au Québec. Résistances, polysémie et instrumentalisation." In *Appartenances religieuses, appartenance citoyenne. Un équilibre en tension*, edited by Paul Eid, Pierre Bosset, Micheline Milot, and Sébastien Lebel-Grenier, 29–74. Quebec City: Presses de l'Université Laval.

Mulcair, Tom. 2020. "Jagmeet Singh Calls MP 'Racist,' but Has He Forgotten about Bill 21?" *Maclean's*, July 1. https://www.macleans.ca/opinion/jagmeet-singh-calls-mp-racist-but-has-he-forgotten-about-bill-21/.

Neo, Jaclyn L., Matthias Roßbach, Thio Li-Ann, and Alexander Tischbirek. 2019. "Solidarity in Diversity? State Responses to Religious Diversity in Liberal and Non-Liberal Perspectives." *German Law Journal* 20: 941–48.

Quebec. 2019. *Journal des débats de l'Assemblée nationale*. 42nd Legislature, 1st Session, June 16. http://www.assnat.qc.ca/fr/travaux-parlementaires/assemblee-nationale/42-1/journal-debats/20190616/247401.html#_Toc11766434.

–. N.d. *Immigration, Francisation et Intégration*. https://www.immigration-quebec.gouv.qc.ca.

Turgeon, Luc, Antoine Bilodeau, Stephen W. White, and Ailsa Henderson. 2019. "A Tale of Two Liberalisms? Attitudes toward Minority Religious Symbols in Quebec and Canada." *Canadian Journal of Political Science* 52 (2): 247–65.

Vanbellingen, Léopold. 2015. "L'accommodement raisonnable de la religion dans le secteur public: analyse du cadre juridique belge au regard de l'expérience canadienne." *Revue interdisciplinaire d'études juridiques* 75 (2): 221–48.

Willaime, Jean-Paul. 2009. "European Integration, Laïcité and Religion." *Religion, State and Society* 37 (1–2): 23–35.

–. 2017. "Polarisation autour du religieux en francophonie? Les nouveaux défis de la laïcité." *Francophonie d'Amérique* 44–45: 137–62.

Beyond Defending Religious Symbols 2

The Desire to Put Quebec in Its Place

LUCIA FERRETTI

The Act Respecting the Laicity of the State (Bill 21) raises important questions.[1] What does the bill change, and what does it not change? How are opponents of Bill 21 reacting to it? What is the Canadian model of managing religious symbols? What do critics of this model say? What position could Quebec adopt once the courts have rendered their verdict? However, we should begin by recalling a few facts, drawing on the analyses of several experts on all these subjects. But perhaps the most important question is the following: how legitimate would it be for the state of Quebec to enforce an Act adopted by the National Assembly with the support of a significant majority of Quebeckers, even if that law were subsequently to be stricken down by Canadian courts?

The Act Respecting the Laicity of the State: Limited in Scope, Democratically Legitimate

Let us begin by clarifying the scope of the Act Respecting the Laicity of the State with respect to freedom of conscience and religion (Rousseau 2020). We should first make clear what it does not do and then focus on what it does accomplish. Bill 21 obviously does not diminish freedom of conscience, which, according to the most widely accepted formulation, is the freedom to believe or not to believe, to change religion, or to not profess a religion. The act does not limit freedom of religion, which the International Covenant on Civil and Political Rights defines as "the freedom, either individually or in community with others in public or private, to manifest his religion or belief, in worship, observance, practice and teaching" within the limits provided for by this major international text and others of a similar nature.[2] It does not restrict the freedom of parents to provide a religious and moral education to their children. It does not question the neutrality of the Quebec state, which treats all religions equally. It does not call into question the public funding of private religious schools. It keeps in place the rules governing the state's relationship with the four or five thousand charities registered in the name of religious corporations in Quebec – rules that exempt these organizations from taxation and allow them to receive donations in exchange for tax deductions. It does not alter the registered charitable status of religious corporations themselves or the benefits flowing from this status in the name of the "advancement of religion." It does not in any way prohibit the wearing of religious symbols or face coverings for religious reasons in the public sphere, in unsubsidized childcare facilities, or in private schools (even subsidized ones).

So, what does the Act Respecting the Laicity of the State actually do? It prohibits state employees in positions of authority, which extends to principals, vice-principals, and teachers in public schools, from wearing any religious symbol during their working hours. This prohibition is tempered, however, by a grandfather clause, which requires employees of public bodies and certain other occupations to perform their duties with their faces uncovered. It requires that people presenting themselves in person to receive a public service must also uncover their faces. However, this obligation is strictly limited: it applies only if it is necessary to verify their identity or for security reasons and only during those times when they are interacting or communicating with a staff member of an organization in the performance of their duties. Clearly, Bill 21 has a limited purpose and limited objectives.

Nonetheless, opposition to the bill has proven to be so vehement and immediate that the Quebec government has had to resort to every tool at its disposal to get the bill adopted and then to try to protect it. The Liberal Party of Quebec and Québec solidaire were so determined to prevent the bill's adoption before the end of the parliamentary session in the spring of 2019 that the government resorted to the gag order. Moreover, the Quebec government resorted to the notwithstanding clause from the outset to ensure that Bill 21 did not suffer the same fate as the Act to Foster Adherence to State Religious Neutrality (Bill 62), which was suspended in 2017 by the Superior Court of Quebec even before the section regulating uncovered faces could be applied.[3] The notwithstanding clause is provided for in section 52 of the Quebec Charter of Human Rights and Freedoms (Quebec Charter).[4] It is also an integral part of the Canadian Charter of Rights and Freedoms (Canadian Charter) in section 33, which was inserted at the time of the negotiations between the federal government and the English-speaking provinces on the patriation of the Constitution.[5] The purpose of this "notwithstanding" clause was to protect parliamentary sovereignty, which is one of the two fundamental pillars of democracy along with universal suffrage, against what is known as "government by judges" (Mandel 1989).

It should be noted that Quebec is not the only state to regulate the wearing of religious symbols or face coverings. Several other democracies have adopted much more restrictive legislation on these two points as well as on regulating their relations with religious organizations. We need only think of Germany and France, two Group of Seven countries, as well as Belgium and Denmark, among many others (European Court of Human Rights 2011, 2018, 2019; Barnett 2013). It should also be remembered that Bill 21 was adopted as the culmination of a major social debate that took place over approximately fifteen years. The act fulfills a key promise made by the Coalition Avenir Québec during the 2018 election campaign, at the end of which this party won a majority of seats in the National Assembly and the largest number of votes. Among the members of the National Assembly, those from the Coalition Avenir Québec and the Parti Québécois voted in favour of its adoption. In total, these two parties won 54.5 percent of the vote in this election. In addition, poll after poll showed that 62–64 percent of Quebeckers of all origins and languages supported the law (*Journal de Québec* 2020). The adoption of the Act Respecting the Laicity of the State is a case where parliamentary sovereignty has been exercised in line with the clearly demonstrated will of the people. The adoption of the act thus corresponds to the classic definition of democracy.

The Reaction of Opponents: Putting Quebec in Its Place

This major social debate on religious symbols has been going on in Quebec since the year 2000. It is striking for the contrast it offers between the modest objectives of the various bills drafted to regulate religious symbols and the sheer scale of opposition to them. Without rehashing the history of this debate, we should nevertheless take note of some of the debate's highlights. Throughout the reasonable accommodation crisis of the first decade of the twenty-first century, Quebeckers were repeatedly accused of intolerance and an "identity counter-reaction movement" not only by English Canada but also by some intellectuals in Quebec itself as well as by supporters of Quebec's liberal-minded political parties on both the Right and Left (Bouchard and Taylor 2008, 186). So much so that a French expert on the place of religion in contemporary societies, Jean Baubérot (2009), has observed that Quebec's liberal intellectuals are at odds with their nation on this issue. In *Le Devoir*, the cartoonist Garnotte summarized the Bouchard-Taylor Commission's overriding message to these intellectuals as follows: "Open up! And shut up!" (*Le Devoir* 2008).

Since that time, confusion has set in between immigration and religion. And Quebeckers have continued to be subject to slander. In 2010, when the Charest government introduced Bill 94, the Federation of Canadian Muslims accused the government of "succumbing to Islamophobia and racism" (*Le Devoir* 2010).[6] Then, in 2012, when the Marois government's Bill 60, the so-called Charter of Values, was tabled, the prominent Canadian military historian Jack Granatstein (*National Post* 2012), interim Quebec Liberal Party leader Jean-Marc Fournier (*Le Devoir* 2013) and philosopher Charles Taylor (*Journal de Montréal* 2013) used the expressions "original German," "Kristallnacht," and "Vladimir Putin's Russia" to describe the events.[7] Ultimately, neither Bill 94 nor Bill 60 was adopted. As mentioned above, Bill 62, tabled by the Couillard government, was neutralized before ever coming into effect and was widely denounced in English Canada and described as "racist" (in particular, *La Presse* 2017). This continuous barrage of opposition helps to explain why the Quebec government has worked hard at adopting and then protecting the Act Respecting the Laicity of the State.

Once again, some critics have been outspoken. When the bill was tabled in the National Assembly, Hamstead Mayor William Steinberg referred to "ethnic cleansing" and then "peaceful ethnic cleansing" and never apologized for his remarks (*Radio-Canada* 2019a). Several English-speaking cities and Montreal's two English-speaking school boards announced their intention to break the law, although these institutions participate in the governance of Quebec (*Le Devoir* 2019). At the same time as a group of opponents went to court to try to have the law's provisions suspended, which is discussed in more detail below, Quebec Court of Appeal Chief Justice Nicole Duval Hesler bluntly suggested that they mount a challenge to which, supposedly, the notwithstanding clause would not apply, while presenting Bill 21 as a remedy for the "visual allergies" to religious symbols that Quebeckers have supposedly developed (*La Presse* 2019). For their part, two Supreme Court of Canada justices, Russell Brown and Rosalie Abella, agreed to participate in a fundraising event for the Lord Reading Law Association, an advocacy group for Jewish jurists otherwise actively engaged in challenging the act before the Quebec Superior Court; it took a public outcry and the threat of a complaint to the Judicial Council for this event to be postponed (*Radio-Canada* 2020). To sum up, hate propaganda, the promotion of lawlessness, and the lack of impartiality or at least the appearance of a lack of impartiality has been evident in the actions of the judges of the highest court in Quebec and in the highest court in Canada.

Moreover, outside Quebec, starting before the adoption of the Act Respecting the Laicity of the State and continuing without a break since that time, the *Globe and Mail* and the *National Post* have both undertaken a campaign against Bill 21, against the Quebec government, and against Quebeckers in general (see in particular *Globe and Mail* 2019; Selley 2019a, 2019b). The premiers of several provinces and the mayors of several cities have denounced the "racism" of the law (*Le Monde* 2019). In Ontario, the legislature passed a motion calling on the government of that province to participate in a potential Supreme Court of Canada challenge to the law (*Radio-Canada* 2019b). As for Prime Minister Justin Trudeau, he has not closed the door on the federal government's involvement in such a challenge (*Le Nouvelliste* 2019). Opponents have even gone so far as to contact international bodies, such as the United Nations, the Inter-American Commission on Human Rights, and the Organization for Security and Cooperation in Europe, without much success (*La Presse* 2020). This campaign against Bill 21 has amounted to "Quebec bashing," with the intention of damaging the reputation of Quebec and especially of French-speaking Quebeckers in the eyes of Quebec's ethnic and religious minorities, in English Canada, and around the world. At the same time, English Canadian legislatures are upholding a "government of judges" above a law adopted by Quebec's National Assembly.

Two Ontario-based organizations, the National Council of Canadian Muslims and the Canadian Civil Liberties Association, were encouraged by their previous success in blocking Bill 62. Once Bill 21 was adopted, these organizations quickly moved to support student teacher Ichrak Nourel Hak's petition to the Ontario Superior Court to suspend the bill's application.[8] The Superior Court rejected the request, as did the Ontario Court of Appeal, despite the dissent of its chief justice. The Supreme Court of Canada, in turn, refused to hear the case. All these courts are reserving judgment on the merits of the law.

At the same time, between June and November 2019, and precisely on the merits, the law was targeted by four legal challenges. The first challenge was undertaken by the same student, supported by the same two organizations. The second involved three teachers (two of them Muslim and the other Catholic) with backing from the Coalition Inclusion Québec. The English Montreal School Board and the Fédération autonome de l'enseignement each initiated a legal challenge on their own. It is worth noting that the English Montreal School Board applied for and received $125,000 from the federal Court Challenges Program, in violation of the Act Respecting the Ministère du Conseil exécutif – a Quebec law – without first obtaining or seeking permission from the Quebec government.[9] Given the public outcry, the English Montreal School Board chose not to accept federal funding in this case (*La Presse*

2020). In other words, the English Montreal School Board acted illegally and managed to line up indirect support from the federal government to challenge a law meeting all the requirements of democracy.

So much for the actions. Now for the arguments. Opponents of Bill 21 have deployed an impressive range of arguments in the hopes of having the bill stricken down. According to some opponents, the law breaks with the spirit of the Quebec Act of 1774.[10] Some hold that the act concerns freedom of religion, which is an exclusively federal jurisdiction. Other arguments suggest that it violates freedom of conscience and religion and also undermines several sections of the Canadian Charter to which the "notwithstanding" clause does not apply: section 6 on freedom of movement and settlement, section 23 on minority language education rights, and section 28 on the equal rights of men and women. Such arguments hold that, in any case, the use of the notwithstanding clause should itself be declared illegitimate as the jurisprudence on the notwithstanding clause should be reviewed in light of the guidelines set for the use of similar clauses in the International Covenant on Civil and Political Rights and the European Convention on Human Rights.[11] In short, according to these opinions, Bill 21 flies in the face of history, the division of powers, and many of the sections of the Canadian Charter not affected by the "notwithstanding" clause, and it may even call for an amendment to the Constitution.

The unleashing of this legal firepower is revealing because the issue at stake goes far beyond the defence of the wearing of religious symbols by a few teachers and public servants. One cannot help but see this artillery barrage as a sign that English Canada and those Quebeckers who follow the Canadian model are determined to put Quebec in its place as an internal colony. Quebec should not have the latitude to regulate the wearing of religious symbols and face coverings differently than the rest of Canada, even in its own public schools and the government apparatus.

The Canadian Model Promotes Maximalist, Very Liberal, and Multiculturalist Management of Religious Freedom

We should first make a clarification. We are not questioning Canada's right to choose its own model for managing religion. We are rather noting that Canada is constitutionally a federal state. We could therefore expect Canada to respect the model for managing religion that Quebec wishes to apply, even though this latter model is more different on a conceptual level than it is in terms of its actual impact on the population. The Canadian Charter came into effect in 1982. As attested by an exhaustive survey of the literature, the jurisprudence developed since that time has resulted in Canada opting for a maximalist, very liberal, and multiculturalist management of church and state relations and religious freedom. In our view, and we will explain why shortly, the most recent decisions rendered by the Canadian courts cannot really be interpreted as the beginning of greater moderation in this respect.

A Benevolent Neutrality

To ensure that the state governs with benign neutrality, the courts have acted on two fronts. On the one hand, the courts have been careful to remove from the laws as well as from the rituals of public administration any vestige of "Christian privilege" (Seljak 2012). To cite a famous example, the Supreme Court of Canada declared the Lord's Day Act unconstitutional in 1985.[12] On the other hand, the courts have supported the state's willingness – the federal state, of course, but not just the federal state – "to open up laws to the particular needs of faith-based" minorities (Barnett 2013). In the first half of the 1990s, the Dhillon case on the wearing of turbans by officers in the Royal Canadian Mounted Police stirred public passions in English Canada. Since that time, jurisprudence has established that users of federal public services cannot claim that being exposed to the religious affiliation of state officials infringes on their own right to religious freedom (Ontario Human Rights Commission 2012). In their interactions with the federal government and the English-speaking provinces, these users, on the other hand, enjoy the greatest latitude. After minimal verification, they can wear religious symbols at any time; they can even wear a niqab when taking a citizenship oath; under certain conditions, they can do so during a criminal trial; in federal elections, in order to vote, they need only solemnly declare that they are eligible to do so, while keeping their faces covered; and the kirpan is now allowed in Canadian embassies, courthouses, and parliamentary buildings. Sikhs have also been granted permission by the federal government to ride on airplanes with a small kirpan and, in several provinces, to ride motorcycles without helmets.

An English Canadian consensus has emerged over the past forty years or so as a result of several rulings by many courts in a wide variety of cases as well as the cumulative effect of regulatory changes, legislative amendments, and the adoption of new laws. This consensus is very solid in political and legal institutions and quite solid in civil society. It holds that, while religion should not be institutionalized in the state, individuals can and are encouraged to display their religious preferences not only in the public sphere but also within the government apparatus. Along these lines, in 2015, the Supreme Court of Canada prohibited the recitation of a non-denominational prayer before the City of Saguenay Municipal Council in the name of the religious neutrality of the state. This decision surprised many people in English Canada where such public prayers are common (Grammond 2016, 258). The plaintiff in this case was an atheist supported by the Mouvement laïque québécois. It is important to note that the Supreme Court carefully argued that this decision should not be seen as "a position for atheism or agnosticism" at the expense of religion (Walker 2015).

Canadian neutrality does not require individuals to show discretion in religious matters. In addition to the examples provided earlier, there was the case in 2016 where the Supreme Court of Canada allowed a Sikh child in Montreal to wear his kirpan to a public school as long as it was contained in a secure package. Moreover, Canadian neutrality values and encourages contact between religions. In 2012, the same court ruled against Catholic parents in Drummondville who wanted to exempt their public school children from the Ethics and Religious Culture program for fear, among other things, that exposure to several religions at the same time would end up confusing these youngsters about their own faith: in the court's opinion, the parents' position "amounts to a rejection of Canada's multicultural reality" (*Le Devoir* 2012). Later in this chapter, we discuss a similar case brought by a publicly funded English-language private school, in which the decision was quite different.

The Active Recognition of the Religious Fact

The courts have constructed an extremely broad definition of religion, including personal religion, as well as an equally broad definition of belief, provided only that it be a religious belief. The protection afforded by the courts is no less extensive. A sincere belief is sufficient to render a contract null and void – no matter how personal, subjective, and recent that belief may be – where the contract has the effect of preventing the performance of a ritual, and this is the case even when religious authorities deem that the ritual can be adapted and that the contract was signed knowingly and willingly.[13] The courts have ruled that, in addition to individuals, legal entities can also assert religious rights. A company used a freedom of religion argument to have the Lord's Day Act declared unconstitutional.[14] In this case, the Supreme Court of Canada overturned two of its own rulings on the same law in 1985, including one based on the Canadian Bill of Rights.[15]

Many rulings have set out stringent obligations for employers with respect to reasonable accommodation. In order to prohibit the display of religious symbols during working hours, employers have had to demonstrate to the satisfaction of the judges that the health or safety – in other words, the very life – of their devout employee and their companions was at stake. Employers also had to demonstrate having made every attempt, within reasonable – but very narrow – limits, to restrict the number of tasks and the length of time that the devout employee was required to do without these religious symbols or at least to make some accommodation as to the manner in which they are worn. For example, shipping companies operating in Montreal's container terminals were able to demonstrate that they had reorganized the work of some of their Sikh truck drivers so that they only had to get out of their vehicles for ten or fifteen minutes at a time. Meanwhile, the truck drivers did not have to remove their turbans but simply wore helmets over them. In 2020, the Supreme Court of Canada refused to hear the truck drivers' appeal, thus ending a dispute that had lasted no less than fifteen years (*Le Devoir* 2020). Beyond these borderline cases, employees wishing to display their religious symbols almost always win in court.

The same goes for the arrangement of work schedules and religious holidays. Once again, employers must show that everything, up to a high degree of undue hardship, has been done to accommodate their religious employees: this can go as far as paying them more days off than their colleagues so that they can perform their religious duties.[16] The Supreme Court of Canada ensures that private religious organizations, even those receiving public subsidies, are subject to the law in a way that interferes in the least possible way with how they conduct their affairs. For example, Loyola High School, a private English-language high school that is subsidized 60 to 70 percent by the Quebec Ministry of Education, nevertheless won a case against the ministry, thereby obtaining the right to adapt its ethics and religious culture course in order to teach Catholicism from a Catholic perspective (*La Presse* 2015).

Finally, to avoid having to rule in favour of one fundamental right or the other in cases that appear to place two rights in conflict, the Supreme Court of Canada has sometimes reframed the dispute so that it can claim that, on the merits, it does not actually involve a conflict of rights. In 2001, in *Trinity Western v British Columbia College of Teachers*, the court drew a distinction between belief, on the one hand, and conduct consistent with that belief, on the other.[17] The court found no evidence that graduates of this evangelical university, in believing homosexuality to be a serious sin, would act in accordance with this belief and would discriminate against homosexual students. As a result, the court ordered the province's College of Teachers to license them to teach.[18]

The De Facto Primacy of Religious Freedom over Other Fundamental Rights

The right to religious freedom is not unlimited in Canada. Section 1 of the Canadian Charter provides that, like any other right, freedom of religion is subject only to such reasonable limits prescribed by law as can be demonstrably justified in a free and democratic society. In private litigation, a different test applies – religious freedom may be limited if the measure challenged by the plaintiffs is, in the opinion of the justices, only "negligible or insignificantly harmful" to them.[19] The Supreme Court of Canada dismissed the Hutterites' 2009 application for a driver's licence that did not require the driver's photo, invoking the concern of the Alberta government to counter the potential for loopholes in its campaign to combat identity theft.

In general, however, it actually takes nothing less than a risk to the life or physical safety of others for the courts to impose limits on religious freedom. For example, they have not consented to the petitions of Jehovah's Witness parents to refuse blood transfusions for their minor-age children who might otherwise die. The Supreme Court of Canada has allowed a man convicted of conspiracy to commit a terrorist attack to remain in prison without being moved on the grounds that this terrorist activity was a way for him to express his religious beliefs (Ontario Human Rights Commission 2012). And, to the relief of the BC government, the Supreme Court of British Columbia in 2011 ruled in favour of the constitutionality of the federal law prohibiting polygamy, which was passed in the early twentieth century to criminalize polygamy in the Mormon community. In the case of Bountiful, the evidence left no doubt that the polygamy of community leaders was directly responsible for the sexual assault and abuse of women and children. (Nonetheless, in 2018, the same court chose leniency for the two leaders: rather than applying the five-year prison sentence provided for by the law, it merely placed them under house arrest, one for six months and the other for three months [*Journal de Montréal* 2018].)

In the 2007 decision in *Bruker v Marcovitz*, the Supreme Court of Canada ruled against a Jewish man who had waited fifteen years after the divorce to grant his ex-wife the *get*[20] despite his contractual commitment to do so without delay.[21] In this case, the criterion of negligible or insignificant inconvenience to the husband's freedom of religion was applied in comparison to the harm suffered by his ex-wife, who, without the get, was unable to remarry religiously for all those years. Some legal scholars believe that Justice Rosalie Abella, the drafter of the majority judgment, sought to use the power of the Supreme Court to correct what she saw as clear discrimination against women in Jewish divorce law. They see this as an interventionist and exceptional departure from the court's very liberal tradition (Astengo 2008; Langevin et al. 2008). In this case, the judge went even further, changing the common understanding of the Canadian Charter that Canadians should not be arbitrarily disadvantaged because of their religion: there is no other case where a woman has been protected by Canadian courts from discrimination within her own faith.

Notwithstanding these and other examples, many legal scholars have concluded that the courts' repeated assertion that there is no hierarchy of fundamental rights in Canada does not tally with the facts. Louis-Philippe Lampron (2011, 396) defended his doctoral dissertation on this issue and concluded that a "substantive (or systemic) legal hierarchy" of constitutional rights does exist in this country:

> Comparative analysis of the scope that was attributed, over time, to the two selected groups of fundamental rights – on the one hand, the provisions protecting religious beliefs and, on the other, the rest of the set of fundamental rights of a constitutional nature in Canada – enabled us to observe a generalized qualitative imbalance favouring religious beliefs as the object of protection of laws concerning fundamental rights."

Accordingly, for Lampron, the courts are faced with a choice. They must either correct this systemic imbalance if they truly value the principle of non-hierarchy among fundamental rights or, if they consider such a principle to be legitimate, they must start by conceding it publicly and then account for their position – in effect, justifying the primacy they give to religious freedom. Furthermore, they must accept that legislators may, as they see fit, prefer to give primacy to another fundamental right, such as the equality between women and men.

Criticisms of the Canadian Model

As we have noted above, the Canadian model of the management of religion has developed as a result of the decisions of the courts as well as the action of legislators and public administrators in a dialectical movement that has ended up building a broad consensus in English Canada. This model also appeals to Quebec's liberal-minded intellectuals and politicians on the Right and the Left. This model is no doubt subject to criticism in Canada as well as in Quebec.

Inability to Protect the Religious Core of First Nations Culture

In 2017, the Supreme Court of Canada, in its role as a defender of religious freedom, upheld the BC government's approval of a private company's plan to build a ski resort on a mountain considered sacred by the Ktunaxa First Nation, which was also part of a territory they claimed as ancestral. The members of the Ktunaxa First Nation maintained that they sincerely believed such a project would drive out the Spirit of the Bear that resides there, thus rendering their religious practices unnecessary. But the court did not take this into account. For the court, the state has no obligation to protect religion: it only has the obligation to protect the freedom of individuals to believe in religion (*Le Devoir* 2017). This is an example of the inability (or unwillingness) of the Canadian legal system to protect the religion and culture of First Nations.

The State's Adoption of the Concept of Religious Freedom as Developed by Religious Organizations

According to the prevailing liberal perspective in Canada, the important thing is not that the state assert and enforce its independence from religious organizations but, rather, that it allows them the greatest freedom with respect to the state (Lévesque 2019). Indeed, for many critics, the Canadian model adopts far too closely the point of view of religious organizations that see freedom of religion as giving them the right to develop as they see fit, without hindrance. The de facto primacy given by the courts to religious freedom contributes to the very high legitimacy of religious belief systems. The substantial public funding of religious charities and the favourable tax treatment of religious organizations also help them to become increasingly important not only in the community life of faith groups but also in society at large and even within the state, from which they receive some of the means to influence governments and public administrations. While the Harper government was in power, much was said at the time about how close that government was to the evangelical churches (Villeneuve 2008). In fact, all religious organizations seek to introduce their own standards into the apparatus of the state (Ben Saad 2016). Religious organizations, especially the most determined among them, can only view Canada's extreme benevolence towards them with satisfaction.

Encouraging Fundamentalists

As jurist Pierre Bosset (2005), then director of research and strategic planning at the Commission des droits de la personne et des droits de la jeunesse (Quebec Human Rights and Youth Rights Commission), noted close to twenty years ago, there is no denying that certain militant religious groups are determined to have their specific character recognized and have therefore adopted a strategy of resorting to the courts. Moreover, an analysis of the complaints received by the commission shows that applicants seeking accommodation generally belong to the most orthodox currents, not to mention the fundamentalist movements, of the religious denominations to which they belong. The defenders of reasonable accommodation may claim that the obligation of reasonable accommodation and, therefore, the authorization to evade common norms leads to better social integration, but, actually, it "acts as a political legitimization of the fundamentalist group closing in on itself" (Eid 2009, 205). There is no reason to believe that the petitioners taking accommodation cases before the courts have a different personal profile from the applicants who have come before the Human Rights Commission.

Promoting Multiculturalism under the Guise of Protecting Religious Freedom

Religious freedom is defined so broadly in Canada that it has ended up reversing the spirit of the major international covenants on rights and freedoms.[22] Instead of freedom of religion being understood as a right stemming from freedom of conscience, Canadian jurisprudence has ensured that freedom of conscience is, on the contrary, subsumed under freedom of religion. Moreover, the courts too often consider as true religious practices or requirements what are actually cultural practices or requirements. In so doing, the courts end up offering protections to the latter that go well beyond what is required by these major international covenants (Milot 2008). This dual preference of the courts leads them to grant freedom of religion not only to devout individuals but also to ethno-confessional groups. As a result, Canadian institutions invoke religious freedom, whereas what they are really trying to do is promote multiculturalism.

The Supremacy of Special Interests as Promoted by the "Government of Judges" over the Common Good as Defined by Parliamentary Democracy

Certain ethno-confessional groups and religious organizations are not content with the sphere that governments and courts in Canada are willing to concede to them outright, however vast that sphere may be. In their desire to occupy more and more space in the public and political sphere, certain ethno-confessional groups present their political claims as claims for individual protection since this allows them greater access to the courts. Indeed, the judicial system seems more receptive than the parliamentary system to the advancement of their interests. But this process of judicialization undermines the mediation of opposing interests and the search for compromise on religious as well as other issues, which are both the hallmarks of politics (Lebel-Grenier 2009). Moreover, by chalking up gains of a constitutional nature from judges that they can then impose on legislators, these ethno-confessional groups and organizations succeed in evading the common will: their particular interests are endorsed by the courts and end up prevailing over the general interest of the population as expressed by universal suffrage and the legislative activity of parliaments (Mandel 1989; Manfredi 2001).

A Liberal Conception of Women's Equality Rights

During the twentieth century, feminists made strong demands for equality between men and women. They saw equality not as an end but, rather, as a means for women to gain access to freedom, defined as the accepted and recognized power to take decisions about one's own personal life and to co-define the rules of the social game. The struggles led by feminists changed society, and they also provided the foundation of sections on equality in the Quebec and Canadian Charters. Without entirely replacing this so-called universalist feminism, a new feminism has emerged in recent years. This so-called identity-based and particularist feminism redefines equality and freedom in a way that is quite congruent with liberal ideology: the right to equality is somehow merged with the right to freedom so that women's equality simply becomes their freedom to make individual choices (Lamoureux 2016).

The pursuit of equality as a means of acquiring freedom requires the active intervention of the state in order to create or help create the material and cultural conditions making it possible for women to free themselves from the traditional constraints that weigh particularly on them: pay equity laws, legal recognition of parental equality, penalty-free maternity leave, affordable childcare, and other measures of the state. However, the liberal identification of equality with individual freedom of choice makes it easier for the state to offload the responsibilities with which it has been charged by society and that it had recognized as its own during the welfare-state era. Thus, in the name of women's autonomy and individual preferences, Canada in the early twenty-first century, in good conscience, may be forgetting that some Canadian women are subject to more religious, cultural, and social pressures than others and that their "choices" are not always real choices as a result.

With respect to religious freedom, Bosset (2005, 91) writes that the country lacks "strategic thinking around the central issue of gender equality." This is also the recent opinion of a network of feminist groups published by the Canadian Centre for Policy Alternatives (2019). Lampron (2011, 403), for his part, notes that it seems "difficult, to say the least, to reconcile the current substantive primacy accorded to provisions protecting religious beliefs in Canadian law with the strong interventions of the Quebec legislator in recent years, the proven objective of which has been to strengthen the foundations of the right to equality between men and women within the broadest catalogue of rights and freedoms protected in Quebec." It will be important to monitor the courts' interpretation carefully, particularly given the suggestion made by the chief justice of the Quebec Court of Appeal, Nicole Duval Hesler, to opponents of Bill 21 that they invoke section 28 of the Canadian Charter as a defence and also given that this suggestion has been adopted in at least one court case.

English Canadian feminists wanted section 28 to be inserted into the Canadian Charter since it specifically recognizes that "notwithstanding anything in this Charter, the rights and freedoms referred to in it are guaranteed equally to male and female persons" and they were concerned about section 27 of the Canadian Charter, which states that any interpretation of the charter "shall be interpreted in a manner consistent with the preservation and enhancement of the multicultural heritage of Canadians" (Proulx 1988; Pelchat 2019). We know that equality for women is a long way off in any religion or culture and in some even less than in others. We also know that head coverings or face coverings worn by Muslim women are primarily cultural practices and, increasingly, are even claimed by some women as simply individual preferences (Emnus 2016; Fall 2019). Forty years later, it remains to be seen whether section 28 means that individual clothing preferences or certain cultural practices have become rights and that rights take precedence over the responsibility assumed by the Quebec state, in line with the will of the people, to promote the formal and substantive equality of women, regardless of their religious affiliation.

If It Turns Out Quebec's Refusal to Comply Is Illegal, Could It Nonetheless Be Considered Legitimate?

Canadian Model Fuels Tensions in Quebec

Starting in the 1960s, Quebec underwent a series of major socio-cultural changes that included the gradual withdrawal of many Quebeckers from the Catholic Church. However, this change did not immediately affect relations between religious organizations and the state, with the possible exception in the fields of health and social services, which became secularized at the same time that they became public. For the rest of the province, very little has changed – for example, the state has continued to recognize the role of religious organizations as civil registrars, and the confessional nature of the public school system was enshrined. In fact, if there was any change, it was along the lines of strengthening the ties between the Quebec state and the religious denominations. Not only did public funding of private schools increase, but it was also extended to ethno-confessional schools of religious minorities. The Quebec state also agreed to fund 100 percent of the Jewish health and social services network, which refused all adjustments proposed in order to integrate it into the new Quebec-wide public structure.

The effects of the secularization of Quebec culture only gradually began to be felt. For example, in the early 1980s, with the exception of marriage, the functions of the civil registrar were withdrawn from religious organizations. And, at the end of the twentieth century, a constitutional amendment made it possible to de-confessionalize the school system. In 1999, the Proulx report recommended replacing denominational religious education with a course in the cultural teaching of religions, and this recommendation was implemented in 2008. In other words, since the Quiet Revolution, Quebec has established its own new model for regulating religion: the state wanted to distance the educational structures and pedagogical content from Christian normativity and to treat all religions equally and with benevolence (Ferretti 2010, 2011). The way this was done and the results obtained were virtually unopposed in Quebec for almost forty years.

Since the 1990s, however, and especially in the 2000s, we have witnessed the increase of demands from religious groups seeking to take up greater visibility in the public sphere or to adapt this public sphere to their own religious norms. Consider, for instance, the case of the frosted windows in a Montreal YMCA; the repeated violations, justified on religious grounds, of the parking code of the city of Outremont; the episode where ambulance drivers were expelled from the kosher cafeteria of a hospital; the refusal of a woman to take her driving test with an examiner of the opposite sex; and a young soccer player wearing a hijab (Tremblay and Cherblanc 2019). Sometimes individuals have gone all the way to court to challenge the Quebec model of managing religion. Under the Quebec model, the state provides financial support to faith-based organizations well beyond what is done elsewhere in Canada. Moreover, this model requires everyone to voluntarily restrain their religious claims and displays of their religious affiliation in public schools and in their interactions with the state; however, this is something these plaintiffs have refused to do. The opponents of the Quebec consensus on secularism have benefited from the financial support of special interest groups with the wherewithal to sustain lengthy legal battles, and they have found an unwavering ally in the Supreme Court of Canada.

The Supreme Court of Canada has made no bones about overturning several decisions of the Quebec Superior Court and the Quebec Court of Appeal in order to impose its own vision of religious freedom and its definition of "reasonable accommodation" and to promote, at all costs, the Canadian goal of multiculturalism. It has also undermined the opinion of Supreme Court justices from Quebec to the extent that they have often dissented in judgments.[23] In the early 2000s, Quebec justices on the Supreme Court even sometimes criticized their colleagues for misrepresenting the Quebec Charter to invalidate court of appeal judgments (Rousseau Houle 2016). The majority judgments of the Supreme Court have thus resolutely set aside Quebec's vision of religion and of the religious neutrality of the state (Grammond 2009). The result has been that the Supreme Court has helped to break down a consensus that has held for forty years, has aggravated the issue of reasonable accommodation, and has inflamed the public debate. The Supreme Court is thus a factor of tension in the contemporary relationship between Quebeckers and religion (Lampron 2011).

Canada's highest court has come to realize that the frequent dissent of its Quebec judges and the repeated reversals of court of appeal rulings are causing it to lose credibility in Quebec. Yet its response has not been to take better account of the Quebec model but, rather, to coalesce around the Canadian model (Bosset 2018). Supreme Court justices from Quebec have fallen in line, but how can this attitude be explained: "The act of handing down court decisions has become a political act, particularly since the advent of charters. [One can no longer deny] the participation of legal decisions in the debates that animate and mark out the public sphere, that is, the political sphere" (Rousseau Houle 2016, 238). Even though the democratic legitimacy of the "government of judges" is an institution of the rule of law, and has been strengthened by the Constitution Act, 1982, it is nonetheless weak, even in English Canada.[24] After all, why exactly would the "government of judges" be deemed more legitimate than the government of parliamentarians elected by universal suffrage?

Under these conditions, jurist Andrée Lajoie (2000) suggests, the Supreme Court of Canada has no other options for consolidating its legitimacy and maintaining an appearance of fairness than to judge in a manner that is consistent with the values of the majority of the country's citizens – values that it also helps to shape. As Stéphane Bernatchez (2000) writes, the only way to argue that a government of judges is democratic is to change the definition of democracy. Until such time as that comes to pass, the Supreme Court derives democratic legitimacy solely from its general alignment with the English Canadian consensus or at least with the way in which English Canada wishes to see itself. That it has begun to take better account of the Quebec model of religious management could have been misunderstood in English Canada. The Supreme Court and the Quebec judges have had to choose between the court's legitimacy as an institution of the rule of law in English Canada and its credibility in Quebec. They have chosen, but not in a way that favours Quebec.

It is probably futile to make a case for the civil law tradition of Quebec or to ask Canadian courts, and particularly the Supreme Court of Canada, to show more restraint, more legal certainty, and more willingness to interpret the law in line with the will of the legislator while acting less as a law-creating institution of its own. At least in matters dealing with the relationship between the state and religious organizations, the Supreme Court has held to the common law tradition that guides judges in "making" the law (Lavoie 2016). It is probably just as futile to argue that in Quebec, perhaps because of its predominantly Catholic and now secularized culture, there is a tendency to entrust social cohesion and the organization of collective life, including the place of religion in the public and state sphere, to institutions rather than to individuals themselves: liberalism is based on a Protestant worldview that is now secularized as well and very much in evidence in the Canadian Charter (Gauthier 2017). When it comes to relations between the Quebec state and religious organizations, it seems as if Quebec has no right to be what it really is.

Quebec Is by No Means a Stakeholder in Upcoming Judicial Decisions

On the other side of the Atlantic, when cases are brought before the European Court of Human Rights, the court chooses judicial restraint. Out of respect for parliamentary sovereignty, for the history and culture of the European peoples, and for the institutions of each of the member states of the European Union, the court's overriding principle and practice is to allow member states a wide margin of appreciation in setting the parameters for their relations with religious individuals and organizations (European Court of Human Rights 2011, 2018, 2019; Barnett 2013). Nothing of the sort has happened in Canada.

The same activist strategy deployed by the Supreme Court of Canada to impose the Canadian model of management of religion on Quebec was deployed during the 1980s in another crucial area of Quebec society's collective life and social cohesion – namely, the defence of the French language. In dismembering Bill 101, the Supreme Court had at its disposal section 23 of the Canadian Charter, precisely because section 23 was designed to address Quebec language legislation (Proulx 1985). The Supreme Court has most often, if not always, spoken with one voice on language in this legislation (Choudhry 2013). Clearly, Quebec's special character is very poorly tolerated by the highest court in the land (Grammond 2009).

Let us stop here, but not before making a few remarks. Canada's courts are the least federal of all the country's federal institutions (Brouillet 2011): the judges who will render decisions about Bill 21 in the Quebec Superior Court, the Federal Court of Appeal, and the Supreme Court of Canada have all been appointed solely by the federal government. The Canadian Charter and the Constitution Act, 1982 were imposed on Quebec, which has still not signed it forty years later. There is nothing in the Canadian Charter or the Constitution that recognizes the country's plurinational reality or Quebec's cultural distinctiveness (Guénette 2016). Under these circumstances, why exactly should Quebec submit to the decisions of Canadian courts? Why exactly should it accept that these courts once again invalidate the legitimacy of the Quebec state to align with Quebec society and to represent its aspirations? Can we still speak of the rule of law when the application of this rule of law to Quebec appears to have so little concern for democracy?

Notes

1 Act Respecting the Laicity of the State, SQ 2019, c. 12.

2 International Covenant on Civil and Political Rights, 1966, 999 UNTS 171 (ICCPR). Notably, the issue of the wearing of religious symbols or head coverings by government employees is not addressed. See United Nations Human Rights Committee, *General Comment no. 22 on Article 18 of the Covenant,* Doc.CCPR/Ch1/Rev.r/Add. 4, July 20, 1993, para. 4.

3 Act to Foster Adherence to State Religious Neutrality and, in Particular, to Provide a Framework for Requests for Accommodations on Religious Grounds in Certain Bodies, SQ 2017, c. 19.

4 Charter of Human Rights and Freedoms, RSQ 1977, c. C-12.

5 Canadian Charter of Rights and Freedoms, Part 1 of the Constitution Act, 1982, being Schedule B to the Canada Act 1982 (UK), 1982, c. 11 (Canadian Charter).

6 Bill 94, An Act to Establish Guidelines for Requests for Accommodation within the Administration and Certain Institutions, 2010, which was introduced during the 39th Legislature, 1st Session and was reinstated during the 39th Legislature, 2nd Session on February 24, 2011 (Kathleen Weil, Minister of Justice).

7 Bill 60, Charter Affirming the Values of State Secularism and Religious Neutrality and of Equality between Women and Men, and Providing a Framework for Accommodation Requests, November 7, 2013, which was introduced during the 40th Legislature, 1st Session (Bernard Drainville, Minister responsible for Democratic Institutions and Active Citizenship).

8 Quebec Superior Court, *Application for Judicial Review (Declaration of Invalidity and Application for an Interim Stay),* File no. 500–17–108353–17, June 17, 2019.

9 Act Respecting the Ministère du Conseil exécutif, SQ, c. M-30.

10 Quebec Act 1774 (UK), 14 Geo. III, c. 83.

11 ICCPR; Convention for the Protection of Human Rights and Fundamental Freedoms 1950, 213 UNTS 222.

12 Lord's Day Act, RSC 1970, c. L-13.

13 See *Syndicat Northcrest v Amselem,* [2004] 2 SCR 551 (*Amselem*).

14 *R. v Big Drug Mart,* [1985] 1 SCR 295.

15 Canadian Bill of Rights, SC 1960, c. 44.x

16 *Commission scolaire régionale de Chambly v Bergevin,* [1994] 2 SCR 525 (*Bergevin*).

17 *Trinity Western University v British Columbia College of Teachers,* [2001] 1 SCR 772.

18 On the other hand, in 2018, the same court ruled that Trinity Western College's regulation prohibiting students from having sex outside of heterosexual marriage discriminated against lesbian, gay, bisexual, and transgender people. Accordingly, it granted the request of the Law Society of two provinces not to issue licenses to practise to its law graduates (*Radio-Canada* 2018). In other words, the graduates were penalized because of their university's regulations. These two judgments on Trinity Western College and the other two on the ethics and religious culture course illustrate the point made by legal scholars who note the lesser legal security in common law than in civil law (Lavoie 2016). Litigants may have the impression that the personal values and opinions of common law judges – their practice of "judge-made law" rather than primarily interpreting the law – play a role in the judgments rendered.

19 Canadian Charter, section 2(a).

20 "According to biblical law, a married couple is only released from the matrimonial bond through the transmission of a divorce document given by the husband to

the wife. This document, commonly called by its Aramaic name 'get' is more than proof of the dissolution of the marriage ... it is what effects the divorce. Although Jewish law requires that one follow the law of the land, and thus also implies the need for a civil divorce, the latter is no substitute for a halakhic (i.e., Jewish law-compliant) get. Without a get, even if a couple has been separated for a long time and dozens of civil documents have been drawn up regarding their divorce, in the eyes of Jewish law, they remain 100% married." "Le divorce juif en bref," *Chabad*, https://fr.chabad.org/.

21 *Bruker v Marcovitz*, [2007] 3 SCR 607 (*Bruker*).

22 International Covenant on Civil and Political Rights, 1966, 999 UNTS 171; International Covenant on Economic, Social and Cultural Rights, 1966, 993 UNTS 3.

23 See *Bruker*; see also *Bergevin; Anselem*.

24 Constitution Act, 1982, Schedule B to the Canada Act 1982 (UK), c. 11.

References

Astengo, Francesco. 2008. "Commentaire d'arrêt. Liberté de religion ou égalité entre les sexes? La Cour suprême du Canada se prononce sur un cas de divorce." *Revue de droit de l'Université de Sherbrooke* 39: 507–10. https://canlii.ca/t/2s1k.

Barnett, Laura. 2013. *Freedom of Religion and Religious Signs in the Public Sphere*. Research publication no. 2011–60-F. 2nd rev. ed. Ottawa: Library of Parliament. https://publications.gc.ca/collections/collection_2013/bdp-lop/bp/2011-60-1-eng.pdf.

Baubérot, Jean. 2009. "Liberté, laïcité, diversité; la France multiculturelle." In *Appartenances religieuses, appartenance citoyenne. Un équilibre en tension*, edited by Eid et al., 13–27. Quebec City: Les Presses de l'Université Laval.

Ben Saad, Safa. 2016. "Quelle analyse juridique de la religion?" *Droit-Inc*, February 12. https://www.droit-inc.com/article17177-Quelle-analyse-juridique-de-la-religion.

Bernatchez, Stéphane. 2000. "La controverse doctrinale sur la légitimité du juge constitutionnel canadien." *Politique et sociétés* 19 (2–3): 89–113.

Bosset, Pierre. 2005. "Le droit et la régulation de la diversité religieuse en France et au Québec: une même problématique, deux approches." *Bulletin d'histoire politique* 13 (3): 79–95.

–. 2018. "La neutralité de l'État en matière religieuse: méandres d'une notion." *Revue juridique Thémis* 51 (2–3): 305–35. https://canlii.ca/t/x9fz.

Bouchard, Gérard, and Charles Taylor. 2008. *Building the Future. A Time for Reconciliation*. Quebec City: Commission de consultation sur les pratiques d'accommodement reliées aux différences culturelles. https://numerique.banq.qc.ca/patrimoine/details/52327/1565995.

Brouillet, Eugénie. 2011. "La légitimité fédérative du processus de nomination des juges à la Cour suprême du Canada." *Revue générale de droit* 41 (1): 279–93.

Canadian Centre for Policy Alternatives. 2019. *Travail inachevé: Un rapport parallèle sur la mise en œuvre de la Déclaration et du Programme d'action de Beijing*. Ottawa: Canadian Centre for Policy Alternatives. http://www.policyalternatives.ca.

Choudhry, Sujit. 2013. "Rights Adjudication in a Plurinational State: The Supreme Court of Canada, Freedom of Religion, and the Politics of Reasonable Accommodation." *Osgoode Hall Law Journal* 50 (3): 575–608. https://digitalcommons.osgoode.yorku.ca/ohlj/vol50/iss3/5.

Eid, Paul. 2009. "La ferveur religieuse et les demandes d'accommodement religieux. Une comparaison intergroupe." In *Appartenances religieuses, appartenance citoyenne. Un équilibre en tension*, edited by Eid et al., 283–323. Quebec City: Les Presses de l'Université Laval.

Eid Paul, Pierre Bosset, Micheline Milot, and Sébastien Lebel-Grenier, eds. 2009. *Appartenances religieuses, appartenance citoyenne. Un équilibre en tension*. Quebec City: Les Presses de l'Université Laval.

Emnus (alias). 2016. "Ma réponse aux quatorze arguments les plus courants contre le voile." *Lällab Magazine*, December 20. https://www.lallab.org/ma-reponse-aux-14-arguments-les-plus-courants-contre-le-voile/.

European Court of Human Rights. 2011. *Aperçu de la jurisprudence de la Cour en matière de liberté de religion*. Strasbourg, France: European Council/European Court of Human Rights. January. https://www.refworld.org/pdfid/4ee0f4452.pdf.

–. 2018. *Factsheet: Religious Symbols and Clothing*. December. https://www.echr.coe.int/documents/fs_religious_symbols_eng.pdf.

–. 2019. *Factsheet: Freedom of Religion*. October. https://www.echr.coe.int/documents/fs_freedom_religion_eng.pdf.

Fall, Khadiyatoulah. 2019. "Le voile islamique: mieux comprendre pour agir." *Le Soleil*, April 17.

Ferretti, Lucia. 2010. "Les relations entre les organisations religieuses et l'État au Québec: vers une reconfiguration de leur régime d'association." In *Modernité et religion au Québec. Où en sommes-nous*, edited by Robert Mager and Serge Cantin, 239–52. Quebec City: Presses de l'Université Laval.

–. 2011. "L'État québécois et les organisations religieuses sous la Révolution tranquille: continuités et changements." *Possibles* 35 (1): 44–52. http://classiques.uqac.ca/contemporains/ferretti_lucia/Etat_qc_organisations_religieuses_Rev_tranquille/Etat_qc_texte.html.

Gauthier, François. 2017. "Républicanisme vs libéralisme. Les régimes de laïcité et leur mise à l'épreuve." *Revue du Mouvement anti-utilitariste dans les sciences sociales* 49 (1): 269–90. https://www.cairn.info/revue-du-mauss-2017-1-page-269.htm.

Globe and Mail. 2019. "Editorial." October 28.

Grammond, Sébastien. 2009. "Conception canadienne et québécoise des droits fondamentaux et de la religion: convergence ou conflit?" *Revue juridique Thémis* 43 (1): 83–108.

–. 2016. "Louis LeBel et la société distincte." *Les Cahiers de droit* 57 (2): 251–67. https://doi-org.biblioproxy.uqtr.ca/10.7202/1036484ar.

Guénette, Dave. 2016. "La Cour suprême du Canada et la pluralité démotique de l'État canadien. Des traces de consociationalisme dans la jurisprudence constitutionnelle." *Revue générale de droit* 46 (1): 215–52.

Journal de Montréal. 2013. "Signes religieux interdits. Charles Taylor fait un parallèle avec la Russie de Vladimir Poutine." August 20.

–. 2018. "Deux prédicateurs mormons canadiens assignés à résidence pour polygamie." June 26.

Journal de Quebec. 2020. "Décevante récupération politique." January 31.

Lajoie, Andrée. 2000. "La primauté du droit et la légitimité démocratique comme enjeux du Renvoi sur la sécession du Québec." *Politique et Sociétés* 19 (2–3): 31–41.

Lamoureux, Diane. 2016. *Les possibles du féminisme. Agir sans "nous."* Montreal: Éditions du Remue-ménage.

Lampron, Louis-Philippe. 2011. "L'existence d'une hiérarchie juridique favorisant la protection des convictions religieuses au sein des droits fondamentaux canadiens." PhD diss., Université Laval / Université d'Avignon et des Pays de Vaucluse.

Langevin, Louise, Louis-Philippe Lampron, Christelle Landheer-Cieslak, Alain Prujiner, and Patrick Taillon. 2008. "L'affaire *x*: variations sur un thème." *Les Cahiers de droit* 49 (4): 655–708.

Lavoie, Bertrand. 2016. "La tension sociojuridique entre laïcité et multiculturalisme: le bijuridisme comme clé de compréhension des débats québécois sur le rapport entre le droit et la religion." *Recherches sociographiques* 57 (2–3): 333–49.

Lebel-Grenier, Sébastien. 2009. "La religion comme véhicule d'affirmation identitaire: un défi à la logique des droits fondamentaux." In Eid et al. 2009, 123–39.

Le Devoir. 2008. "Ouvrez-vous! Et fermez-la!" May 23.

–. 2010. "Accommodements dans l'administration publique: Le projet de loi soulève des craintes de racisme." May 20.

–. 2012. "La Cour suprême déboute les parents." February 18.

–. 2013. "Fournier se défend d'avoir tissé un lien entre la charte et le nazisme." November 13.

–. 2017. "L'Esprit de l'ours grizzly' débouté en Cour suprême." November 2.

–. 2019. "Une coalition appelle à la mobilisation contre le projet de loi sur la laïcité." April 4.

–. 2020. "Les camionneurs sikhs devront porter le casque au port de Montréal." April 30.

Le Monde. 2019. "Canada: la laïcité à la québécoise critiquée par les autres provinces." December 16.

Le Nouvelliste. 2019. "La demande oubliée." September 18.

La Presse. 2015. "Cours d'éthique religieuse: l'école Loyola a gain de cause en Cour suprême." March 19.

–. 2017. "La loi 62 attaquée dans le reste du Canada." October 20.

–. 2019. "Une plainte contre la juge en chef de la Cour d'appel." December 2.

–. 2020. "Trois instances internationales font part de leurs inquiétudes à Ottawa." February 6.

Lévesque, Gérard. 2019. *La laïcité en harmonie avec la liberté religieuse*. Montreal: Liber.

Mandel, Michaël. 1989. *The Charter of Rights and the Legalization of Politics in Canada*. Toronto: Wall and Thompson.

Manfredi, Christopher. 2001. *Judicial Power and the Charter: Canada and the Paradox of Liberal Constitutionalism*, 2nd rev. ed. New York: Oxford University Press.

Milot, Jean-René. 2008. "La polygamie au nom de la religion au Canada: L'islam est-il en cause?" *Cahiers de recherche sociologique* 46: 123–33.

National Post. 2012. "J.L. Granatstein: How a Separate Quebec Would Transform Our Defence Policy." September 7.

Ontario Human Rights Commission. 2012. *Creed Case Law Review*. May. https://www.ohrc.on.ca/en/creed-case-law-review

Pelchat, Christiane. 2019. *Projet de loi n° 21. Loi sur la laïcité de l'État.* May 9. https://www.assnat.qc.ca/fr/video-audio/archives-parlementaires/travaux-commissions/AudioVideo-80369.html.

Proulx, Daniel. 1985. "La Loi 101, la clause-Québec et la Charte canadienne devant la Cour suprême: un cas d'espèce?" *Revue générale de droit* 16 (1): 167–93.

–. 1988. "L'objet des droits constitutionnels à l'égalité." *Les Cahiers de droit* 29 (3): 567–98.

Radio-Canada. 2018. "L'université chrétienne Trinity Western perd la lutte pour son école de droit." June 15.

–. 2019a. "'Nettoyage ethnique': pressé de s'excuser, le maire de Hampstead en rajoute." April 9.

–. 2019b. "Laïcité: les élus à Queen's Park réclament l'abrogation de la loi 21." November 25.

–. 2020. "Loi 21: la conférence de l'Association Lord Reading reportée pour une deuxième fois." January 24.

Rousseau, Guillaume, et al. 2020. *Loi sur la laïcité de l'État commentée et annotée: philosophie, genèse, interprétation et application*. Sherbrooke: Éditions Revue de droit de l'Université de Sherbrooke.

Rousseau Houle, Thérèse. 2016. "L'art de juger: sources et méthodologie. Ce que révèle l'œuvre du juge LeBel." *Les Cahiers de droit* 57 (2): 231–50.

Seljak, David. 2012. *Protecting Religious Freedom in a Multicultural Canada*. Toronto: Ontario Human Rights Commission. https://www.ohrc.on.ca/en/creed-freedom-religion-and-human-rights-special-issue-diversity-magazine-volume-93-summer-2012/protecting-religious-freedom-multicultural-canada.

Selley, Chris. 2019a. "Why Isn't 'Unthinkable' Quebec's Religious Symbols Ban a Federal Election Issue?" *National Post*, August 28.

–. 2019b. "Latest Trial Balloon from Quebec Is Another Attack on Minority Rights." *National Post,* November 6.

Tremblay, Stéphanie, and Jacques Cherblanc. 2019. "Aux frontières de la nation: les trois temps de la laïcité québécoise." *Studies in Religion / Sciences religieuses* (October): 528–52. https://doi.org/10.1177/0008429819872974.

Villeneuve, Hubert. 2008. "Analyse et réflexion sur la présence évangélique contemporaine dans la sphère sociale et politique au Canada." *Bulletin d'histoire politique* 16 (3): 183–98.

Walker, Julian. 2015. *Mouvement laïque québécois v Saguenay (City): Freedom of Religion and the State's Duty of Neutrality*. Ottawa: Research publications program, Library of Parliament of Canada. May 12. https://scc-csc.lexum.com/scc-csc/scc-csc/en/item/15288/index.do.

Part 2
Historical and Sociological Perspectives

3

Quebec

Under the Rule of Its Two Cities

MARC CHEVRIER

The title of this chapter refers to the two cities depicted by Saint Augustine in *The City of God* – namely, the heavenly city of love and the earthly city of pride. People often forget that these two cities did not set the church against Rome or spiritual power against political authority at a given moment in time. In fact, they were two ideal cities, each of them driven by its own principle and movement. No matter how much these two cities were projected into the Platonic world of ideas, the two cities ultimately came down to the human world and took concrete historical forms, either in the form of a church ready to govern political society or at least to organize it or in the form of a secular power intruding on the church's affairs. Quebec has not escaped this great political-theological dilemma, and I propose to study two key moments. In addition, I will focus my attention on the nature of the other city – the political one – which seeks to circumscribe religions, without having to favour any single religion, by means of the debates arising from the Act Respecting the Laicity of the State (Bill 21).[1]

The Church, a Political Form for Human Government

Rather than engaging in a critique of clericalism, I propose to consider the church politically – that is, to understand it as a true human association within which believers govern themselves in dealing with both secular and spiritual matters. In the course of history, the church has taken on the form of a government by turns competing with, complementing, and negating civil government, without succeeding in replacing it. This government of the church has directed the religious society that it founded, which was superimposed on a civil society politically governed by weak or powerful secular powers, depending on the prevailing conditions at the time. In this sense, no matter how far the church has gone in governing the human world, it has always needed a civil power deploying its own resources to elevate the church, recognize it, tolerate it, and support it. In short, the religious society governed by the church has never succeeded in totally absorbing political society.

Two authors will guide the present reflection: the historian François Guizot, a leading figure of French liberalism at the beginning of the nineteenth century, and the contemporary philosopher Pierre Manent, who has renewed political thought in recent years with his theory of political forms. Manent owes much to Guizot in the formulation of this theory, which has the original feature of trying to outline a grammar of political forms, while including, along with the empire, the city, and the nation, the church, whose appearance in history has profoundly disturbed ancient forms such as the city and the empire and has long prevented the formation of a stable civil power in Europe. Indeed, Europe has only emerged from this historical dead-end by creating a new form that is midway between the city and the empire and able to stand up to the church – namely, the nation (Manent 2001, ch. 2, 4, 5; Chevrier 2019, ch. 16).

During his masterclasses at the Sorbonne between 1828 and 1830, Guizot (1985) established that the Christian church, which reigned triumphant between the fifth and twelfth centuries in Europe, presented the characteristics of a government of its own. The church was placed at the head of an "independent and strongly constituted society, interposed between the sovereigns or masters of the world who wielded temporal power, on the one hand, and the people, on the other hand. Indeed, the church served as a link between sovereigns and subjects and acted on all of them" (132). In this sense, the church can be understood as a true principle of association, whereas many people in Guizot's time, and probably still nowadays, persist in seeing religion as the simple expression of an individual feeling of a "fluid and questionable" nature. According to Guizot, the church brought men together "bound by common religious precepts" in creating a community led by an educated elite (135). Guizot was convinced that the church, in the same way as civil government, but without resorting to force, could "discover the truth which has the right to govern society, and then introduce this truth into people's minds and have them adopt it voluntarily and freely" (137). According to Guizot, government was a matter of intelligence and discernment rather than of military coaction – hence, the crucial role played by an intellectually gifted elite, capable of solving "the challenges of human destiny" (138).

Over time, however, two other principles had the effect of undermining the church, causing it to exceed the limits of its competencies. The first was "the denial of the rights of individual reason," by which the church claimed that faith was handed down to the faithful from above. The second was the right of constraint – of "coaction" that the church had arrogated to itself – by transforming itself into a judicial body enforcing morality in the name of a code of sins. However, Guizot was observing the church from the outside, without inquiring into how it understood itself. Manent (2010) points out that the church does not see itself as an association forming a part of, and inserted into, a larger, all-encompassing community, guaranteed by the state. On the contrary, the church sees itself "as a complete society with its own principle and whose purpose infinitely outweighs that of any other society – the Church sees itself as the *respublica perfecta* whose independence is not merely functional but ontological, and which therefore cannot be subordinated to any other body, including the secular State" (283). This quote summarizes the church's historical position with respect to secular power; it also reveals the church's fundamentally political nature.

A Catholic City of Public Law in America

In Canada, the most radical elements of the church – particularly, the ultramontane fringe – characterizes the church as a complete society divinely constituted to govern and even to exercise all powers over men. As Abbé Louis-François Laflèche (1866, 15) wrote in 1866, "the Pope, the bishops and all priests under their guidance know and teach that they are divinely entrusted with the government of the kingdom of God in this world, and are responsible for the souls of all those entrusted to them." Writing in the *Revue Canadienne* in 1871, the lawyer François-Xavier Anselme Trudel (1871) attacked liberal Gallicanism, which had been condemned by Pope Pius IX. Trudel defended the fundamental rights of the church, upholding its nature as a "true and perfect" society, possessing sovereignty, independence, and freedom: "Based on the principle that the Church is endowed with sovereign authority and complete independence from all civil power ... it necessarily follows that the Church possesses the sovereign power to govern, to legislate and to judge. Without the perfect exercise of these three powers, namely the administrative, legislative and judicial, no society is possible" (218). Monseigneur Louis-Adolphe Paquet, a theologian at Laval University, even quarrelled with Guizot in claiming that the church was endowed with its own fundamental public law. He criticized Guizot for recognizing that the church only constituted a society starting in the fourth century. For Paquet (1916, 59), the church had from the very day of its foundation the "characteristic features of a society properly so called: namely a multitude gathered together, a common end, identical means, a legally constituted authority: nothing was missing."

But these claims regarding the universal sovereignty of the church in Canadian lands risk misleading us as to the real status that the church acquired following the British Conquest. In actual fact, the real church turned out to be far less powerful than ultramontane supporters would have people believe. The church was itself subject to political domination. There was never a theocracy in Canada, either during New France or during British rule, although the church certainly enjoyed a privileged status that gave it considerable influence and pre-eminence over its followers.[2] The church was a religious city competing with the civil city, formed and grafted onto the civil city on which it depended for its survival. Some authors have even evoked the construction in Quebec or French Canada of a "Christendom" (Arès 1981; Ferretti 1999, 67–79). This term is usually applied to socio-political forms emerging from periods experiencing the narrow unity of politics and religion, such as after the time of Constantine in Rome or from Charlemagne onwards

(Maldamé 2018, 61–66). However, the Catholic city built in French Canada and subsequently in Quebec proved to be neither complete, as the ultramontanes would have preferred, nor universal, since it was limited to Catholics alone, who were imperfectly united among themselves. And the church was not born alone since the secular power contributed to its impetus, even if that meant assigning the church a precise place within the state or within society.

This dual construction began as early as the time of New France. In 1663, the French Gallican monarchy integrated the church into the colonial government by means of the Sovereign Council. The founders of New France may have been mystics who nourished dreams of theocracy, but it was the administrative law of the French kingdom that authorized or ratified the system of parishes that crisscrossed settled territory. In 1679, a royal edict established tithes payable to the parish priest, while making *seigneurs* and inhabitants responsible for the construction and maintenance of presbyteries and cemeteries (Lareau 1888, 429–30). In 1722, a civil regulation delineated the boundaries of the parishes. Throughout New France, a dual system of government was established, and this system had both civil and Catholic dimensions. In a treatise on ecclesiastical law, Justice Joseph Ubalde Baudry (1870, 26) described these two closely intertwined cities in terms that merged the parish with the seigneury:

> For civil purposes, the district was in fact the parish. The particular *seigneurs*, who had succeeded to the obligations of the first companies, were obliged to provide religious assistance to their inhabitants or *censitaires*, and almost everywhere the limits of the parish were the same as those of the seigneury. The *seigneur* in this district was the military commander; he had the right to administer justice and to appoint the judges and the clerk, as well as the officers of the road system. The inhabitants of each seigneury thus formed a community which, by law, was represented by churchwardens for the purposes of worship and by the *seigneur* or by a trustee for temporal matters.

The whole system was based on accepting "the intervention of the civil authority ... for the erection of parishes and the delineation of their boundaries" (Baudry 1870, 26). The British Conquest destroyed the French colonial state but preserved these two institutions – the parish and the seigneury – around which revolved the social life of the new subjects of his British majesty, to whom the capitulations and the 1763 Treaty of Paris conceded the free exercise of their Catholic faith "in so far as the laws of Great Britain permit it."[3] This was simple tolerance that a Protestant conqueror deigned to accord to his new Catholic subjects. British rule did little to undo the duplication of local government, civil and ecclesiastical. Indeed, it would eventually give its *imprimatur* to this duplication and even a new lease on life. The British authorities certainly tried to gain control of the Catholic hierarchy and the civil erection of parishes in the colony; they did not hesitate to seize the property of the Jesuits, and to try to induce the young generation to become Protestant by osmosis, in establishing schools by means of the Royal Institution of 1801.

As early as 1793, King George III created an Anglican diocese in Quebec City; the Anglican bishop had the privilege of being a member of the Legislative Council in Lower and Upper Canada (Lareau 1889, 436). However, the war of 1812–15 against the United States and the representations of Monseigneur Plessis (who went all the way to London to defend the rights of the church) convinced the British government to set aside the spiritual supremacy that the Quebec Act of 1774 had accorded to the king over Catholic worship (Walsh 1958, 370). As a result, Plessis received an increase in salary, an appointment to the Legislative Council, and the official title of bishop (Ferretti 1999, 41–43). According to historian Michel Brunet (1969, 48), "the first steps" in the new alliance between the church and the colonial power were taken thanks to the intense legislative work of the "Special Council for Lower Canada" and the help it gave to the church's educational and hospital institutions.

Indeed, the Special Council governed Lower Canada under an exceptional regime for nearly thirty-three months following the Rebellions of 1837–38 – rebellions that John Stuart Mill saw as a failed war of liberation. The Special Council adopted the ordinances needed to create this new alliance and displayed the characteristic features of a constitutional dictatorship by concentrating in the hands of the governor and Council members the sovereignty delegated by London over the constitutionally dissolved Lower Canada (Chevrier 2019, ch. 10). This government by committee was small in numbers. It only included about twenty people hand-picked by successive governors, of whom Lord Durham was the most illustrious. It began each sitting with a prayer to the glory of God, Her Majesty, and the empire (Perrault 1943, 12). This dictatorship transformed the diocese of Montreal into a civil corporation,[4] confirmed Sulpician ownership of its property, constituted as legal persons all existing parishes, missions, or societies of Christians, and also confirmed rights to their property. Similarly, the dictatorship provided the colony under trusteeship with a more comprehensive law on parish *fabriques*[5] than the one previously passed by the Assembly of Lower Canada in 1831: this new law covered the future civil erections of parishes and did not merely serve to ratify parishes that the church had already established on its own (Lareau 1889, 443–45). As a result, this ordinance on fabriques shaped Quebec public law governing parishes during the Act of Union (creating the Province of Canada in 1841) and long after the Canadian Confederation of 1867 (Perrault 1943). From then on, parishes provided the basic unit of "the entire administration of the country, both religious and secular" (Baudry 1870, 28), which is what Gilles Leclerc (2002, 283) referred to as "the marriage of Priesthood and Empire."[6]

The dual character of the cities in French Canada can be seen in the dualities ordering each of these cities as well as in their mutual relations. Thus, the entities of the Catholic city generally followed the principle of the dual institution. By this means, the church started by constituting its corporations, orders, and other entities; most often, civil law then intervened to validate what the church had established by decree. This dual institution resorted to two systems of law at the same time: canon law, which predefined religious bodies and decisions of the clergy, and the civil and political law of the state, which gave it effect in its juridical order before the courts by means of certain obligations, such as the payment of tithes. The dual institution governed by two laws led to a dual civil membership for Catholics. They were both citizens of the civil city, which granted them, like all other citizens, rights and prescribed obligations, and they were citizens of the other city, particularly as parishioners exercising their prerogatives and responsibilities through parish assemblies. This second citizenship was for men "who owned property on the territory of the parish" (Baudry 1870, 63).

According to Guizot (1985, 140), throughout its history, the church made appointments based on two principles: first, "by means of the election of the inferior by the superior, choice, nomination" and, second, "by means of the election of the superior by the subordinates, or of an election itself, as we conceive it today." These two principles had been combined and fought over throughout the history of the church; however, as Guizot noted, the first principle had prevailed over the second. Quebec was no exception in this regard; the civil power allowed Rome to exercise its power over the appointment of the high clergy, bishops, and cardinals and over the institution of monastic orders and higher educational establishments, universities, and seminaries.[7] But within the parishes and even within the congregations, there was a form of democracy, whereby parishioners elected each other to occupy positions in the administration of the parish, and members of the congregations chose their superiors from among themselves (Roy 1950).

This system also brought together a territoriality partly dependent on the law of the church, which subdivided its circumscriptions into provinces and parishes, as well as an extraterritoriality, which reflected the decisions of the Holy See in Lower Canada and then in Quebec after 1867. The Holy See conducted a genuine foreign policy that was concerned with protecting American and British interests in North America and was seeking to reconcile the contradictory opinions of the high French Canadian clergy and the powerful Anglo-Saxon episcopates, while favouring the Anglo-Irish, assimilative vision of North American Catholicism (Perin 1993). In fact, from the outset, Rome did not recognize the Catholic Church of Quebec as a national church, preferring, at least towards the end of the nineteenth century, to consider it as part of the Catholic Church of England (Dumas 2019, 19). This is why the Catholic city became plurinational in Quebec, where parish law allowed for the possibility of erecting "national" or "linguistic" parishes for the exclusive use of particular ethnic or linguistic groups.[8] In fact, parish law reproduced the logic of imperial differentialism that undermined the territorial universalism of the church; in 1872, the Vatican itself, following pressure from the influential D'Arcy McGee, ordered the creation of a system of separate ethnic parishes for the benefit of the Irish in Montreal, and the Italians later took advantage of this precedent (Perin 1993, 47–48; Ferretti 1999, 76; Trigger 2001, 553–72).[9]

There can be no government without corresponding fiscal power. The Catholic city was financed, among other things, by tithes, payable by Catholics in Lower Canada and Quebec unless they formally abjured their Catholic faith or could demonstrate their adherence to the Protestant faith (Baudry 1870, 98). The Civil Code of Lower Canada treated tithes as a civil debt, enforceable before the courts and capable of encumbering a building with a legal servitude, just like municipal and school taxes. In addition, parishioners could order the levying of dues for the construction or renovation of buildings needed for worship. As soon as assessments were determined, they were binding on all parishioners domiciled in the parish. The system of parish dues lasted until the 1965 revision of the Act Respecting Fabriques, which limited the rights of contribution to the financing of outstanding debts, a partial system that ended in 1981 (Noppen and Morisset 2005, 75–77).[10]

In sum, until 1965, the parish resembled a parallel form of local government: it levied its own taxes in addition to civil levies. The governmental dimension of the parish is also reflected in the fact that it had long been empowered by law to establish schools within its territory, to which it could allocate one-quarter of its revenues (Baudry 1870, 269). Until the First World War, notes historian Lucia Ferretti (1992, 15), the state and the church considered assistance to the poor, health, and education to be "almost exclusively a parochial responsibility." In reality, the church, through the social and educational work of its congregations, offered a kind of public assistance coverage financed by charity and public subscriptions, which complemented the action of its parishes. It was not until the Taschereau government's adoption of the so-called Public Assistance Act in 1921 that the Quebec state itself supplemented, albeit timidly, the action of the congregations, which by then were overwhelmed by the needs of society (Ferretti 2011, 19).[11] The territorial framework of the parish, however, was more appropriate for the countryside than for the city. In reaching working-class and urban areas, the church relied on the work of Catholic Action movements, which accorded a greater place to the laity (Guindon 1999, 15).

In several published works up to the dawn of the Quiet Revolution, the parish was considered to be the primary unit of social life and thus took its place among normal local institutions, alongside municipalities and school boards, whose territory and sometimes whose names were based on those of the parishes.[12] In 1870, Justice Joseph Ubalde Baudry published a Code des Curés, marguilliers et paroissiens (Code of Priests, Churchwardens and Parishioners), and Hector Langevin (1863), a future key player in Canadian Confederation in 1867, preceded him in 1863 by bringing out a collection entitled Droit administratif ou manuel des paroisses et fabriques (Adminstrative Law or Manual of Parishes and Fabriques), which followed the customary designation under the French regime by considering the law governing religious corporations to be administrative law (Affre 1827).

The first major syntheses published on Canadian or Quebec law after 1867, such as those of Edmond Lareau (1888, 1889) and Simon Pagnuelo (1872), examined the relationship between the state and the church and the canonical and civil organization of parishes. Both clerics and lay jurists explored this relationship. A civics textbook published in 1907 for teachers who had graduated from normal school as well as their students placed the ecclesiastical organization of Quebec on the same level as administrative and political institutions (Magnan 1907). At the beginning of the twentieth century, the education of a Catholic schoolboy naturally included learning how a parish functioned and what the rights of the parish priest were. As late as 1957, Émile Morin (1957), former Quebec deputy minister of municipal affairs, wrote a booklet intended for the public service, explaining the workings of local Quebec institutions, including the religious and civil parish.

The Church in Quebec: Between Implicit Union with the State and an English-style Establishment

But how did these jurists represent the close intertwining of the two cities? Baudry provided a key to interpretation: this was a union of the two authorities – civil and Catholic – along the lines of what a *Concordat* signed directly with the Vatican would have been, were it not for the absence of diplomatic relations between Rome and London. It was a union by virtue of which the legislative power of Lower Canada, of United Canada, and then of Quebec, succeeding the French authority in regulating the temporal affairs of the church, continued to legislate on this matter, often at the request of the episcopate itself. As a result, wrote Baudry (1870, 5), "it may be said, by virtue of an agreement and a mutual deference by which, on the one hand, [that] the Church consents to this secular legislation, and on the other, [that] the civil authority protects the Catholic religion and assures it privileges and a particular preponderance." As Baudry observed, several provisions of the Civil Code of 1866 endorsed this implicit union. An order of the imperial authorities, probably adopted in July 1868, gave precedence in an official protocol to the archbishops and bishops, immediately after the representatives of the army and the monarchy but before members of the executive, judicial, and legislative branches.[13] In sum, this system received the civil blessing both of the imperial and Canadian authorities.

In many respects, this system of implicit union resembled that of an established church in the British sense of the term – that is, a church that the civil power recognized and to which it granted favoured treatment, even if that meant submitting it partially or completely dependent to the civil authority. In fact, the British concept of an established church is rather vague; the jurist François Borella (2008, 338) sees in "the establishment of a religion" a "formula very close to a State religion, but which avoids proclaiming that the State, a legal person without individual conscience, can be considered as professing a religion." The emerging status of the church in Canada was judged with this notion in mind. Chief Justice Jonathan Sewell, a strong proponent of the union of the two Canadas in 1822, criticized the Lower Canadian Catholic Church for its established character (Kennedy 1930, 243–44). One might think that with the passage of the Rectories Act in 1852 and another Act in 1854 on the abolition of the Protestant clergy reserves in the United Province of Canada, there would no longer be an established church in the colony.

However, these laws only liquidated the reserves that had been set aside for the use of the Protestant clergy and got rid of any appearance of an alliance between the state and the Anglican Church in United Canada.[14] They also left intact the entire legal system that had supported the growth of the Catholic city in Lower Canada, particularly since the ordinances of the Special Council. In the famous *Guibord* case, the Judicial Committee of the London Privy Council considered the possibility of the Catholic Church being an established church, while not making a final decision on the matter.[15] However, the members of the Imperial Court conceded two things: first, since the British Conquest, the Catholic Church had ceased to be established in the full sense of the word, although it continued to be recognized by the state, retaining its possessions and some of its enforceable rights under the law, and, second, in many respects, it differed substantially from voluntary religious associations, such as the Anglican Church in the colonies or the Catholic Church in England.

Many observers would later consider the Catholic Church in Quebec, in the form it took until at least the 1960s, as an established or semi-established church (Walsh 1958, 378; Ferretti 1999, 39–41).[16] Elsewhere in Canada, other churches also seem to have benefited from some form of establishment. A 1990 article in an Ontario law review argued that under section 93 of the Constitution Act, 1867 and section 29 of the Canadian Charter of Rights and Freedoms, which protects the rights of separate or denominational schools, the Catholic Church in Ontario enjoys a status equivalent to that of a semi-established church, in part because of the privileged status accorded to its schools.[17] And, since 1867, the Catholic religion has become the most practised in Ontario (Ogilvie 1990). The author also points out the established character of the Anglican Church in the Maritimes and the Catholic Church in Lower Canada, at least before 1867; indeed, the Anglican Church was established in Nova Scotia as early as 1758 but with the guarantee of freedom of conscience offered to dissenting Protestant denominations (Walsh 1958, 366). In short, the idea of the established church has taken several different forms. In the United Kingdom, the Scottish Presbyterian Church, also established alongside the Anglican Church, is considered to have retained a semi-established status, even after Westminster granted autonomy to the Scottish Presbyterian Church in 1921 (Munro 1997).

The Civil Organization of Religions: A Constitutional Jurisdiction Mainly Exercised by Quebec and the Other Provinces

Ultimately, the implicit concordant union between the Catholic Church and the civil powers of Quebec and Canada does not imply that they have merged together. The clergy may have celebrated in the Catholic city the idealized survival of a Middle Ages steeped in religious and political unity (Gingras 1880). However, the fact remains that Quebec, which achieved federated autonomy in 1867 under pressure from the British imperial city, also placed itself at the service of the leading Protestant denominations, which headed parallel religious societies. Quebec therefore granted them the legal facilities they needed, which stemmed, among other things, from the constitutional obligations that Quebec had to observe between 1867 and 1997 – obligations ensuring that Protestants had separate educational institutions, with distinct socio-religious institutions thereby removed from the orbit of the Catholic Church.[18]

Surprising as it may seem, once the imperial power had tried to "establish" the Anglican Church in the two Canadas, and then had changed its mind by abolishing the reserves for the maintenance of the Protestant clergy, Quebec took over from the imperial legislator and then from the Province of Canada (1841–67) in regulating the temporal affairs of the Protestant churches on its territory. Quebec adopted multiple public and private laws to confer legal personality on them, modifying their status and internal management, and authorizing their ministers to carry out civil acts.[19] Quebec also exercised jurisdiction over the Jewish faith, the Mennonites, other Christian churches such as the Greek Ruthenian Church, and the Muslim faith, mainly through private bills.[20] The other provinces followed the same path in regulating the temporal affairs of their churches and religious denominations – that is, conferring legal personality on their parishes, bishoprics, missions, and congregations, often determining the setting up of their religious entities and even their social vocation, regulating religious properties and lands, as well as empowering the ministers of religion to administer civil acts.[21] It can be seen that neither the Catholic Church, nor the Protestant churches, nor any other major religious denomination are in themselves all-encompassing legal entities; they exist civilly through a myriad of civil entities incorporated by the state, albeit under a common theological framework.

The multiplicity of churches legally incorporated by Quebec went hand in hand, at least until the Quiet Revolution, with the differentiation of the social action of these churches. The Catholic Church relied mainly on its congregations to provide assistance to its faithful through its hospitals, schools, reformatories, orphanages, hospices, and asylums, some of which became Anglicized to serve Catholics of Irish origin. Meanwhile the Protestant churches feared that their congregations would seek Catholic assistance and relied instead on the patronage of the Anglo-Montreal bourgeoisie and volunteer groups. As a result, by 1900, there were thirty-three Protestant social organizations other than hospitals, some of which targeted a specific ethnic community (Harvey 2003).

In short, this legislative overview shows that the civil organization of religions in Canada is mainly the responsibility of the provinces, much as in Germany and Switzerland, where it is the responsibility of the federated *Länder* (states or cantons). The constitutional scholar Gérald Beaudoin (1984, 595) could have been more precise in writing: "The public authorities also had to legislate in areas such as religious education, the *Act on Fabriques,* episcopal corporations, the non-taxation of land and dwellings used for worship, Roman Catholic cemeteries, etc." In fact, all these questions fell under the responsibility of the Quebec legislature. The other provinces adopted their own measures, with the federal Parliament playing only a marginal role, in particular, in incorporating, by private laws, religious entities that had given themselves a pan-Canadian or interprovincial legal superstructure. Canada is thus quite distinct from highly centralized federations such as Mexico, Argentina, and Austria, where the civil organization of religions is primarily the responsibility of the federal state.

Moving beyond Canada, we can see how Quebec is unique in America. Quebec has built a Catholic city through general laws, which give its religious corporations a status of public law. In the United States, many states have established a Protestant denomination, even after 1787, despite the adoption of the First Amendment prohibiting the establishment of religion. The US Supreme Court did not apply this amendment at the state level until 1947. For the most part, American states have moved away from the legal incorporation of churches by special executive or legislative acts to a general legislative regime of private law, which grants churches the status of associations or fiduciary corporations (Kauper and Ellis 1970). However, during the colonial period, Massachusetts, Connecticut, and Maine had established a system of territorial, public law parishes that levied their own taxes. They were considered the "spiritual arm of the State" and were subject to judicial review. These public law parishes existed until the states decided to disestablish their religion (1507).

In Mexico, a country with a strong Catholic presence, liberal and revolutionary elites have long refused to recognize the Catholic Church, which has benefited from a civil personality since the constitutional reform of 1992 (Martinez de Codes 2001). In Argentina, we find a regime dedicated to the protection of the Catholic Church, a responsibility assigned to the federal government by Article 2 of the 1853 Constitution, renewed in 1994. This review of different jurisdictions around the world sheds light on the paradoxical nature of Quebec's jurisdiction over religions. On the one hand, Quebec has exercised sovereignty in regulating the temporal affairs of its religious denominations, without confining itself to Christian denominations, acting as a broker of religious franchises; on the other hand, it has long conceded its own inferiority with respect to the Catholic Church, which is superior in terms of intellectual qualities, objectives, and works and with respect to the imperial order, which has also had an impact on Quebec's internal domain.

Westphalia in Canada

Let us now turn to some of the debates arising from the Act Respecting the Laicity of the State, which shed some light on the nature of the other political city under whose umbrella Quebec society sought to place itself, once the church had been "brought to heel" following an ongoing drive against tradition since the post–Second World War period (Guindon 1999).[22] In matters of religion, the question of the division of legislative powers arose. Some would like to have Bill 21 declared *ultra vires* on the grounds that all religious freedom falls under the jurisdiction of the federal Parliament, either under its criminal law jurisdiction or under its general jurisdiction over peace, order, and good government. Professor Maxime St-Hilaire (2019) has made several arguments in support of this thesis in an article published on the Canadian Bar Association website. In particular, he cites the precedent of the Supreme Court of Canada's decision in the 1953 *Saumur* case,[23] in which a Jehovah's Witness challenged the validity of a municipal bylaw that made the distribution of publications subject to the prior approval of the chief of police. Also at issue was the Freedom of Worship Act,[24] a consolidation of the Rectories Act of 1852 by the Quebec legislature, which adapted it in its own way to regulate good order in places of worship.

The justices signed several separate opinions; a narrow majority struck down the bylaw or declared it inapplicable to the plaintiff, but another narrow majority upheld Quebec's jurisdiction to delegate to municipalities the power to enact such bylaws. Four of the nine judges ruled that the bylaw was outside Quebec's jurisdiction since freedom of religion would fall under federal, general, or criminal jurisdiction (a fifth judge, Justice Patrick Kerwin, declared the bylaw unenforceable but recognized Quebec's jurisdiction over freedom of religion). One of the four justices even associated this freedom with the preamble of the Constitution Act, 1867, which would be a source of innumerable individual rights. But the fact remains that five justices agreed that Quebec had constitutional jurisdiction over freedom of religion or worship or at least over the pursuit of activities related to the practice of religion.[25]

I will not undertake an in-depth analysis of the judgment here. One element, however, deserves particular attention – namely, the arguments put forward by justices supporting the centralist view of religious freedom. Consider, for example, Justice Ivan Rand's reasoning:

> The Christian religion, its practices and profession, exhibiting in Europe and America an organic continuity, stands in the first rank of social, political and juristic importance. The *Articles of Capitulation* in 1760, the *Treaty of Paris* in 1763, and the *Quebec Act* of 1774, all contain special provisions placing safeguards against restrictions on its freedom, which were in fact liberations from the law in force

> at the time in England. The *Quebec Act,* by sec. 5, declared that His Majesty's subjects, professing the religion of the Church of Rome of and in the said Province of Quebec, may have, hold and enjoy, the free exercise of the religion of the Church of Rome, subject to the King's supremacy ... and, by sec. 15, that no ordnance [sic] touching religion ... shall be of any force or effect until the saine shall have received His Majesty's approbation.[26]

Justice Willard Estey also went back to the Treaty of Paris of 1763 to establish that the guarantee of religious freedom – for conquered Catholics, first of all – was a pure emanation of British sovereignty and a condition of peace that would shape all subsequent regimes governing Canadians until the creation of the Dominion in 1867. In fact, both justices adopted a line of reasoning similar to the one followed by the Privy Council in London in the *Guibord* case, which also went back to the articles of the Capitulation of Montreal to rule on the legal status of the Catholic Church.

Justice Rand's reasoning proceeds from a general proposition – the pre-eminence of Christianity organically uniting Europe and America – to the less obvious proposition that it is the legal Acts resulting from the military conquest of New France (the Quebec Act of 1774 explicitly mentions the conquest) that provide the primary and overarching foundation for religious freedom.[27] Justice Rand even transforms the conquest into a liberating religious war since it is said to have saved her majesty's new Catholic subjects from the empire of English laws, which were then vexatious and debilitating for Catholics in the British Isles. In a book devoted to the long history of secularism in France over a period of at least a thousand years, the Orthodox theologian and publisher Jean-François Colosimo (2019) highlights some surprising features about secularism in Canada. In his day, Aristide Briand (1905), rapporteur of the French Law of Separation of Churches and State, considered Canada to be a trailblazer of secularism.[28]

But Colosimo (2019, 115) finds that Canada has actually been heir to the "Wars of Religion" in trying to settle the relations between French-speaking Catholics and English-speaking Protestants along the lines of the Treaties of Westphalia, the famous treaties in 1648 that brought an end to the Thirty Years' War, which had long torn apart the Catholics and Protestants of central Europe. These treaties, as Valentine Zuber (2019, 194) reminds us, "reserved for the princes the right to impose their own religious choice on all their subjects and made the religious domain a prerogative of the sovereign State, which had the right to manage it freely without fear of international constraint." According to the Westphalian model that Colosimo discusses in relation to Canada, the religion of the subjects – whether treated as a privilege, a tolerance, a right, or a restriction – is of direct interest to the sovereignty of the state – indeed, it challenges the most fundamental aspect of state sovereignty by forming the condition, set by the state, for reinstating peace after war.

These treaties affirmed the religious prerogative of the princes and recognized private devotion and freedom of emigration between the territories concerned (Baubérot 2008a, 55). The Seven Years' War was also, in many respects, a war of religion. This war led to a series of capitulations bearing the signatures of the belligerents and, finally, to the Treaty of Paris of 1763. The historian Edmond Dziembowski (2015, 295–302) reminds us that the Seven Years' War, the first war to have truly worldwide ramifications, was motivated, among other things, by the British and Americans' fear that the Protestant citadel could be besieged by the Papist enemy. It was resolved in New France by granting concessions for the Catholic faith of the conquered subjects and a right to emigration in exchange for the British Crown's total control of their territory and collective destiny. Moreover, the Treaty of Paris of 1763 states in Article 2 that the Treaties of Westphalia of 1648 "serve as a basis and foundation to the peace, and to the present treaty."

In addition to the Westphalian heritage underlying the reasoning of some of the justices in the *Saumur* case, there is another surprising aspect to consider: the Hobbesian language underpinning their analysis. According to Thomas Hobbes, the state comes into being both by contract between equal citizens and through war; in both cases, the same logic prevails that the subject renounces his natural freedom in order to submit to a sovereign power under the guarantee that his life and personal safety will be preserved by it. And for Hobbes (2000, 663), a consenting pact or surrender creates irrevocably, and thus for all time, a sovereign state whose prerogatives extend to everything, even spiritual matters. For Hobbes, the distinction between temporal and spiritual government is irrelevant: "Temporal and spiritual government are but two words brought into the world to make men see double and mistake their lawful sovereign." The British Leviathan, which had claimed to be an empire at least since the sixteenth-century reign of King Henry VIII, did not see "double": there was no "spiritual" domain behind it, capable of confronting and overwhelming it. The church and the state constituted the spiritual and temporal counterparts of one and the same body, a "body politic," as English jurists wrote, brought together under the reign of a sacred sovereign who was both the defender of the faith and the defender of the liberties of the kingdom (Buckler 1941). This bivalent "body politic" thus absorbed everything, including spiritual matters – that is, the creation of churches, their doctrines, and religious freedom and observance, which also fell under the body politic's sovereignty, as exercised by the civil sovereign – "the chief pastor," in the words of Hobbes. The civil sovereign could then make all the laws he deemed expedient with respect to religion; he could distribute the masses and the spiritual rights that were needed for civil peace. He acquired this supreme power by war or by founding contract.

In Canada's case, it appears that some justices of the Supreme Court of Canada – and, before that, of the Privy Council – saw the Canadian federal state as the direct successor of the conqueror and thereby acquired jurisdiction over religious freedoms and observances by virtue of a war title.[29] It is not clear that this doctrine will prevail in determining legislative jurisdiction over religion or the rights of the state and the individual in this regard. This doctrine still finds favour with some legal scholars. It brings to the forefront a fundamental reality that Canadian constitutional law likes to ignore or claim that we have somehow moved beyond: the British Conquest. According to this doctrine, the conquest is the first of Canada's constitutions because it precedes, provides the foundation for, and structures all subsequent constitutions. The British Conquest stands outside the law, and yet it penetrates throughout the laws of Canada. In the Canadian legal imagination, religious freedom and observance call on the pacifying violence of the state, notably through criminal law, to which Canadian and British judges have linked these matters.[30]

In the 1955 *Henry Birks & Sons* case, Justice Rand referred back to the Norman Conquest of 1066, noting that the criminal law's regulation of religious observance arose out of the church-state conflicts in Great Britain between the fourteenth and eighteenth centuries, which had required the use of corporal punishment to shape public behaviour.[31] Justice Roy Kellock referred back to an English statute passed under King Henry VI in 1448 and another enacted in 1551 under King Edward VI, the son of King Henry VIII (who came to the throne at the age of nine), to establish that the observance of religious holidays, in the English tradition, was a matter of criminal law. The first law was passed a few years before the outbreak of the War of the Roses. The second law followed the imposition in 1649 of the *Book of Common Prayer*, which replaced the Latin liturgy with English at the cost of rebellions that were suppressed throughout the country. During the short reign of King Edward VI (1547–53) additional measures were taken, particularly of a penal nature, to enshrine a State Protestantism inspired by Calvinism (Chassaigne 2001, 92–94).

In sum, these two justices determined what constituted a criminal law by referring to a precedent from close to five hundred years ago, at a time when English kingship was bound together with a national religion and the sovereign practised religious intolerance by sword and by law. It was on this basis that the Quebec legislature was not allowed to delegate to municipal councils the power to set closing days for stores. As a result, the Montreal municipal council could not order businesses to observe essentially religious holidays since, according to Supreme Court of Canada Justice Gérald Fauteux, "legislation to compel the observance, even the relative observance, of religious holidays belongs to the branch of criminal law."[32] Even today, while Canada is supposed to have no official religion and praises religious tolerance and constitutionalized individual rights, it is nevertheless astonishing that some jurists determine the criminal scope of a law by looking to a precedent from the reign of a Tudor king whose rule was the very antithesis of religious tolerance.

In Canada several individual rights also appear to have a peculiar origin, given that the British Conquest of 1759–63 is taken by some jurists to be a fountain of rights. This can be understood if we consider that the conquest reduced a conquered people to the status of atomized individual subjects, stripping them of their citizenship, their state, and their primary allegiance, which the conqueror nevertheless recognized in their pure humanity, even if it meant granting them rights that would follow the conquered over several generations but without ever restoring their original collective identity, which was lost forever. The granting of individual rights proves to be an invaluable tool for sealing a collective dispossession that never ends and for which there is no remedy. Moreover, this same logic was repeated in 1898, also in Paris, with the signing of the peace treaty between the United States and Spain, which ceded the Philippines, Cuba, Puerto Rico, and the island of Guam, with the assurance that the inhabitants of these "ceded" territories would retain the free exercise of their religion.[33] The Treaty of Utrecht of 1713, by which France ceded peninsular Acadia and Hudson Bay to Great Britain, had also guaranteed "the exercise of the Roman religion" and the right of emigration for subjects remaining in the conquered colonies. The deportation of the Acadians in 1755 demonstrates that these guarantees were purely theoretical.

For those justices in the *Saumur* case who drew inspiration from the Westphalian treaties, the religious rights resulting from the legal texts generated by the British Conquest formed a category of their own: as a result of the Capitulations of 1759 and 1760, religious rights would therefore not fall within the notion of "property and civil rights" and would thus be removed from the jurisdiction of the provincial states (provinces) in matters of civil law. It is also a Lutheran or Calvinist way of conceiving freedom of religion, which is seen as a freedom located outside of society and which postulates the self-sufficiency of the individual in his or her relationship to God and is therefore not exercised through social relationships governed by civil law.[34]

Is the Deconfessionalization of the School Systems in Quebec and Newfoundland Another Example of Constitutional Asymmetry?

These justices certainly did not only base their opinions on texts going back to the British Conquest. They also invoked another argument – namely, section 93 of the Constitution Act, 1867, on denominational education rights, which they saw as illustrating the principle that religious freedom and observance are a federal responsibility since this section provides for a right of appeal to the federal Cabinet of decisions made by a provincial authority affecting the education rights of Catholics and Protestants in a "minority" situation within the province concerned. Since 1997, however, this argument no longer holds water since Quebec has obtained, through a bilateral constitutional amendment, complete exemption from the system of denominational education rights provided for in paragraphs 1–4 of this section. Quebec can therefore enact legislation relating to education without any restriction and without being subject to a right of review by the federal Cabinet.

This amendment completes the deconfessionalization of the Quebec public school system. Its significance is best understood by comparing it to the constitutional amendments obtained by Newfoundland, which held two referendums. In 1949, the terms of Newfoundland's union with Canada maintained a school system that virtually entrusted school governance to six denominations, to which a seventh was added through a bilateral constitutional amendment in 1987. But, eventually, a section of Newfoundland public opinion and Newfoundland governments sought to reform this cumbersome system and to give Newfoundland a free hand to deconfessionalize its public school system (Ellis Fenin et al. 2001). The first amendment, passed in 1997, sought to undo the denominational regime, but it maintained varying guarantees for the existing denominations, the interpretation of which led to confusion.[35] The Newfoundland government returned to the fray in 1998 with a new amendment replacing the previous one and providing two restrictions on the exercise of Newfoundland's exclusive jurisdiction over education: "(2) In and for the Province of Newfoundland, the Legislature shall have exclusive authority to make laws in relation to education but shall provide for courses in religion that are not specific to a religious denomination; (3) Religious observances shall be permitted in a school where requested by parents."[36]

The contrast with Quebec's bilateral amendment is telling. Newfoundland has been given exclusive jurisdiction over education but with two conditions: the introduction of general religious education and the observance of a religion at the request of parents. Neither of these restrictions is attached to the exercise of Quebec's jurisdiction over education. We can draw a few conclusions from this situation. First, the Canadian Constitution clearly creates a new asymmetry in the religious regime of school systems. Newfoundland must guarantee a minimal religious configuration in its schools through the content of its teachings and the practices of religious observance, which may vary from one school to another depending on requests made by parents. Quebec is under no obligation to allow religion to penetrate through its schools. It can logically be inferred from this that Quebec has been granted the constitutional power not to provide for any religious instruction in its schools – or, on the contrary, to specify such instruction – as well as to decide whether or not it is appropriate to guarantee the observance of a religion or of religions in general. Ontario, on the other hand, continues to be subject to the four paragraphs of section 93 on educational rights. Second, if it is true, as Westphalian judges and jurists have argued, that religious freedom and observance are strictly within federal jurisdiction (Scott 1959), even within educational institutions, it is not clear why the framers of the Constitution would have bothered to specify that parents in Newfoundland have the right to demand religious observance in public schools. This latter obligation only makes sense to the extent that religious observance in public schools is understood to be a provincial responsibility.

There is also evidence that Quebec, since 1997, has not felt constitutionally obliged to consider the public school as a place of religious observance. In 2005, the National Assembly, on the initiative of Liberal Minister Jean-Marc Fournier, amended section 41 of the Quebec Charter of Human Rights and Freedoms, which deals with the right to religious education.[37] The original 1975 version of this charter reads as follows: "41. Parents or persons acting in their stead have a right to require that, in the public educational establishments, their children receive a religious or moral instruction in conformity with their convictions, within the curricula provided for by law." The new version adopted in 2005 reads as follows: "41. Parents or the persons acting in their stead have a right to give their children a religious and moral education in keeping with their convictions and with proper regard for their children's rights and interests." The legislator has thus decided that the right to religious education of parents or legal guardians will no longer have public schools as its obligatory locus. Moreover, this parental right is now tempered by the rights of the child and their interests, which gives the legislator the responsibility of reconciling the rights of the former with those of the latter. Moreover, the new section 41 no longer refers to religious education curricula provided for by law, which opens up the possibility that the Quebec state will not maintain any of them, that they will be moved to a schedule outside of school hours, or that they will be reserved for private institutions instead.

Towards a Canadian Civil Religion?

The Newfoundland constitutional amendment illustrates another issue that goes beyond the analysis of positive law. It makes apparent some aspects of what might be called a "Canadian civil religion" that would appear to have developed since the constitutional reform of 1982. But what does the term "civil religion" mean? In 1993, Andrew Kim (1993), a sociologist at the University of Toronto, published an article with a revealing title: "The Absence of Pan-Canadian Civil Religion." The author starts from the observation, made by American sociologists Robert Bellah and Martin Lipset, that Canada, unlike its neighbour to the south, has not succeeded in developing a civil religion, made up of symbols, rites, and heroes. American sociologists blame this absence of a Canadian "national" mythology on the country's Loyalist past as well as its linguistic and cultural diversity. Moreover, Canada turned its back on revolution and never had to recover from the devastation of a civil war. Kim agrees with the analysis of these sociologists, in that for him the strength of regionalism and biculturalism has prevented the emergence of a distinctively pan-Canadian civil religion. However, Kim does not rule out the possibility of there actually being two competing civil religions in Canada – the one in English Canada marked by the influence of the Protestant churches and the other in Quebec marked by the influence of the Catholic Church (270). In this sense, religions in Canada, rather than coalescing into a unifying civil religion, appear to have fostered the creation of competing identities and loyalties. However, the analyses made by Kim (1993, 271) and also by Bellah and Lipset seem to assume that the absence of a civil religion in Canada indicates an anomaly, or even a debilitating deficiency, since linguistic and cultural heterogeneity throws up formidable "barriers preventing the formation of a common civil religion."

The concept of civil religion gained some currency in the United States with the publication in 1967 of "Civil Religion in America" by Bellah (2005). His essay reflects on the significance of the ever-present references to God by Presidents John Kennedy and Lyndon Johnson in their speeches and ceremonies. For Bellah, it would be a mistake to see these references to the divine as merely anecdotal or ritualistic. Instead, they reflect the fact that religion has continued to strengthen, inspire, and guide American political society, even though the US Constitution prohibits the establishment of religion while protecting religious freedom. In fact, according to Bellah, the separation of state and church in the United States has not deprived politics of its religious foundations, which remain in place to this day. Of course, Bellah did not invent the concept of civil religion. He acknowledges his debt to Jean-Jacques Rousseau, who discusses it in the *Social Contract*, in extolling the usefulness for the state of maintaining a civil religion that guarantees the loyalty of citizens and enshrines the "sanctity of the social contract and of the laws" (Rousseau 1971, 220).

For Bellah, civil religion draws its substance from Christianity or, rather, Judeo-Christianity: in the United States, powerful biblical archetypes still generate prophets and martyrs in social life as well as new sacred places and symbols that contribute to civil religion. For Bellah, however, the God underlying this civil religion has no clear identity but can be reconciled with the notions of God professed by different religious denominations. This God is, in short, generic – a "God disconnected from the churches,"[38] a supreme being who overshadows political life and who comforts Americans with the grandiose idea that they serve as a Shining City on a Hill, in accordance with His will, enlightening the world. For Bellah, civil religion revolves around a universal God, understood differently by each of the various religious denominations that make up American society; in France, a case can also be made for the existence of a republican civil religion, but one focused on human rights, without reaching a consensus on the nature of its foundations, whether natural or divine (Zuber 2014, 362–66).

In 2023, about thirty years after Kim's diagnosis, it is questionable whether Canada can still be distinguished from the United States by the absence of a unifying civil religion. In 2014, one political scientist even suggested that Canada had long cultivated its own civil religion: first, in the form of Christian civic piety, which has been Catholic in Quebec and Protestant elsewhere in Canada. Second, federal policies of bilingualism and multiculturalism, and even the secularization of Quebec society since the Quiet Revolution, have all combined to crystallize a new civil religion in the form of a pan-Canadian democratic faith based on the Canadian Charter of Rights and Freedoms, which apparently the Supreme Court of Canada wishes to enlighten through the beacon of its "conscience" (Hofsink 2014). This new civil religion would seem to rely more on the state than the old religion, which was dependent on society.

Moreover, this Canadian-style civil religion would appear to possess many of the features that Rousseau (1971) recommends. As he wrote, the dogmas of the civil religion "ought to be simple, few in number, stated with precision, without explanations or commentary" (220). The dogmas that Rousseau favoured resemble the pithy articles found in the Canadian Charter of Rights and Freedoms, whose preamble proclaims the supremacy of God. Civil religion, according to Rousseau, must affirm "the existence of a mighty, intelligent and beneficent Divinity" (220). In addition to its positive dogmas, civil religion rests on an essential exclusive dogma – namely, the exclusion of intolerance, which precludes the maintenance of an "exclusive national religion" and obliges all religions to tolerate one another. This purely civil religion, according to Rousseau, inspires "social sentiments that are needed to be a good citizen and a faithful subject." Since preservation of this "civil profession of faith" is the responsibility of the state, it can for this reason banish anyone who defies the articles of this religion, "not for impiety but for being antisocial." Quoting Hobbes, Rousseau advocated civil religion because governing oneself in a Christian city, and, in particular, in a Catholic city, proved to be an untenable solution for him. Indeed, this city "gives men two codes of law, two rulers, two homelands, subjects them to contradictory duties and makes it impossible for them to be believers and citizens" (214). In other words, civil religion appears as the solution to the dual cities, one spiritual and the other temporal, observed in the Western world.

All in all, there is an important feature of the debate on the Act Respecting the Laicity of the State and of the debates before it on the proposed Charter of Values and on "reasonable accommodation," as examined by the Bouchard-Taylor Commission's report: Quebec is far from adhering "*en bloc*" to this still theoretical civil religion in Canada – a civil religion that would seem to celebrate the unity of a patriotism of rights that is blind to national differences but not to denominational affiliations (Bouchard and Taylor 2008). Many Quebeckers want to break with the overpowering Catholic city of former times, but they have no wish to replace this Catholic city with a new religious city; from here onwards, they wish to govern themselves through a state that is free of the influence of religion. However, other Quebeckers, many of them intellectuals and academics, defend a close relationship between religion and the state that would include even educational institutions. For this latter group of Quebeckers, religious freedom and observance seem to derive from the sovereign individual, who is not comfortable with any restrictions that the state may adopt on their faith for the public good, social cohesion, or the guarantee of other freedoms. As Colosimo (2019) argues, this vision of religious freedom seems to be more concerned with separating the application of the law from religious faith (in order to neutralize any effect that could offend the practice and sincere self-perception of believers) than with separating religions and the state.

Outside of Quebec, Canadian public authorities tend to promote the presence of religion in their everyday operations – from para-public services to the central organs of power – and they do this by means of prayers, rites, references, vestimentary, or symbolic externalizations. In short, the new Canadian city, which is said to be "open" to all religions, relies on a kind of multi-faith piety, which would seem to be part of the Canadian civic identity and of the staging of public action. This new Canadian city is convinced of the positive role of religions, which play "a role of socialization and civilization" on the basis of what seems to be a general act of faith – but this act of faith is not universally shared within Quebec itself (Baubérot 2008b, 252). True, there is a community in Quebec that embraces this Canadian civil religion and even actively promotes it. However, there is another community in Quebec – in all likelihood a majority of the population – that resists this Canadian civil religion: instead, this latter community rallies around the idea of secularism in order to free the Quebec state from the impact of religious belief and proselytizing, while protecting freedom of conscience and of thought, in addition to freedom of religion.

The Newfoundland constitutional amendment of 1998 is interesting in that it makes visible two aspects of the Canadian civil religion in the making: 1) the provincial state must provide a general education on religions, without promoting any of them, on the grounds that these religions are presumed to be beneficial for the moral and civic formation of students and 2) the school is an institution bound to respect some religious observance, even in a public setting. Since 1997, Quebec has more or less adhered to the first of these aspects by offering the ethics and religious culture course, which, in the face of public criticism, the Coalition Avenir Québec government decided to abolish and replace. As for the second aspect, some people would like Quebec's public schools to be recognized places of worship, which would benefit both parents and teachers. This is a way of maintaining that the stronger Newfoundland clauses should apply in Quebec, even if the Constitution says nothing about the matter. This is also a way of admitting that Canada – and Quebec, in particular – remains subject to the old Westphalian order that has morphed once more into "a sublimated ideology of otherness and diversity," to quote Colosimo (2019, 115). Time will tell whether Quebec, having left the Catholic city, will be able to shape the free city it wants or whether it will instead have to profess its faith in a new spiritual body.

Notes

1 Act Respecting the Laicity of the State, SQ 2019, c. 12.

2 Historians such as Francis Parkman have popularized the idea that New France was under an "oppressive theocracy," but this is an exaggeration that obscures the fact that the church remained the daughter of a monarchy that had asserted its independence from Rome (Jaenen 1985, 3).

3 See Treaty of Paris, February 10, 1763, s. 4, https://www.uottawa.ca/clmc/treaty-paris-1763.

4 According to lawyer Antonio Perrault (1943), the civil incorporation of the Montreal bishopric was the work of Governor John Colborne himself, not the Special Council, which issued letters patent in August 1839. But this detail does not change the fact of the direct involvement of the British power in the civil institutionalization of the church.

5 Translator's note: A "*fabrique*" in Quebec is a legal entity consisting of the Roman Catholic parish priest and the churchwardens of the parish – the definition of "fabrique" has changed over time and is still subject to the Act Respecting Fabriques, LQ 1965, c. 76, which was adopted in 1965 and revised in 1993.

6 Gilles Leclerc (2002, 284) reveals that he had originally planned to incorporate three long chapters into his *Journal d'un inquisiteur* that were later deleted: they were devoted to the marriage between the church and the empire, "which will have completed before long the complete degradation of the human person of the French Canadian." According to Leclerc, this marriage enslaved the church to the state, and, in consenting to it, the church signed "the death warrant of its original nobility."

7 Michel Brunet (1969, 42) discusses this as well: "The Catholic Church in Lower Canada ... had always enjoyed both the privileges of aristocratic continuity and the advantages of democratic recruitment."

8 See Act Respecting Fabriques, art. 1(m) and (n).

9 Born in 1825 in Ireland, D'Arcy McGee opposed the British rule in his youth and left for the United States in 1848, where he changed his mind over Irish republicanism. Established in the Province of Canada from 1857, he advocated collaboration between Catholics and Protestants and promoted the federal union of Canada in 1867. He was assassinated in 1868.

10 Act Respecting Fabriques.

11 An Act to Establish the Quebec Bureau of Public Charities (UK), 1921, 11 Geo. V, c. 79.

12 The territorial and administrative organization of Quebec still bears the mark of the parish system, as Louis Georges Deschênes (2018) shows. See also section 11 of the Act Respecting Elections and Referendums in Municipalities, RLRQ, c. E-2.2.

13 See *Ordre de préséance établi par les autorités impériales pour les réunions d'un caractère officiel dans la puissance du Canada,* reprinted in Montigny 1878, 234–35.

14 The two original laws were An Act to Repeal So Much of the Act of the Parliament of Great Britain Passed in the Thirty-First Year of the Reign of King George the Third, and Chapter Thirty-One, As Relates to Rectories, and the Presentation of Incumbents to the Same, and for Other Purposes Connected with Such Rectories (UK), 1852, 14 & 15 Vict. c. 175; An Act to Make Better Provision for the Appropriation of Money Arising from Lands Heretofore Known As the Clergy Reserves, by Rendering Them Available for Municipal Purpose (UK), 1854, 18 Vict. c. 2. These laws were consolidated under the following titles during the Union: Rectories Act, SRC 1859, c. 74; Act Respecting Clergy Reserves, RSC 1859, c. 25.

15 *Brown v Les Curé et Marguilliers de l'Œuvre et Fabrique de la Paroisse de Notre-Dame de Montréal*, (1874) LR 6, PC 157.

16 In fact, the question of Catholic establishment in conquered Canada arose during the adoption by the British Parliament of the Quebec Act (UK), 1774, 14 Geo. III, c. 83. Several parliamentarians mentioned this establishment, such as the "solicitor general" of the time: "First, I agree that the Roman Catholic religion ought to be the established religion of that country in its present state; the clergymen of which are paid by the landed revenue of that country." But this establishment applied only to Catholics; Protestants enjoyed their separate worship under British protection. Edmund Burke opposed such an establishment on philosophical grounds. Power cannot establish religion in itself: power can only confirm it. The relevant excerpts from the debates are reproduced in O'Sullivan 1890, 122–28.

17 Constitution Act, 1867 (UK), 30 & 31 Vict., c. 3; Canadian Charter of Rights and Freedoms, Part 1 of the Constitution Act, 1982, being Schedule B to the Canada Act 1982 (UK), 1982, c. 11.

18 In addition to the protections provided in section 93, this community enjoyed other safeguards confirming its privileged status: a second legislative chamber, where it was understood that the executive would appoint its representatives, and a provision that twelve protected electoral districts could not be changed without the consent of the representatives of those districts. The system was abolished in 1970. See Constitution Act, 1867, former s. 80. The Legislative Council ceased to exist at the very end of 1968.

19 See, in particular, Act Respecting Protestant Churches Authorized to Keep Civil Status Registers, RS 1964, c. 331 (repealed in 1992); Act Respecting the Constitution of Certain Churches, RLRQ, c. C-63. As early as 1871, the Quebec legislature legislated, by private act, for the legal status of the United Church of England and Ireland within its territory. See An Act to Empower the Synod of the Diocese of Montreal to Subdivide the Parishes Erected for Ecclesiastical Purposes by Royal Letters Patent (UK), 1871, 35 Vict., c. 19; see also An Act to Extend the Powers Granted to the Provincial Synod of the Anglican Church, by the Act of the Late Province of Canada, 29 and 30 Vict., c. 15 to the Synod of the Diocese of Quebec, in So Far As They Relate to the Property of the Church in the Said Diocese (UK), 1879, 42–43 Vict., c. 69; see also An Act to Amend the Act (UK), 14–15 Vict., c. 176, respecting the Temporal Property of the United Church of England and Ireland in the Diocese of Montreal (UK), 1890, 53 Vict., c. 123; a much more recent statute is the statute entitled Relating to the Presbyterian Church: An Act Respecting the Presbyterian College, Montreal, SQ 2010, c. 48.

20 An Act Respecting the Mennonite Church and the Canadian Conference of the Mennonite Brethren Church in North America, SQ 1962, c. 109; An Act to Incorporate the Centre Islamique du Québec-El Markaz Islami, SQ 1965, c. 133; An Act Respecting the Education of Certain Children in Montreal and

Outremont, SQ 1931, c. 63; An Act Respecting the Erection in This Province of Parishes and Missions of the Ruthenian Greek Catholic Church in Communion with Rome, SQ 1916, c. 117.

21 There is extensive legislation relating to this matter. For example, the Anglican Church Act, SNB 2003, c. 39.

22 As Hubert Guindon (1999, 23) points out, this criticism of tradition can be explained in part by the internalization by Quebec intellectuals of the vision that Anglo-Canadians have long held of Quebec society – namely, of "a church-ridden monolithic and archaic society, whose economic underdevelopment dates from the French feudal regime and from the values inculcated by Catholicism." See also Dumas 2019, 5.

23 *Saumur v Ville de Québec*, [1953] 2 SCR 299 (*Saumur*).

24 An Act Respecting Freedom of Worship and Good Order in and around Churches, RSQ 1941, c. 307.

25 *Saumur*, 387 (see the opinion of Justices Cartwright and Fauteux).

26 *Saumur*, 327.

27 Quebec Act 1774 (UK), 14 Geo. III, c. 83.

28 In a comparative table of foreign laws, Aristide Briand (1905, 168) mentions Canada in the following terms: "Canada (where a law of 1854 secularized certain ecclesiastics and removed any official character from the Anglican Church)."

29 Jurists are not the only ones to go back to the British Conquest in search of the legal foundation of freedom of religion and even the idea of secularism. A sociologist of religion has done just this in one of his articles (Koussens 2013).

30 *A.-G. Ont. v Hamilton Street Railway*, [1903] AC 524; *Henry Birks & Sons v Montreal*, [1955] SCR 799 (*Henry Birks & Sons*).

31 *Henry Birks & Sons*, 812–13.

32 *Henry Birks & Sons*, 809.

33 Treaty of Peace between the United States and Spain, 1898, art. 10, https://avalon.law.yale.edu.

34 On the Calvinist mindset that influences religious culture in English Canada, see Walsh 1958. On the Lutheran and Calvinist visions of faith, see Dumont 1981.

35 Constitutional Amendment, 1997 (Newfoundland Act), SI/97–55, May 2, 1997.

36 Constitutional Amendment, 1998 (Newfoundland Act), special edition, vol. 132, no. 1, SI/98–25, January 14, 1998.

37 Charter of Human Rights and Freedoms, RSQ 1977, c. C-12; see Act to Amend Various Legislative Provisions of a Confessional Nature in the Education Field, SQ 2005, c. 20, s. 13.

38 This expression regarding American civil religion is not from Robert Bellah (2005) but, rather, from Jean Baubérot (2008a, 63), who says American civil religion endorses "the Nation in a religious but not a clerical way."

References

Affre, Denis-Auguste. 1827. *Traité de l'administration temporelle des paroisses*. Paris: A. Le Clère.

Arès, Richard. 1981. "L'évolution de l'Église au Canada français de 1940 à 1975. Survivance et déclin d'une chrétienté." In *Idéologies au Canada français, 1940–1976*, vol. 3: *Les partis politiques: L'Église*, edited by Fernand Dumont, Jean-Paul Montminy, and Jean Hamelin, 267–97. Quebec City: Les Presses de l'Université Laval.

Baubérot, Jean. 2008a. *Petite histoire du christianisme*. Paris: Édition J'ai lu.

–. 2008b. *Une laïcité interculturelle*. Paris: Éditions de l'Aube.

Baudry, Joseph Ubalde. 1870. *Code des curés, marguilliers et paroisses*. Montreal: Des presses à vapeur de la Minerve.

Beaudoin, Gérald A. 1984. "Considérations sur l'influence de la religion en droit public au Canada." *Revue générale de droit* 15 (3): 589–602.

Bellah, Robert. 2005. "Civil Religion in America." *Daedalus* 134 (4): 40–55.

Borella, François. 2008. *Éléments de droit constitutionnel.* Paris: Presses de la Fondation nationale de science politique.

Bouchard, Gérard, and Charles Taylor. 2008. *Building the Future. A Time for Reconciliation*. Quebec City: Commission de consultation sur les pratiques d'accommodement reliées aux différences culturelles. https://numerique.banq.qc.ca/patrimoine/details/52327/1565995.

Briand, Aristide. 1905. *Rapport fait au nom de la commission relative à la séparation des Églises et de l'État et à la dénonciation du concordat chargée d'examiner le projet de loi et les diverses propositions de loi concernant la Séparation des Églises et de l'État.* Paris: Assemblée nationale de France, annexe au procès-verbal de la 2e séance du 4 mars 1905.

Brunet, Michel. 1969. "L'Église catholique du Bas-Canada et le partage du pouvoir à l'heure d'une nouvelle donne (1837–1854)." *Historical Papers/Communications historiques* 4 (1): 37–51.

Buckler, F.W. 1941. "The Establishment of the Church of England: Its Constitutional and Legal Significance." *Church History* 10 (4): 299–346.

Chassaigne, Philippe. 2001. *Histoire de l'Angleterre des origines à nos jours*. Paris: Flammarion.

Chevrier, Marc. 2019. *L'Empire en marche. Des peuples sans qualités, de Vienne à Ottawa*. Quebec City: Presses de l'Université Laval.

Colosimo, Jean-François. 2019. *La religion française*. Paris: Les éditions du Cerf.

De Montigny, B.-A.T. 1878. *Catéchisme politique*. Montreal: Beauchemin and Valois, libraires-imprimeurs.

Deschênes, Louis Georges. 2018. "L'empreinte du catholicisme dans l'organisation territoriale et administrative du Québec." In *Les catholiques québécois et la laïcité*, edited by David Koussens and Catherine Foisy, 165–93. Quebec City: Presses de l'Université Laval.

Dumas, Alexandre. 2019. *L'Église et la politique québécoise, de Taschereau à Duplessis.* Montreal and Kingston: McGill-Queen's University Press.

Dumont, Louis. 1981. "La genèse chrétienne de l'individualisme moderne." *Le Débat* 8 (15): 124–46.

Dziembowski, Edmond. 2015. *La guerre de Sept Ans, 1756–1763.* Paris: Perrin.

Ellis Fenin, Scott, Sharon A. Gibb, E. Vance Randall, and Ellen Stuck. 2001. "From Sectarian to Secular Control of Education: The Case of Newfoundland." *Journal of Research on Christian Education* 10 (2): 411–30.

Ferretti, Lucia. 1992. *Entre voisins. La société paroissiale en milieu urbain. Saint-Pierre-Apôtre de Montréal (1848–1930).* Montreal: Boréal.

–. 1999. *Brève histoire de l'Église catholique au Québec.* Montreal: Boréal.

–. 2011. "Du 'devoir de charité' au 'droit à l'aide publique': la naissance de l'État-providence au Québec." Université de Montréal, Les Conférences Gérard Parizeau, 11e Conférence, October 5.

Gingras, Jos. Apollinaire. 1880. *Le Bas-Canada entre le Moyen Âge et l'âge moderne.* Quebec City: L'Imprimerie du "Canadien."

Guindon, Hubert. 1999. "La révolution tranquille et ses effets pervers." *Sociétés* 20–21: 1–38.

Guizot, François. 1985. *Histoire de la civilisation en Europe.* Paris: Hachette.

Harvey, Janice. 2003. "Les Églises protestantes et l'assistance aux pauvres à Montréal au XIXe siècle." *Études d'histoire religieuse* 69: 53–54.

Hobbes, Thomas. 2000. *Léviathan.* Paris: Gallimard.

Hofsink, Clarence Gerald. 2014. "From God to Mammon: The Metamorphosis of Civil Religion in Canada." Master's thesis, University of Northern British Columbia.

Jaenen, Cornelius J. 1985. *Le rôle de l'Église en Nouvelle-France.* Brochure historique no. 40, Société historique du Canada.

Kauper, Paul G., and Stephen C. Ellis. 1970. "Religious Corporations and the Law." *Michigan Law Review* 71: 1499–1574.

Kennedy, W.P.M. 1930. *Statutes, Treaties and Documents of the Canadian Constitution, 1713–1929.* Toronto: Oxford University Press.

Koussens, David. 2013. "Une mise en scène nationaliste de la laïcité en porte-à-faux avec la réalité des aménagements laïques canadiens." *Revue de droit de l'Université de Sherbrooke* (Special edition): 195–98.

Kim, Andrew E. 1993. "The Absence of Pan-Canadian Civil Religion: Plurality, Duality and Conflict in Symbols of Canadian Culture." *Sociology of Religion* 54 (3): 257–75.

Laflèche, Louis-François. 1866. *Quelques considérations sur les rapports de la société civile avec la religion et la famille.* Montreal: Eusèbe-Sénécal.

Langevin, Hector Louis. 1863. *Droit administratif ou manuel des paroisses et fabriques.* Quebec City: Desbarats et Derbishire.

Lareau, Edmond. 1888. *Histoire du droit canadien.* Vol. 1. Montreal: A. Périard.

–. 1889. *Histoire du droit canadien*. Vol. 2. Montreal: A. Périard.
Leclerc, Gilles. 2002. *Journal d'un inquisiteur*. Montreal: Lux.
Magnan, Charles Joseph. 1907. *Manuel d'instruction civique*. Quebec City: J.-L. Langeais et Fils.
Maldamé, Jean-Michel. 2018. *Monothéisme et violence*. Paris: Les Éditions du Cerf.
Manent, Pierre. 2001. *Cours familier de philosophie politique*. Paris: Gallimard.
–. 2010. *Les métamorphoses de la cité*. Paris: Flammarion.
Martínez de Codes, Rosa María. 2001. "La libertad religiosa en México." *Anales de Historia Contemporánea* 17: 525–29.
Morin, Émile. 1957. *La municipalité, la municipalité scolaire, la paroisse religieuse et civile, le comté*. Montreal: Service d'éducation, Syndicat national des fonctionnaires municipaux de Montréal.
Munro, C.R. 1997. "Does Scotland Have an Established Church?" *Ecclesiastical Law Journal* 4 (20): 643–44.
Noppen, Luc, and Lucie K. Morisset. 2005. *Les églises du Québec*. Quebec City: Presses de l'Université du Québec.
O'Sullivan, D.A. 1890. *Essays on the Church in Canada*. Toronto: Catholic Truth Society.
Ogilvie, M.H. 1990. "What Is a Church by Law Established?" *Osgoode Hall Law Journal* 28 (1): 179–236.
Pagnuelo, Simon. 1872. Études historiques et légales sur la liberté religieuse en Canada. Montreal: Éditions C.O. Beauchemin et Valois.
Paquet, Louis-Adolphe. 1916. *Droit public de l'Église. Principes généraux.* 2nd ed. Quebec City: J.-A.K. Laflamme.
Perrault, Antonio. 1943. *Le Conseil spécial, 1838–1841*. Quebec City: [unnamed publisher].
Perin, Roberto. 1993. *Rome et le Canada*. Montreal: Boréal.
Rousseau, Jean-Jacques. 1971. *Du contrat social*. Paris: Union générale d'éditions.
Roy, Maurice. 1950. *Paroisse et démocratie*. Montreal: L'œuvre des tracts no. 379.
Scott, Frank. 1959. "The Bill of Rights and Quebec law." *Revue du Barreau canadien* 37: 135–46.
St-Hilaire, Maxime. 2019. "Projet de loi sur la laïcité: dérogatoire à la charte ou contraire à la répartition des compétences?" *ABC National*, April 1.
Trigger, Rosalyn. 2001. "The Geopolitics of the Irish-Catholic Parish in Nineteenth-century Montreal." *Journal of Historical Geography* 27 (4): 553–72.
Trudel, François-Xavier Anselme. 1871. "Quelques réflexions sur les rapports de l'Église et de l'État." *La Revue canadienne* 8: 202–20, 252–72, 359–74.
Walsh, Henry H. 1958. "A Survey of Church History." *The Americas* 14 (4): 361–82.
Zuber, Valentine. 2014. *Le culte des droits de l'homme*. Paris: Gallimard.
–. 2019. "La laïcité française, une exception historique, des principes partagés." *Revue du droit des religions* 7: 193–205. http://journals.openedition.org/rdr/305.

The Difficult Search for a Quebec Model of Laicity

4

MICHELINE LABELLE

Quebec society has undergone a long drawn-out process – from the birth of the Mouvement laïque québécois (Secular Movement of Quebec) in the 1960s and the deconfessionalization of Catholic and Protestant school boards in 1997, under the Parti Québécois government led by Lucien Bouchard, right up to the National Assembly's adoption of the Act Respecting the Laicity of the State (Bill 21) on June 16, 2019.[1] And this process has been accompanied by a lively debate, much along the lines of the debate surrounding the Charter of the French Language (Bill 101) in 1977.[2]

The Act Respecting the Laicity of the State amends the Quebec Charter of Human Rights and Freedoms (Quebec Charter), which now states that "in exercising his fundamental freedoms and rights, a person shall maintain a proper regard for democratic values, State laicity, public order and the general well-being of the citizens of Quebec."[3] And the act affirms that "the Quebec nation has its own characteristics ... and a specific history that have led it to develop a particular attachment to State laicity." Quebec has developed a model of its own, taking into account its history and its national traditions, values, and aspirations. It is true, however, that this model is closer to the models shared by other democratic states with a civil law tradition, such as France, Luxemburg, and Switzerland, than it is to the multiculturalist and communitarian state prevailing in countries with a common law tradition, such as Canada and the United Kingdom.

According to a Léger poll published in the *Journal de Montréal* on September 16, 2019, approximately two out of three Quebeckers supported Bill 21 at the time of its adoption (75 percent of francophones and 46 percent of allophones, with the majority of all age groups supporting the regulation of the wearing of religious symbols). Nonetheless, critics have characterized the bill as discriminatory, even claiming it has fostered systemic racism. A petition signed by 250 university professors came out against it. In response, Micheline Labelle and Daniel Turp (2019) launched a petition in favour of the act, which by April 2019 had been signed by over 6,235 people. These events illustrate the fact that civil society is more united than is often claimed in the face of a very vocal minority benefiting from media coverage. Despite the act's detractors, the few opinion polls conducted on Bill 21 before its adoption show that it reflected a strong social consensus.

A journalist from France made the following observation with astonishment:

> But what has the Quebec government done to trigger such strong reactions? What has Premier François Legault done to be accused of preparing a campaign of "ethnic cleansing," of drawing inspiration from *Mein Kampf,* and even of paving the way for an attack on Canada? ... An initiative supported by a large majority of Quebeckers (around 65% in opinion polls), which nevertheless earned Legault a cascade of insults and slander, revealing the sensitivity of the question of the relationship to religions in Quebec, but also Quebec's place as a French-speaking province in Canada. (Mathoux 2019)

Hadrien Mathoux (2019) also emphasized how the reaction to the act has brought three pillars together: the religious, a fraction of the Left, and liberals in favour of multiculturalism. This chapter presents a critical view of the debates surrounding the Act Respecting the Laicity of the State. The first part focuses on the arguments in favour of "unqualified" secularism versus "open" secularism. The second part deals with

Canadian multiculturalism, which some opponents of Bill 21 are sure to invoke in the context of the legal challenge looming on the horizon. I take special note of the challenge and critical theories of multiculturalism and communitarianism. A third part examines some of the arguments raised by opponents of Bill 21 in the Ichrak Nourel Hak case filed in the Quebec Superior Court.[4]

Towards the Separation of Church and State without Qualification

The struggle for laicity in Quebec means that we have a duty to remember the past. Bill 21 is part of a long historical movement that has seen Quebec progressively secularize its public institutions, especially with the creation of a Ministry of Education, the creation of a non-denominational junior college system, the adoption in 1981 of the secular Civil Code of Quebec, and the deconfessionalization of Quebec's school boards and public schools.[5] The struggle has been historic and political. In his book *L'heure de vérité. La laïcité québécoise à l'épreuve de l'histoire,* historian Yvan Lamonde (2010, 172) writes that in order to understand the domination of the Catholic Church until the Quiet Revolution of the 1960s, one must recall its political foundations: "The founding stone of clericalism in Quebec was that the Church supported, for spiritual reasons and reasons of power, the English colonial political power following the Conquest of New France." The Catholic Church therefore interfered at many levels in democracy itself – in elections, constitutional regimes, printed matter, associations, freedom, and especially in the school, which was "a crucial power issue" (172).

The public space became a realm of conspicuous religious symbolism – from the names of streets, parishes, and roads to domestic and private space as well as the sacralization of time. Lamonde (2010, 180) notes the importance of the religious symbol: "The religious experience of Quebeckers is rich in examples where the wearing of a symbol gave a strong message. Otherwise, why would anyone want to wear a symbol if that symbol were devoid of an intention?" This sacralization was accompanied by the Catholic Church's power to resort to the index, to excommunicate, to intrude into private and political life. And this was a kind of institutional violence that did not operate on a purely symbolic level. An overbearing power relationship was in place, which countered and sought to stifle a strong current of secular tradition. Although this secular tradition suffered oppression, it reached its peak between 1830 and 1879, then was maintained and strengthened in the 1950s, and continued during the Quiet Revolution until the present day (12). The process of secularization has a long tradition in Quebec, going back to the Patriots of the 1830s because the idea of separation of state and church was contained in the 1838 Declaration of Independence proclaimed by the Patriots. Contrary to what some people are inclined to believe, secularization did not suddenly appear in the 2000s as a remedy for the unease of Quebeckers about religious accommodation in public institutions.

Lamonde (2010), like Guy Rocher (2013), regrets that the Bouchard-Taylor Commission did not take into account the historical and political dimensions of the struggle for secularism. The commission was after all set up to reflect on the issue of cultural and religious accommodations. Yet it hesitated to highlight the limits of an ethical and philosophical debate that has tended to focus on the individual and not on the collective interest. And it was partly by virtue of this political compromise that the report emerging from the commission recommended a model of "open secularism" while promoting a misguided conception of the opposition of the majority and minorities in Quebec and reducing the core function of the state to, merely, a coercive power over the citizens (Bouchard and Taylor 2008). The two commissioners stayed in the headlines long after the report was tabled, and they used separate or converging arguments in a bid to prevent passage of Bill 21. One of the commissioners even did an abrupt about-face, arguing against one of the key recommendations he had previously endorsed – namely, concerning the prohibition of the wearing of religious symbols by certain public employees.

In 2010, a major controversy arose in the press between the Manifeste pour un Québec pluraliste (which had about one thousand signatures), written by Pierre Bosset and colleagues (2010), and the Declaration of Intellectuals for Secularism (which had 3,400 signatures), written by anthropologist Daniel Baril and Guy Rocher (2013). The manifesto denounced two currents of thought that it claimed were at odds with the pluralist orientations of modern Quebec: the "conservative nationalist" current and the current of secularism described by the authors of the manifesto as "strict." According to the signatories of the manifesto, "the pure and simple prohibition of any manifestation of religious affiliation would not meet any social need" and would have "a discriminatory effect because it would only target believers belonging to religions with dress or food prescriptions" (Bosset et al. 2010, 2). The authors of the Declaration of Intellectuals for Secularism swiftly replied that "for a society to be authentically pluralist, that is, respectful of all religious convictions, the State and its institutions need to display total neutrality with respect to these convictions." Moreover, the neutrality of the state "is communicated by the neutrality displayed by its representatives," the "religious symbol being a non-verbal symbol identifying the faith, beliefs, religious affiliation and code of values of the person wearing it" (Baril and Lamonde 2013, 8–9).

Sociologist Guy Rocher (2013, 32–34) also argues for a form of secularism "without qualification" where public institutions are concerned. His first argument is that of historical continuity. In particular, Rocher recalls that the clergy agreed during the Quiet Revolution that they would no longer wear their distinctive religious symbols. At the same time, the feminist movement reinforced the process of deconfessionalization. Francine Descarries (2019), a sociologist specializing in feminist studies, reminds us that the sexism of religions is an obstacle to the full citizenship of women and that gender equality cannot be achieved in a context of open secularism and religious accommodations, both of which stem from cultural relativism. Politically, secularism without qualification can only promote fair and transparent management for the administrators of public institutions and contribute to social peace (Rocher 2010, 13). And, above all, laicity adheres to a "common value" reaffirmed by all Quebec governments for decades in the absence of any explicit law to this effect. It is a moderate response to the social unease that was raging in Quebec over reasonable accommodation and that led to the creation of the Bouchard-Taylor Commission. Laicity could help stem the growth of radical groups. Moreover, European courts have validated similar and even more restrictive measures than those provided for in section 6 of Bill 21 on the grounds that such measures ensure social cohesion (Lemire 2019).

Sociologically speaking, religions are social institutions: they are social facts inscribed in the social hierarchy. The decision whether to utter a public prayer, obtain special status, or wear a religious symbol in a school "depends on the power relations between a group or an authority (a municipal council) and citizens" (Rocher 2013, 36). Religious symbols themselves are not neutral: on the contrary, they convey a message. To see the wearing of a religious symbol simply as a personal choice "is to sever it from its social reality, from the discourse it addresses to the entire environment, from the testimony it bears on the power relations between a particular belief and the public institution" (37). When Gérard Bouchard and Québec solidaire asked Guy Rocher for evidence that the wearing of religious symbols had an influence on students, he retorted that their claim was "without scientific basis" and that it was "methodologically impossible to establish its scientific validity" (Barbeau 2019).

Defenders of "open" secularism, some of whom were particularly influential during the hearings of the Bouchard-Taylor Commission, have been at pains to distinguish between state institutions or structures, on the one hand, and social agents, on the other. They draw this distinction on the grounds that only structures should be neutral. From a sociological point of view, says Rocher (2013, 37), this distinction is nonsense: "The State ... is not an abstraction ... The State exists and acts above all by means of the people, the men and women who form it, who make it act, who maintain it." The state intervenes and governs through the institutions and structures (ministries, agencies, and so on) that embody it and that ensure its impact. I would add that public servants are already required to demonstrate a duty of reserve and political neutrality under the Public Service Act.[6] And even university professors are bound by this constraint, with rare exceptions.

Finally, as the Mouvement laïque québécois points out, according to section 41 of the Quebec Charter, priority must be given to the freedom of conscience and the freedom of religion of parents and students.[7] Bill 21 has been the subject of controversy and has come under attack much the way that the Charter of the French Language did. Four political scientists have recently demonstrated that, in Quebec, a citizen who defends liberal social values is more inclined to support restrictions on the wearing of religious symbols in the public service. This is not the case in the rest of Canada, where a citizen who defends these same liberal values is more likely to oppose any restrictions on the wearing of religious symbols. This conclusion was reached by four academics in a research project launched in 2014 in the wake of the debate surrounding Quebec's proposed Charter of Values (Turgeon et al. 2019). Let us recall that Quebeckers, probably because of their history and their national situation and, moreover, their minority status have an unwavering attachment to the collective interest and what they share in common. Laicity, let us remember, reaches beyond individual choice.

Does multiculturalism-communitarianism have anything to do with the fact that Quebeckers and Canadians take contrary positions on these issues? We will look more carefully at this question, to which the experts and lawyers in the Ichrak Nourel Hak case certainly have referred in court.[8]

The Pillar of Multiculturalism

For ages, confusion has persisted in Quebec debates as to the meaning of multiculturalism. Simply put, it can be a public policy as it exists in Canada and Australia, or it can be a more widely held political philosophy.[9]

Canadian Public Policy

In 1971, Prime Minister Pierre Elliott Trudeau instituted the public policy of multiculturalism, thereby denying the Aboriginal and Quebec national questions: "Each ethnic group has the right to preserve and promote its own culture and values within the Canadian context. For although there are two official languages, there is no official culture, nor does any ethnic group take precedence over another."[10] Aboriginal people and Quebeckers were thus reduced from nations to mere ethnic groups. The Canadian Constitution was repatriated from London by the Trudeau government in 1982. This repatriation was undertaken without Quebec's consent, and it allowed multiculturalism to be enshrined in the Canadian Charter of Rights and Freedoms (Canadian Charter).[11] The Parliament of Canada subsequently passed the Canadian Multiculturalism Act in 1988, which recognizes "that multiculturalism is a fundamental characteristic of the Canadian heritage and identity and that it provides an invaluable resource in the shaping of Canada's future ... to preserve and enhance the use of languages other than English and French, while strengthening the status and use of the official languages of Canada."[12] It is based on two premises: "to recognize and promote the understanding that multiculturalism reflects the cultural and racial diversity of Canadian society and acknowledges the freedom of all members of Canadian society to preserve, enhance and share their cultural heritage" and to "foster the recognition and appreciation of the diverse cultures of Canadian society and promote the reflection and the evolving expressions of those cultures."[13] The first premise erroneously assumes the existence of "races" within Canadian society, which is a considerable scientific error since races do not exist. The second is based on an undefined view of culture, which gives the courts the power to strike down provincial laws (such as the Quebec Charter of the French Language), purportedly in the name of defending human rights.

Yet the federal multiculturalism policy has been disavowed by all Quebec governments – Liberal and Parti Québécois – since 1971 because it denies the "distinct" or "national" character of Quebec. On the other hand, a Quebec policy of interculturalism was gradually developed, focusing on cultural dialogue, the French language, and the sense of belonging to Quebec, without any legislation on the subject. Starting in the 1970s, the policy of multiculturalism has been subject to sustained criticism across Canada. For some observers, the multiculturalism policy constitutes an obstacle to integration or assimilation. For others, it ignores the legacy of British and French colonialism. Some critics say it stigmatizes "visible minorities" while maintaining a folkloric and condescending view of minorities, masking inequalities and doing little to encourage accession to Canadian citizenship. There has been so much criticism that the Canadian minister of citizenship and immigration eventually declared that multiculturalism must not become a "rigid religion." Heritage Canada was concerned at the time about social exclusion, radicalization, and the formation of ethnic enclaves (Labelle 2015a, 37). Practices such as honour killings, female circumcision, and polygamy became a real concern over time. Under the influence of the philosopher

Will Kymlicka (2003), the idea of dialogue was even borrowed from Quebec's model of interculturalism. Commenting on these illiberal practices, Kymlicka refers to the need for intercultural dialogue: "Proponents of intercultural education today are quite aware of this danger, and so emphasize the need for a deeper understanding, dialogue and appreciation between the members of different groups" (163). In their expert report to the Bouchard-Taylor Commission, François Rocher, Micheline Labelle, and Anne-Marie Field (2007) documented in depth the importance of this notion of intercultural dialogue, which has been at the heart of Quebec's public policies since the late 1970s. On the theoretical level, Micheline Labelle and Xavier Dionne (2011) have also analyzed the foundations of interculturalism that oppose multiculturalism, whose visions are debated by specialists in the philosophy of multiculturalism in Canada and elsewhere.

Then the paradigms changed. For some researchers, Canada is now in a post-national and post-multicultural era. The world is now made up of "connections and flows that cross multiple universes, transcending borders and challenging the authority of post-national states," and the profusion of belongings and allegiances no longer has anything to do with the mosaic model of multiculturalism that applied to a society composed of well-differentiated "ethnic groups" (Fleras 2012, 39). The notion of super-diversity has taken hold in the academic literature and within the Canadian state. This notion corresponds to the dynamic interplay of variables among a growing number of "immigrants, of multiple origins, transnationally connected, socio-economically differentiated and with highly differentiated legal status" (Vertovec 2007).[14]

Not surprisingly, during the media furor over Bill 21, many English Canadian jurists attacked the legislation, claiming that it violated Ottawa's promotion of the Canadian multiculturalism policy. But what visions of Canadian multiculturalism, if any, inspire these jurists and their Quebec colleagues in defending the *Hak* case: the visions of the 1970s or the visions disparaged by the thinkers of super-diversity, anti-racism, and intersectional feminism?[15] It does not really matter in the end because they are always inspired by multiculturalism, whose foundation is the rejection of all national issues and collective rights.

Post-Multiculturalism

During the 1990s and 2000s, several factors complicated the interpretation and promotion of multiculturalism as a political philosophy: the resurgence of religion, different strains of religious fundamentalism, Islamist terrorism, populism, the extreme right, and post-colonial reinterpretations of national identities, to make a long list short. In Europe as well as in Canada, there has been a call to order from critical theorists of multiculturalism. A fundamental question arises. Is it legitimate for a democratic society to seek to restrict cultural or religious expressions, or should it instead defend cultural relativism the way classical colonial anthropology does, on the grounds that these expressions have a social function in a given setting? In answering this question, political theorist Bikhu Parekh (2006, 271) recommends a bifocal dialogue between majorities and minorities. While all cultures are worthy of respect, the majority in the host society has the right to defend its "core common values" against a minority whose practices it finds unacceptable. Every society has the right and the duty to reject or disavow practices that run counter to this core set of values.

Philosophers have sought to defend a "complex cultural dialogue" insofar as struggles for recognition and identity movements aim for democratic inclusion, social and political justice, and cultural fluidity. According to Seyla Benhabib (2002), a political scientist and philosopher at Yale University, fundamentalist, essentialist, or traditionalist movements that advocate the purity of cultures are irreconcilable with basic epistemological and democratic considerations. Interculturalism is also being debated. In 2012, the *Journal of Intercultural Studies* brought out a special issue devoted to the merits and shortcomings of both political ideologies. Radical theories such as critical race theory, whiteness studies championed by sociologist Paul Eid (2018), and decoloniality are light years away from multiculturalism and interculturalism. In particular, decoloniality addresses the analysis of systems of sexual, political, epistemic, economic, linguistic, and racial hierarchies and devices of domination and capitalist exploitation on a global scale that have been produced by colonial administrations and whose effects persist in contemporary societies (Grosfoguel 2006).

In its violent form, it is embodied, for example, in the discourse of Houria Bouteldja, spokesperson for the Parti des Indigènes de la République in France and a figure in the decolonial movement. As for the theory of intersectionality, it aims to interpret the complexity and multidimensional nature of inequalities and oppressions based on social class, sex/gender, colour, ethnicity, religion, and disability. It posits their interaction at both the micro-sociological level – that is, the level of individual experience – and the macro-sociological level – that is, the way in which power relations are involved in the production and maintenance of inequalities in social institutions (Bilge 2009). It also raises the issue of the diversity of struggles and coalitions. These currents of thought have had a strong impact on Quebec, and many activists have resorted to them in challenging Bill 21 – for example, the coalitions of First Nations and people from racialized and religious minorities that have come together in the Table de concertation sur le racisme systémique au Québec or the Coalition Inclusion Québec, which is supported by Québec solidaire, Charles Taylor, and other intellectuals who present themselves as authentic "pluralists."

But let us move on to the foundation of religious opposition to the Act Respecting the Laicity of the State.

Religious Opposition, Supported by a Fraction of the Left

The most virulent attacks on the Act Respecting the Laicity of the State come from religious circles (Jews, Sikhs, Muslims, Catholics) as well as from a fraction of the Left and from philosophers who believe they possess, and claim to teach, the virtues of pluralism, inclusion, and openness. However, it should be noted that these attacks also stem from political and ideological struggles within the minorities themselves. And, in this regard, it is important to note the deep division between universalist feminism and differentialist feminism (decolonial, Islamist, Afro-American, and so on), the latter representing a new doxa in universities and social movements.

Secularism is an issue that has nothing intrinsically or in principle to do with immigration. However, the rise of religious forces (states, organizations, sects) on an international scale has meant that democratic states have to deal with politically active rigorist religious groups around the world. For example, at a demonstration organized by the Canadian Anti-Islamophobia Collective and Imam Adil Charkaoui, which featured "decolonial" feminists, young hijab-wearing girls, and demonstrators shouting *Allahu akbar*, Premier François Legault was called a "fascist" and compared to Adolf Hitler. On a previous occasion, Imam Adil Charkaoui praised Canadian multiculturalism, while declaring the Parti Québécois to be anti-pluralist. Similarly, a coalition of elected officials from Montreal's West Island denounced the "institutionalization of discrimination." According to William Steinberg, the mayor of Hampstead (a gilded, English-speaking enclave), Bill 21 is "an attempt to remove those who practise minority religions, leaving only non-believers and Christians in Quebec. This is ethnic cleansing. Not with a gun, but with a law" (Corriveau and Bélair-Cirino 2019). In the face of public outrage and a potential lawsuit over his comments, he modified the expression "ethnic cleansing" to "peaceful ethnic cleansing."

Some women wearing the hijab and challenging Bill 21 have maintained that they left France in order to display their faith freely in Quebec. Other women have stated that Quebec is not a country and that they have emigrated to a land where "Canadian multiculturalism" reigns. These women do not seem much like the oppressed women some intellectuals take them for, in a way that could be considered paternalistic and focused above all on images of misery. From a left-wing perspective, some women emphasize that they belong to the decolonial movement. For example, Alexa Conradi (2019), former president of the Fédération des femmes du Quebec (an organization that split on these issues, leading to the founding of Pour les droits des femmes du Québec), has refuted the republican conception of universalism according to which "principles such as equality, solidarity and freedom apply universally. However, many historically marginalized political and intellectual movements increasingly challenge this way of thinking, making way for better grounded and more contradictory conceptions of the good, the livable or the just life. What was previously held to be true is now the subject of debate." And Amel Zaazaa (2015, 80), who claims to be a proponent of the intersectionality of oppressions and whiteness, argues that "the anti-racist and indigenous movements that are active today are shaking up Quebec by advocating a decolonial vision ... These movements refuse the pluralist veneer as well as this image of the colour-blind Quebec where it is good to live together." And she concludes that the activists of the anti-racist movement are reinventing their struggle "driven by the desire to be grains of sand that will disrupt the well-oiled machine." Displaying her contempt for a "white" National Assembly, it is not surprising that she, like her fellow activists, has come out against the Act Respecting the Laicity of the State, which she arguably perceives as legislation marked by republicanism.

It is in this highly controversial context that Ichrak Nourel Hak, a female student at the Université de Montréal, decided to challenge Bill 21 in court, with backing from the National Council of Canadian Muslims and the Canadian Civil Liberties Association, two Ontario-based organizations. Hak emigrated from Morocco in 1994 and is completing a bachelor's degree in teaching French as a second language, and she was planning to teach French in a high school reception class or an elementary school class in an English-language school. She wears the Islamic veil or hijab, which she says is part of her religious beliefs and identity, and she has explained that she refuses to remove the hijab in order to get a job and feels insulted, hurt, and excluded from Quebec society by Bill 21.[16]

The plaintiffs maintain that Bill 21 violates the equality of women and men under section 28 of the Canadian Charter and section 50.1 of the Quebec Charter on the following grounds: that women fill most of the teaching positions affected by the ban on wearing a religious symbol; that most Muslim women wear a veil; and that the ban on wearing a religious symbol is therefore a denial of the free will, dignity, and autonomy of those women concerned and also stigmatizes women who already suffer from socio-economic disadvantages. This legal reasoning suggests that the experts on behalf of the plaintiff may be invoking the theory of intersectionality as there may be a claim of cumulative inequality and oppression. Yet each category of difference (national origin, social origin, social class, religion, sex/gender, colour, and so on) is in turn characterized by internal diversity, which poses the problem of analysis and interpretation in determining the factors involved as well as in identifying the relative weight to be assigned to each of them, a problem that is well known in sociology.

However, the Act Respecting the Laicity of the State concerns the Jewish kippa as well as the Sikh turban and the Catholic cross. The act applies to all religious symbols, whether worn by women or men. The Lord Reading Law Association, representing Jewish jurists, has been recognized as an intervener in the case. The same is true of the World Sikh Organization. The fact remains that it is a young student who has found herself at the forefront of the legal challenge. Other arguments, some of them actually quite bizarre, have been put forward in the reports of experts on behalf of the plaintiff. For example, according to psychologist Richard Bourhis (2020, 4, para. 6), Bill 21 "heightens the salience of the minority 'Them' categories of Jews, Muslims and Sikhs in relation to the 'Us' of the national majority." He maintains that "the *Act respecting the laicity of the State* adopted by the Quebec government in June 2019 prohibits the wearing of religious symbols by certain categories of people in Quebec State institutions. Among other things, these provisions of the *Act respecting the laicity of the State* have the avowed long-term goal of excluding by attrition all religious minorities wearing religious symbols from the Quebec school system," which will cause them definite psychological harm; "an effect that the Christian and non-believing Quebec majority of the province does not have to suffer" (paras 16, 36, 52). Note the choice of words: "[A] Christian majority in a province." Moreover, Bourhis used obsolete racial categories during the trial (for example, the term "brown" to designate Muslims). With such generalizations, this psychologist overlooks the fact that there is no question in the act of excluding religious minorities who wear religious symbols from the Quebec school system: the objective of the act is rather to ensure that people wearing religious symbols refrain from doing so during working hours in public institutions.

An American scholar, Thomas Dee (2020) argues for the importance of teacher diversity in the US context, focusing on the case of African Americans and Hispanics. And he concludes that the same goes for religious symbols:

> My summative conclusion based on this literature is that a ban on the wearing of religious symbols among primary and secondary teachers is likely to reduce teacher diversity and to have negative

> effects on multiple student outcomes (e.g., engagement, motivation, achievement and, ultimately, longer-run life outcomes), particularly among minority students whose personal, cultural and religious representations within schools would be censored. Moreover, the available research suggests that these effects will occur through multiple reinforcing mechanisms (14, para. 59).

Several problems with his approach are worth noting. For example, he relies on research showing the benefits of so-called racial diversity among teachers in the United States to determine the impact of a ban on wearing religious symbols in Quebec schools. He also assumes that Bill 21 will reduce diversity in Quebec's teaching force without providing any evidence to back up this claim. This statement does not seem relevant in Quebec, which adopted the Act Respecting Equal Access to Employment in Public Bodies in 2000.[17] It is true that this Act is not being implemented as successfully as we would have hoped. Moreover, there is a difference between promoting diversity and promoting religion in a public education system that is already deconfessionalized and is supposed to be secular.

Another expert on behalf of the plaintiff seeks to demonstrate, based on interviews with twenty veiled teenage girls, that the hijab is part of their identity, that they wear it without pressure, and that they consider wearing the hijab to be a matter of agency and freedom (Eid 2020). A methodological problem arises here. Scientific rigour requires that interviewing such a limited number of people in a qualitative study be presented as a non-representative sample and also that the starting point of the "snowball technique" allowing for this interview sample be made explicit. In fact, if we were to test this hypothesis, we would need to construct a mirror sample of teenage girls who wear the veil under pressure from their parents or imams in order to understand and illustrate their situation. This would require courage and skill on the part of the researcher. But Paul Eid concludes: "There is no evidence from existing research that the choice of Quebec and Canadian Muslim women to wear the hijab is dictated by religious institutions, authorities or currents (e.g., Salafism, Wahhabism, Sufism)" (para. 104). This conclusion diverges from the work of researcher Yolande Geadah (2020), who was retained as an expert in the court challenge by the feminist group Pour le droit des femmes, and whose lawyer is Christiane Pelchat, former president of the Conseil du statut de la femme.

What is also problematic about the *Hak* case, briefly outlined here, and the arguments invoked by some experts is the *ad nauseam* repetition of accusations of systemic racism, the opposition of majority and minority, and, finally, the "methodological nationalism" that focuses in its analysis of issues of secularism and pluralism on the case of Quebec alone.

On Racism

In the current context, authors and activists believe that systemic racism is the result of the oppression of majorities over minorities. Racism has become a buzzword applied to all sorts of social groups and inequitable situations. Moreover, this misuse of language has turned groups that define themselves by religion into supposed "races." It is true that the federal Employment Equity Act clearly encourages the racialization of citizens.[18] According to the act, visible minorities are made up of "persons, other than Aboriginal peoples, who are non-Caucasian in race or non-white in colour." This classification applies to the following categories: South Asian, Chinese, Black, Filipino, Latin American, Arab, Southeast Asian, West Asian, Korean, and Japanese. However, this classification is scientifically unacceptable: it lumps together into the category of "race" groups with regional or national identities of origin, which are themselves phenotypically diverse.

What are we to make of this racism? It is certainly not the classic racist and colonial ideology that advocates the biological, spiritual, and intellectual superiority of one population over another. Is it, instead, a question of differentialist racism (also called neo-racism, cultural racism, or symbolic racism, depending on the authors), according to which certain cultures are unassimilable and must therefore be kept at a distance in the name of a natural right to live among themselves? If the state was to segregate, discriminate against, or prevent the immigration of people of Jewish, Muslim, or Sikh faith from particular countries or regions, we could speak of classical racism, as was the case in the selection practised by the Canadian state before 1965, or of differentialist racism in the current period (Labelle 2011). But this is far from being the case in Quebec. Moreover, if there was an element of racism in the state's desire to ban religious symbols in public institutions during working hours, would we consider people from the same minorities who support this ban to be racist or complicit in what is described as systemic racism?

Majorities and minorities are stratified according to various factors: origin, language, social class, culture, phenotype, religion, political beliefs, and so on. I quote a Sephardic Jewish leader speaking about the Jewish community: "The Jews themselves are not aware of all branches of Judaism. They think their own branch is representative of the whole community. There are ultra-Orthodox, Orthodox, Conservative, Reconstructionist and Reform" branches (Labelle and Levy 1995). The same goes for all religious faiths. For this reason, many Muslim women in favour of the Act Respecting the Laicity of the State are active in the Association québécoise des Nord-Africains pour la laïcité, the Mouvement laïque québécois, Pour les droits des femmes du Québec (PDF Québec), and so on. Many male and female citizens have suffered from the expansion of the Wahhabi-Salafist ideology in their country of origin, have fled their home country as refugees, asylum seekers, or regular immigrants, and now have found the same movement in Quebec keeping a watchful eye on women. Clearly, Quebec society is not isolated from the international currents of thought and networks.

To conclude, I would add that the debate on laicity is missing something important: a critique of "methodological nationalism," and this idea forms the basis of my conclusion.

Conclusion

To understand the current debate on secularism, we should not focus exclusively on Quebec society. To do so would be to demonstrate "methodological nationalism" or, in other words, "sedentary bias," an expression borrowed from the sociologist Stephen Castels (2010) in his analyses of international migration. Indeed, globalization forces "us to read history, and the history that is made, politics, geopolitics, war, as well as religion, migratory phenomena, justice, new social movements or the surge of identities by adopting perspectives that are no longer ethnocentric, Western-centric, perspectives that bring everything back to the nation-state," according to American sociologist Greg Calhoun and French sociologist Michel Wieviorka (2013, 12; see also Labelle 2015b).

It seems increasingly important for us to move away from methodological nationalism in analyzing social and national struggles for emancipation involving labour, gender, secularism, and nations. These struggles for emancipation form a disparate whole, they are crossed by diverse currents, and they are waged by social actors with diverse agendas. As Calhoun and Wieviorka (2013) have already pointed out, social movements are distinguished from community movements in that social movements aim to promote a societal objective, whereas community movements are organized on the basis of cultural, ethnic, gendered, racialized, or religious categories, through the identification of an adversary and through a desire to break away that can go as far as fanaticism. And, at the same time, as is always the case in the current international situation, these communitarian struggles are subject to political instrumentalization by ideological currents without borders. In this sense, the debate on secularism is taking place in a context of troubled times.

This new context has changed the situation and raises several questions. How do ideologies circulate? What ideologies and what strategies of action are disseminated within Quebec society through websites, closed discussion groups, and international social networks? These questions are particularly important when it comes to analyzing social forces and power relations. It is important to find a way to penetrate closed environments that are often hostile to the host society's set of values.

Notes

1 Act Respecting the Laicity of the State, SQ 2019, c. 12.

2 Charter of the French Language, SQ 1977, c. 5.

3 Charter of Human Rights and Freedoms, RSQ 1977, c. C-12.

4 Quebec Superior Court, *Hak et al. v P.G. Québec*, Application for Judicial Review (Declaration of Invalidity and Application for an Interim Stay), File no. 500–17–108353–17, June 17, 2019 (*Hak et al.*).

5 Civil Code of Quebec, SQ 1991, c. 64.

6 Public Service Employment Act, SC 2003, c. 22.

7 Quebec Superior Court, *Acte d'intervention volontaire à titre agressif par Djaafar Bouchilaoun (Art 186 C.p.c)*, File no. 500–17–108353–1972, December 18, 2019, para. 18.
8 *Hak et al.*
9 This section is largely inspired by my work and, in particular, by Labelle 2015a.
10 *Débats de la Chambre des communes*, 28th Legislature, 3rd Session, vol. 8, October 8, 1971, 8545, https://parl.canadiana.ca/view/oop.debates_CDC2803_07/699.
11 Canadian Charter of Rights and Freedoms, Part 1 of the Constitution Act, 1982, being Schedule B to the Canada Act 1982 (UK), 1982, c. 11.
12 Canadian Multiculturalism Act, RSC 1985, c. 24 (4th Supp).
13 Canadian Multiculturalism Act, s. 3(1)(a), (h).
14 The original wording is as follows: "among an increased number of new, small and scattered, multiple-origin, transnationally connected, socio-economically differentiated and legally stratified immigrants."
15 *Hak et al.* The Juristes pour la laïcité de l'État (2019) maintain that "if Canada preaches so much about diversity, we submit that it is very much in the interest of society that it first accept the diversity represented by Quebec."
16 *Hak et al.*, paras. 22–23.
17 Act Respecting Equal Access to Employment in Public Bodies, 2000, https://www.legisquebec.gouv.qc.ca/en/document/cs/A-2.01: "This Act establishes a special framework to provide equal access to employment in order to remedy the situation experienced by persons belonging to certain groups discriminated against in employment, namely women, handicapped persons within the meaning of the *act to secure handicapped persons in the exercise of their rights with a view to achieving social, school and workplace integration* (chapter E-20.1), aboriginal peoples, persons who are members of visible minorities because of their race or the colour of their skin and persons whose mother tongue is neither French nor English and who belong to a group other than the aboriginal peoples group or the visible minorities group."
18 Employment Equity Act, SC 1995, c. 44.

References

Barbeau, Bernard. 2019. "Les convictions religieuses des élèves avant celles des enseignants." *Radio Canada*. https://ici.radio-canada.ca/nouvelle/1169702/projet-loi-21-laicite-etat-signes-religieux-consultations-particulieres-guy-rocher.

Baril, Daniel, and Yvan Lamonde, eds. 2013. *Pour une reconnaissance de la laïcité au Québec. Enjeux philosophiques, politiques et juridiques*. Quebec City: Presses de l'Université Laval. https://www.pulaval.com/libreacces/9782763718729.pdf.

Benhabib, Seyla. 2002. *The Claims of Culture: Equality and Diversity in the Global Era*. Princeton, NJ: Princeton University Press.

Bilge, Sirma. 2009. "Théorisations féministes de l'intersectionnalité." *Diogène* 1 (225): 80–88. https://www.erudit.org/en/journals/ps/1900-v1-n1-ps01449/1025584ar/.

Bosset, Pierre, Dominique Leydet, Jocelyn Maclure, Micheline Milot, and Daniel Weinstock. 2010. "Manifeste pour un Québec pluraliste." *Le Devoir,* February 3. https://www.ledevoir.com/opinion/idees/282309/manifeste-pour-un-quebec-pluraliste.

Bouchard, Gérard, and Charles Taylor. 2008. *Building the Future: A Time for Reconciliation*. Quebec City: Commission de consultation sur les pratiques d'accommodement reliées aux différences culturelles. https://numerique.banq.qc.ca/patrimoine/details/52327/1565995.

Bourhis, Richard. 2020. *Rapport d'expertise de Richard Y Bourhis dans le cadre de la contestation de la validité constitutionnelle de la Loi sur la laïcité de l'État.* File no. 500-17-107204-193. Presentation to the Quebec Superior Court, Montreal, 12 May.

Calhoun, Greg, and Michel Wieviorka. 2013. "Manifeste pour les sciences sociales." *Penser Global* 1: 5–39.

Castels, Stephen. 2010. "Understanding Global Migration: A Social Transformation Perspective." *Journal of Ethnic and Migration Studies* 36 (10): 1565–86. https://www.tandfonline.com/doi/abs/10.1080/1369183X.2010.489381.

Conradi, Alexa. 2019. "Oser un féminisme décolonial." *Le Devoir,* May 28. https://www.ledevoir.com/opinion/idees/555394/oser-un-feminisme-decolonial

Corriveau, Jeanne, and Marco Bélair-Cirino. 2019. "Une coalition invite les Québécois à combattre le projet de loi sur la laïcité." *Le Devoir,* 6 April. https://www.ledevoir.com/politique/quebec/551574/une-coalition-appelle-a-la-mobilisation-contre-le-projet-de-loi-sur-la-laicite.

Dee, Thomas. 2020. Expert report presented to the Superior Court of Quebec in the context of the challenge to the constitutional validity of the Act Respecting the Laicity of the State, File no. EMSB-23-47. Presentation to the Quebec Superior Court, Montreal, March 11.

Descarries, Francine. 2013. "Pourquoi les femmes ont-elles besoin d'un État laïque dans leur lutte à l'égalité?" In Baril and Lamonde 2013, 97–108.

Eid, Paul. 2018. "Les majorités nationales ont-elles une couleur? Réflexions sur l'utilité de la catégorie de 'blanchité' pour la sociologie du racisme." *Sociologie et sociétés* 50 (2): 125–49. https://www.erudit.org/fr/revues/socsoc/2018-v50-n2-socsoc05087/1066816ar/.

–. 2020. *Rapport d'expertise présenté à la Cour supérieure du Québec dans le cadre de la contestation de la validité constitutionnelle de la Loi sur la laïcité de l'État*. File no. 500–17–107204193. Presentation to the Quebec Superior Court, Montreal, March 31.

Fleras, Augie. 2012. "From Mosaic to Multiversality: Repriming Multicultural Governance in a Post national Canada." *Canadian Ethnic Studies* 48 (1–2): 17–39.

Geadah, Yolande. 2020. *Rapport d'expertise pour le groupe Pour les droits des femmes PDF,* File no. 500–17–108353–197. Presentation to the Quebec Superior Court, Montreal, March 2020.

Grosfoguel, Ramon. 2006. "Les implications des altérités épistémiques dans la redéfinition du capitalisme global." *Multitudes* 3 (26): 51–74.
Juristes pour la laïcité de l'État, represented by Julie Latour. 2019. "Brief Tabled with the Commission des institutions (in French), National Assembly of Quebec, Special consultations Bill 21 Act respecting the laicity of the State. May 6." *National Assembly*. https://assnat.qc.ca/fr/travaux-parlementaires/commissions/CI/mandats/Mandat-41031/memoires-deposes.html.
Kymlicka, Will. 2003. "Multicultural States and Intercultural Citizens." *Theory and Research in Education* 1 (2): 147–69. https://journals.sagepub.com/doi/10.1177/1477878503001002001.
Labelle, Micheline. 2011. *Racisme et antiracisme. Discours et déclinaisons*. Quebec City: Presses de l'Université du Québec. http://classiques.uqac.ca/contemporains/labelle_micheline/racisme_et_antiracisme_qc/racisme_antiracisme.html.
–. 2015a. "Multiculturalisme, interculturalisme, antiracisme: le traitement de l'altérité." *Revue européenne des migrations internationales* 31 (2): 31–54. http://classiques.uqac.ca/contemporains/labelle_micheline/multiculturalisme_interculturalisme/multiculturalisme_interculturalisme.html.
–. 2015b. "Le paradigme de la mobilité propose-t-il une perspective adéquate de l'immigration internationale?" *Éthique publique* 17 (1): 1–14. http://classiques.uqac.ca/contemporains/labelle_micheline/paradigme_de_la_mobilite/paradigme_de_la_mobilite.html.
Labelle, Micheline, and Xavier Dionne. 2011. *Les fondements théoriques de l'interculturalisme*, Rapport présenté à la Direction de la gestion de la diversité et de l'intégration sociale, Ministère de l'Immigration et des Communautés culturelles du Québec. Montreal: Chaire de recherche en immigration, ethnicité et citoyenneté, Université du Québec à Montréal. https://criec.uqam.ca/upload/files/Rapport%20Inter%20final%2029%20sept%202011.pdf.
Labelle, Micheline, and Joseph J. Lévy. 1995. *Ethnicité et enjeux sociaux. Le Québec vu par les leaders de groupes ethnoculturels*. Montreal: Liber. http://classiques.uqac.ca/contemporains/labelle_micheline/ethnicite_enjeux_sociaux/ethnicite_enjeux_sociaux.html.
Labelle, Micheline, and Daniel Turp. 2019. "Le Projet de loi sur la laïcité. Une avancée tangible." *Le Devoir*, April 11. https://www.ledevoir.com/opinion/idees/551886/projet-de-loi-sur-la-laicite-une-avancee-tangible.
Lamonde, Yvan. 2010. *L'heure de vérité. La laïcité québécoise à l'épreuve de l'histoire*. Montreal: Del Busso Éditeur.
Lemire, Samuel. 2019. "Une marge d'appréciation fédérale pour reconnaître la laïcité québécoise." *La Presse*, December 5. https://plus.lapresse.ca/screens/47e74400-94e3-4282-8a78-8bd9226d0525%7C_0.html.
Mathoux, Hadrien. 2019. "Au Québec, la gauche radicale, les libéraux et les intégristes font alliance contre la laïcité." *Marianne*, April 23. https://www.marianne.

net/monde/au-quebec-la-gauche-radicale-les-liberaux-et-les-integristes-font-alliance-contre-la-laicite.

Parekh, Bhikhu. 2006. *Rethinking Multiculturalism: Cultural Diversity and Political Theory*. Basingstoke, UK: Palgrave Macmillan.

Rocher, Guy. 2010. "Allocution prononcée à la Grande Bibliothèque." Conference organized by the Coalition Laïcité Québec, April 28. https://www.google.ca/books/edition/La_communaute_politique_en_question/hMNwef4B6WgC?hl=fr&gbpv=1&dq=Rocher,+Guy.+2010.+%E2%80%9CAllocution+prononc%C3%A9e+%C3%A0+la+Grande+Biblioth%C3%A8que.%E2%80%9D&pg=PA366&printsec=frontcover.

–. 2013. "La laïcité pour le Québec, quelques arguments." In Baril and Lamonde 2013, 31–39.

Rocher, François, Micheline Labelle, and Anne-Marie Field. 2007. *Le concept d'interculturalisme en contexte québécois: généalogie d'un néologisme*. Montreal: Commission de consultation sur les pratiques d'accommodement reliées aux différences culturelles, Chaire de recherche en immigration, ethnicité et citoyenneté, Université du Québec à Montréal. https://www.mce.gouv.qc.ca/publications/CCPARDC/rapport-3-rocher-francois.pdf.

Turgeon, Luc, Antoine Bilodeau, Stephen E. Blanc, and Ailsa Anderson. 2019. "A Tale of Two Liberalisms? Attitudes toward Minority Religious Symbols in Quebec and Canada." *Canadian Journal of Political Science* 52 (2): 247–65.

Vertovec, Steven. 2007. "Super-Diversity and Its Implications." *Ethnic and Racial Studies* 30 (6): 1024–54. https://www.tandfonline.com/doi/abs/10.1080/01419870701599465.

Zaazaa, Amel. 2019. "Hoodstock ou la réappropriation d'une citoyenneté confisquée." In *11 brefs essais contre le racism,* edited by Amel Zaazzaa and Christian Nadeau, 73–80. Montreal: Éditions Somme toute.

5

Some Muslim Quebec Women and Men Are in Favour of Bill 21

YASMINA CHOUAKRI

The Act Respecting the Laicity of the State (Bill 21) was adopted on June 16, 2019.[1] It is being challenged in the courts on the grounds that it is discriminatory and suppresses religious freedom. It is also being criticized by part of the feminist community movement that is close to the multiculturalist Left, which also considers the law to be discriminatory, specifically with respect to Muslim women. However, something important has emerged from the hue and cry about the act – namely, the view that women should wear the veil to symbolize their adherence to the Muslim religion is driven ultimately by a conservative and dogmatic vision of Islam. It is as if the very definition of a Muslim woman were that she be a veiled woman. This helps propagate a monolithic image of what a Muslim woman must be and, of course, stigmatizes those women who are not veiled, whether they be practising or not.

The majority of so-called Muslim women[2] in Quebec do not wear the veil. Bill 21 is not a problem for them at all. They are emancipated from, or distanced from, an interpretation that sees the veil as a religious obligation. Sometimes, these women even reject the veil because they disagree with the way in which the veil is imposed on women for religious and political reasons in several Muslim countries. These women share a liberal vision of Islam. But I should be clear about one thing: I mean "liberal" in the classical emancipatory sense of the term, which has nothing to do with the conservatism of current liberal thinking in the West. This liberal, emancipatory Islam presents a vision of life that is open to modernity and to the values of equality between women and men. The people challenging and contesting[3] Bill 21 seem only to be taking into account the positions of conservative groups, which are in the minority within the so-called Muslim communities of Quebec. For this reason, we can state that the opposition to Bill 21 is essentially based on a conservative vision of Islam, a vision that is not representative of the majority of Muslim women in Quebec.

What Difference Is There between Conservative Islam and Liberal Islam?

The conservative vision of Islam adheres closely to the religious writings and practices of the Prophet and his following, without providing any contextual interpretation. In returning to the wellspring of Islam, this vision defends an originalist conception of the religion. Some groups adhering to this conservative vision even go so far as to advocate a transformation of the political and social system based on certain precepts of Islam. Obviously, this vision is opposed to the liberal current of Islam, by which I mean a reformist movement that wishes to reconcile modernity and the Muslim religion. This liberal current, also called "progressive," seeks to restore a plurality of interpretations and rationality within Islam. This current is opposed to the rigid interpretation of religious texts conveyed by the most fundamentalist or conservative currents currently dominant in the Arab and Muslim world, such as Wahhabism and Salafism, for example.[4]

Since the era of the nineteenth-century reformers, the liberal current has brought together many thinkers, theologians, and intellectuals from different countries, all of whom have raised issues in society that are taboo for conservative Islam: issues such as the equality of men and women in society and in Islam, the relationship between religion and the state, the defence of secularism, the wearing of the veil as a choice rather than an obligation, the question of jihad, or the rejection of corporal punishment. Nonetheless, this liberal current remains invisible – as much in the Arab and Muslim world as in the Western world – for reasons linked to the immediate political and economic interests of the states concerned.

Why Is the Liberal or Progressive Current of Islam Invisible in the West and in Quebec?

In my opinion, Muslims with a liberal vision of Islam are an invisible presence in Quebec because they feel first and foremost a dual sense of belonging (in their country of origin and in Quebec): they do not have a strictly religious sense of belonging. This feeling probably explains why they lack organizations or any presence in the public sphere, unlike Islamic conservatives whose associations are well organized and, moreover, financially comfortable. My real-world experience in Quebec with so-called Muslim women who have a liberal vision of Islam has allowed me to observe at close hand that the majority of these women do not perceive Bill 21 as discriminatory. Their position is clearly based on the fact that this law bans the wearing of religious symbols for teachers of all religions and not just for Muslim women. Moreover, in all the studies I have conducted over the past twenty years with migrant and immigrant women, so-called Muslim women almost never raise religious concerns as a priority when describing the challenges that they face in integrating socially and economically in Quebec. Indeed, this issue is quite remote from their needs: they are more concerned about structural barriers that persist to this day.

I have conducted many consultations and engaged in field work for various organizations alongside immigrant women from different regions of Quebec, including Muslim women (Chouakri 2019a, 2019b). None of this work has indicated that the representation of women wearing a religious symbol in the public service, and, more specifically, in positions of authority, is a priority issue. The only priority issues are related to socio-economic integration, which includes multiple barriers from isolation, to "francization,"[5] which is often blocked or delayed by a poorly adapted provision of services, the lack of affordable daycare services, the non-recognition of their acquired skills and competencies, the lack of places for socialization, and also racism and discrimination in hiring and employment, which prevent these women from attaining the economic autonomy to which they aspire (Antonius 2008, 2014).

The Quebec Liberal Party was in power for fifteen years. Yet, during this time, the specific needs of immigrant women in immigration and integration policies and programs were never taken into account. However, since the beginning of the twenty-first century, several community organizations have repeatedly called for the implementation of a gender-based analysis in order to create policies adapted to the specific experience of women, which is different from that of men. How can this reluctance to act be explained? It certainly stems from the fear of displeasing a certain ever-vigilant conservative, communitarian male constituency. These coveted male voters have a false perception of the host society in Quebec and consider that women in this province have more rights than men anywhere else in the world; they are also determined that their wives and daughters, and even their communities, should not be contaminated.

Today, as in the past, the goal of most immigrant women and Muslim immigrant women has not changed. They arrive in Quebec aware that this society offers them freedom and equality. These are principles to which they strongly adhere, especially when they come from strictly patriarchal societies (Collectif d'auteurs 2007). The only problem is they need economic autonomy in order to experience freedom and equality, and this requirement proves harder to attain than they expected. These principles therefore remain principles, and they cause a good deal of frustration since the voices of these women have not been heard by successive governments or by opposition parties seeking to appeal to a wider electorate.

The current dominant discourse in Canada on ethnocultural minorities prioritizes other issues. In this respect, it echoes the agenda of the most conservative groups, emphasizing the religious identity of immigrants from certain Muslim-majority countries. It normalizes the most conservative practices of Muslims, especially when it comes to women; it seeks to make the expressions "a Muslim woman" and "a veiled woman" synonymous. This dominant discourse essentializes and stigmatizes Muslim men and women: it eliminates their national or civic affiliation and limits their religious affiliation even though the international and geopolitical context, since September 11, 2001, has not favoured a positive perception of Islam. Do we speak of Orthodox Christians when referring to Greeks or Romanians? No. Do we speak of Catholics when we talk about Poles, French people, or Italians? Obviously not. But when conservative Islam and the multiculturalist Left speak of Algerians, Tunisians, or Egyptians, for example, they speak of Muslims. And, yet, people from Algeria, Tunisia, or Egypt do not all practise in the same way (even if they are all Sunni), they are not necessarily all practising Muslims. Moreover, they may adhere to other faiths or even be atheists.

Why Is the Dominant Perception of a Muslim Woman in Quebec That She Is a Veiled Woman?

Until the nineteenth century, the Western perception of the Arab-Muslim world was influenced by the literary and artistic trend of the Orientalists (Hentsch 1988). Women were often depicted in the nude. Painters and writers developed a compelling vision of an imaginary Orient, which they presented as more open and permissive than the West, which was still often under the yoke of religion. Since the twentieth century, this perception has been gradually replaced by an image of Muslim women completely covered (or veiled). This image is conveyed not so much by art and literature as by the media. This image has become the common Western perception of Muslim women, although it is just as false as the one imagined by the Orientalists of the past.

The current challenge for many so-called Muslim women belonging to the liberal current of Islam is that they need to reappropriate a civic identity, while defending and highlighting their very diverse reality. This identity is actually the diametrical opposite of the prevailing perceptions in a part of Quebec's civil society as well as of the Quebec women's movement, which are simply unable to question how they have been conditioned to maintain a limited and false definition of Muslim women and which are not ready to analyze the oppression experienced by Muslim women within the Muslim religion itself. The dominant perception is far more prejudiced and racist toward Muslim women, whom it essentializes, than the discourse intent on defending equal rights for all women and denouncing the oppressions inherent to the Muslim tradition and religion (Geadah 2007). A new Orient has been constructed by the West: this time, the Arab-Muslim world appears closed, whereas the West is open. So-called Muslim women, whether they live in their countries of origin or in the countries of emigration, can only be the representation of this closed world: veiled women (covered/closed?) to whom, when they live in the West, it is by choice since we are in a democracy and individual rights are sacred there.

On What Grounds Do Critics of Bill 21 Justify Their Position?

In challenging or contesting Bill 21, groups with a conservative vision of Islam often present the act as if it regulates all of the public sphere and "affects" all Muslim women in Quebec. This notion is misleading. One only must see photos of slogans during demonstrations against Bill 21 to understand how much these groups distort the Act Respecting the Laicity of the State, whether intentionally or not. Moreover, these same groups, which present themselves in Quebec as a minority subject to discrimination on the basis of their religion, refuse to recognize that in their country of origin, where the dominant religion is often Islam, they do not defend any discriminated minorities, whether these minorities be defined in terms of religious affiliation or gender or ethnic background. To the dismay of these critics, Bill 21 does not affect the religious practice of all so-called Muslim women in Quebec. The majority of these women belong not to the conservative current but, rather, to the liberal current of Islam. They do not wear veils, they have emancipated themselves from the constraint of the veil, and they even challenge the practice, in Quebec and elsewhere, when they can.

Part of the Feminist Movement, Civil Society, and the Left No Longer Defend the Hard-Won Rights of Women

Intersectional feminist analysis provides a better understanding of the situation of particular groups of women. Nevertheless, this current trend of thought, which is currently dominant and in line with the conservatism of neoliberal ideology, has a perverse effect on Muslim women. Indeed, such an analysis, which is spreading not only in feminist groups but also in civil society and on the Left, no longer questions the religious oppressions suffered by Muslim women, even though these oppressions are a glaring reality. Intersectional feminist analysis refuses to consider the impacts on women, including those who now live in Quebec, of certain practices in countries of the global South. As a result, this analysis ends up legitimizing oppression in the name of respect for religion. An additional problem with intersectional feminist analysis is that it lacks a critical sense and has become dogmatic. For people comfortable with intersectional feminist analysis, the hijab itself has become a meaningless symbol. In their words, the supporters of Bill 21 are "racists." How can the many so-called Muslim women who support this law be cast as "racists?"

Conservative Muslim organizations have appropriated the discourse of emancipatory Islam, for which the wearing of the veil must be a choice and not an obligation. Conservative Islamic groups now claim that wearing the veil is already a personal choice, and, in this perception, they agree with a large part of the Quebec feminist movement. This new conservative discourse manages to cover up the great pressure exerted on Muslim women to wear the veil. Can we speak of choice when honour killings related to the wearing of the veil have taken place in Quebec and Ontario (consider the events involving Aqsa Parvez in 2007 and the Shafia girls in 2009)? Can we speak of choice when veiling ceremonies, in the face of society's indifference, are held in community centres and even in schools for girls as young as eight or nine years old?[6]

Conclusion

As a result, in the current debate on secularism in Quebec, the dominant discourse on Muslim women wearing a religious symbol only essentializes and stigmatizes them. It does the same for immigrant women in general. This discourse does not respond to their real needs, and it does not respond to their aspirations for equality. It only satisfies people who adhere to the conservative current of Islam. We have seen for more than fifteen years now a debate on the wearing of religious symbols in Quebec. We have seen how some political parties use Muslim women as instruments for their own ideological or electoral ends. These parties are ready to portray as standard bearers those Muslim women who identify, whether by choice or not, the conservative brand of Islam of their countries of origin close to the conservative religious Right. At the same time, these political parties seek to cast as victims all those individuals in Quebec who want a more secular state.

These political parties do not listen to the majority of Muslim and immigrant women who actually do not consider the wearing or not wearing of religious signs in positions of authority in the public service and in the world of education as a priority now or in the future. This issue is a distraction. It conceals the real needs and aspirations of these women who want to live in a free and democratic society and have access to meaningful employment. The women of whom I speak do not often speak out publicly. Today, it is almost impossible for them to do so, both individually and collectively. Why? Because they are facing a civil society and feminist movement largely dominated by the ideology of individual and religious rights, without critical analysis or regard for the impacts of the conservative position on immigrant and Muslim women. These women are alone in upholding a liberal or critical vision of the religions to which they adhere; even more alone are those women who cannot speak out without putting themselves at risk within their own communities and who feel neither supported nor represented in civil society organizations.

Notes

1 Act Respecting the Laicity of the State, SQ 2019, c. 12.

2 The term "so-called Muslim women" or "so-called Muslim communities" is used to highlight the fact that they have other affiliations, particularly national ones, and that they often have other ways of practising the Muslim religion than the one that Islamic conservatives seek to impose.

3 When the term "contesting" is used here, it includes legal challenges in court.

4 Wahhabism is a religious doctrine named after Muhammad ibn Abd al-Wahhab (1703–92), a preacher from the Arabian Peninsula. It is a doctrine that seeks to return to the foundations of Islam and advocates a very strict monotheism, while multiplying prohibitions. In terms of legal punishment, for example, it promotes stoning for adultery. Salafism literally means "return to the practices of the pious ancestors" – namely, the generation of the Prophet and the two subsequent generations. This movement, both religious and political, is based on a rigorous interpretation of the Koran and the prophetic tradition" (Valter 2016).

5 Translator's note: the Quebec policy of bringing non-francophone individuals and organizations to learn and publicly use French on a regular basis.

6 *Journal de Montréal* 2014, 8; 2018, 30; Rathle 2018.

References

Antonius, Rachad. 2008. "L'Islam au Québec: les complexités d'un processus de racisation." *Cahiers de recherche sociologique* 46: 11–28.

–. 2014. "L'Islam intégriste, l'hostilité à l'immigration et la droite nationaliste: quels rapports ?" In *Les nationalismes québécois face à la diversité ethnoculturelle*, edited by Micheline Labelle et al., 91–106, 2nd ed. Montreal: Éditions de l'Institut d'études internationales de Montréal.

Chouakri, Yasmina. 2019a. *Analyse qualitative de parcours d'insertion de femmes immigrantes au marché du travail et conditions de réussite observées*. Montreal: Comité consultatif Femmes en développement de la main d'œuvre.

–. 2019b. *Femmes immigrantes nouvellement arrivées et égalité entre les sexes: État de la situation dans la région de Montréal*. Montreal: Table des groupes de femmes de Montréal.

Collectif d'auteurs. 2007. "Lettre d'opinion. Immigrantes: ni aliénées ni soumises." *Le Devoir*, February 26.

Geadah, Yolande. 2007. *Accommodements raisonnables. Droit à la différence et non différence des droits*. Montreal: VLB éditeur.

Hentsch, Thierry. 1988. *L'Orient imaginaire*. Paris: Éditions de Minuit.

Journal de Montréal. 2014. "Une cérémonie du voile pour jeunes filles." May 3.

–. 2018. "Abus de fillettes à la CSDM." April 26.

Rathle, Serge Michel. 2018. "Endoctrinement à l'école Joseph Papineau." Letter addressed to Catherine Harel Bourdon, president of the Commission scolaire de Montréal, May 2. https://www.mlq.qc.ca/wp-content/uploads/2018/05/LettreRathle.pdf.

Valter, Stéphane. 2016. *Qu'appelle-t-on le wahabisme et le salafisme?* Paris: Institut du Monde arabe. https://vous-avez-dit-arabe.webdoc.imarabe.org/.

Part 3

Legal Perspectives

The Laicity of the State 6
The Cornerstone of Individual Civil and Political Rights

JULIE LATOUR

> For knowledge comes through searching for what we are accustomed to call truth.
>
> — Hannah Arendt ([1978] 121)

The principle of laicity, which encompasses the state's duty of religious neutrality, is the primary condition for the existence and thorough exercise of freedom of conscience and freedom of religion. It provides the foundation for equality of all citizens before the law, regardless of their origin or religious beliefs. The laicity of the state allows, upstream, an area of freedom conducive to the development of the autonomy of thought and the deployment of the consubstantial freedoms of thought, opinion, and expression, the combined effect of which allows the exercise of an enlightened citizenship. The gist of this chapter is to explain how the laicity of the state, in becoming a fundamental principle of Quebec, is above all a generator of rights for the citizens of Quebec, both because of its intrinsic structural value and because of the way in which it protects and enriches existing fundamental freedoms and civil rights.

Laicity of the State: A Fundamental Principle of Quebec in the Twenty-first Century

With the adoption of the Act Respecting the Laicity of the State (Bill 21) on June 16, 2019, the Quebec legislator has taken a historic step.[1] This Act affirms that "the State of Quebec is a lay State," it defines the constitutive principles of laicity, and it then embodies laicity in parliamentary, governmental, and judicial institutions. It imposes a corollary duty of reserve on representatives of the authority of the state in the broadest sense with respect to the expression of their religious beliefs in the exercise of their functions: essentially, police officers, justice personnel, school principals, and teachers.[2] The de facto secularism that Quebec has been building for decades is now enshrined in a fundamental law, which is the foundation of a pluralistic society. The principle of secularism and of religious neutrality of the state, which, according to the Supreme Court of Canada, "is based on a democratic imperative,"[3] has gradually developed from incomplete beginnings to engenderment and has acceded to the rank of a fundamental principle in Quebec. The Quebec Charter of Human Rights and Freedoms (Quebec Charter) now states that "the Quebec nation considers State laicity to be of fundamental importance"[4] and specifies that "a person shall maintain a proper regard for State laicity in exercising his human rights and freedoms."[5]

In keeping with the essence of the philosophical and political sources inherent in this notion,[6] the laicity of the state of Quebec is based on four fundamental principles, listed in section 2 of Bill 21. The first two – "(1) the separation of State and religion and (2) the religious neutrality of the State" – represent the structural requirements, which are the guarantors of the corollary rights and freedoms constituted by the second two – "(3) the equality of all citizens and (4) freedom of conscience and freedom of religion." Contrary to a common perception, the Act Respecting the Laicity of the State is above all a generator of rights for the citizens of Quebec. It enhances the guarantees offered by the Quebec Charter as well as existing civil rights and gives rise to a new fundamental right, according to which "all persons have the right to lay parliamentary, government and judicial institutions, and to lay public services."[7]

The principle of the laicity of the state is now elevated to the status of the rights and freedoms protected by the Quebec Charter and therefore enshrines Quebec's distinctive legal and social character. The European Court of Human Rights (ECtHR) has recognized that the principle of secularism and religious neutrality of the state is safeguarded when that principle is a fundamental principle of the state and it has formerly approved strict implementation of that principle.[8] The Act Respecting the Laicity of the State has a forward-looking perspective: it provides a foundation for Quebec leading into the twenty-first century, while establishing a structuring value to this issue beyond the passions of the moment. It is in continuity with existing law, while at the same time carrying an innovative breath that furthers the law.

Laicity: Elaborating Freedom in a Common World

> [T]he common world is what we enter when we are born and what we leave behind when we die. It transcends our lifespan into past and future alike; it was there before we came and will outlast our brief sojourn in it. It is what we have in common not only with those who live with us, but also with those who were here before and with those who will come after us. (Arendt 1998, 55)

More than fifteen years of sustained commitment to further laicity of the state have firmly convinced me that there is a lack of understanding about this fundamental principle of a pluralistic democracy: it is even liable to be distorted by those people opposed to it (Latour 2020). Laicity is a noble aspiration. It is grounded in that universal breadth from which originates the full and complete freedom of the human being. It is deprived of any dogmatic dimension or religious determinism. And it develops in line with the distinctive historical path of a nation-state.[9] Laicity aims to create a sphere of freedom where human beings are fully responsible for themselves, free to change and reinvent themselves over the course of life. Freedom is not something fixed, and, therefore, the full expression of freedom goes beyond the static context of appearances at a given time. The difference between believing oneself to be free and being truly free is the main question raised by philosophy from its very beginning.

Laicity allows the deployment of citizens both free for themselves and open to being together with others, conscious of belonging to a larger political community that is founded on the principle of equality beyond any differences that may exist between individuals. The state must therefore bring together individual identity in all its potentiality as well as civic responsibility, opening the way to the exercise of real citizenship and the maintenance of society as a whole.

Inspired by the Enlightenment, laicity is a democratic philosophical ideal that dates back some 250 years. This ideal has become incorporated into politics and law more recently, with the advent of popular sovereignty and the rule of law. The secular or lay vision of society accords individuals the ability to emancipate themselves. This secular vision opens the way to religious pluralism in the sense that it implies accepting spiritual movement (for example, a person converting to another faith); it also entails granting equal status to non-believers. The secular vision of society is therefore seen by many people as something subversive since it disrupts the truths and revelations on which are based the age-old religious orders of the great monotheistic faiths and their shared ambition for societal pre-eminence. The recognition of religious pluralism has generally been imposed on the established churches or has required concessions from them. At the same time, religious pluralism implies relinquishing the unity of a nation around a single religious affiliation.

Contrary to what one often claims, laicity does not prevent people from displaying their religious belief in society; it provides, instead, the very foundation of societal pluralism by freeing that society from an exclusively theocentric or atheistic vision of the world, while embracing an acceptance of otherness. Laicity does not subtract the sacred from culture; instead, it makes the sacred coexist with a secular political civic sphere, founded on the principle of equality, and this political civic sphere in turn must remain neutral and separated from any spiritual or religious identification. Hence, the importance of the real and concrete neutrality of state institutions so that all citizens can recognize themselves in the state that brings them together. Rather than promise eternal salvation, modern democratic societies must aim to provide temporal equality; rather than preach immutable truths, they should seek to guarantee freedom. And this is precisely what laicity of the state reflects in reconciling both public and private liberties. The national community is open to religious and spiritual pluralism, and, for their part, religious denominations accept otherness and must relinquish their sway over the state and its institutions. From this mutuality of concessions on a political level can arise a reciprocity of exchange and a space for sharing between citizens. The secular vision does not imply renouncing the millennial richness of our societies or the idea of transcendence itself, which is etched on the collective memory of society.

Laicity is a great vector enabling us to join together in our shared humanity. Rather than maintaining a backward-looking vision and bemoaning "the world we have lost" (Raynaud 2019, 229),[10] whatever it may be, laicity invites us to reflect on the world that we are called on to build: a common world. In this sense, it can serve as a fruitful undertaking, a bridge reaching out to the other. In preference to the societal compartmentalization advocated by identity politics and the multiculturalist ideology, which is the source of "liberal" thought, we can only hope for the emergence of a genuine dialogue between the profane and the religious. When properly understood, laicity allows for a productive influx between free thought and religion in order "to keep the civic and spiritual conversation going" (117). The appropriateness, and even the necessity, of legally affirming laicity is widely recognized at the theoretical level. But, in practice, its implementation is often subject to challenge and proves difficult since everyone wants to benefit from the virtues of this fundamental principle without being affected themselves by its inherent structural requirements. Quebec is no exception in this regard. The legal arguments of Bill 21's detractors reflect this essential contradiction for it is, first and foremost, to uphold the integrity of the charters of rights they invoke that state laicity is crucial.

A Fundamental Law That Is Essentially a Generator of Rights

State Laicity: A New Fundamental Right Protected by the Quebec Charter

The secular nature of the state is promoted to the status of rights and freedoms protected by the Quebec Charter, both by the fundamental nature conferred upon Bill 21[11] and by its intrinsic provisions[12] and the protective normative enrichment that it brings to the fundamental freedoms already guaranteed and to existing civil rights.

In Public Law: Increased Protection of the Related Fundamental Freedoms

When laicity of the state is fully embodied, it lays the foundation for the genuine exercise of freedom of conscience and religion, enhancing at the same time, in its ramifications, protection of the consubstantial fundamental freedoms of thought, opinion, and expression as well as freedom of association, which are protected by both the Quebec Charter and the Canadian Charter of Rights and Freedoms (Canadian Charter).[13] These constitute "the body of individual civil and political rights guaranteed at the international level since the Second World War" that the state must protect in order to allow for "the exercise of real citizenship" (Zuber 2017, 187). The indissociable character of these fundamental freedoms lies particularly in the autonomy of thought – hence, the importance of education, which engages the faculty of emancipation as well as the potentiality of the human being. It belongs to the field of education to introduce the individual to the freedom of thought, to instill in that individual a critical spirit and autonomous judgment, free of any imposed dogma. The state must provide a neutral education that is separate from religion.

In Private Law: A Protective Bridge between the Civil Code of Quebec and the Quebec Charter

The Act Respecting the Laicity of the State is a quasi-constitutional statute. Along with the Quebec Charter and the Civil Code of Quebec, the fundamental normative instrument that sets out the "*jus commune,*" the act forms a triptych in the Quebec constitutional order.[14] Indeed, according to its preliminary provision, "the *Civil Code of Quebec,* in harmony with the *Charter of Human Rights and Freedoms* (chapter C-12) and the general principles of law, governs persons, relations between persons, and property." The principle of laicity enables all persons to be treated equally. The Act Respecting the Laicity of the State therefore aims to create a normative and interpretative bridge between the Civil Code of Quebec and the Quebec Charter, given the intertwining of the laicity of the state with civil rights and fundamental rights and freedoms in a number of areas, ranging from the integrity to the capacity of persons, to family, succession, and contracts.

This should further protect the integrity of the civil law when faced with religious claims, while preventing decisions such as the one rendered in 2005 in *Gabriel v Directeur de l'état civil.*[15] In its decision, the Quebec Superior Court agreed to give civil sanction to a married woman's request to change her name to that of her husband, thereby renouncing her own identity, based exclusively on religious grounds, although this was contrary to the public norm of equality between spouses enshrined in the 1981 family law reform by Article 393 of the Civil Code of Quebec, according to which, "In marriage, both spouses retain their respective names, and exercise their respective civil rights under those names."[16] In support of her convictions, the plaintiff in the *Gabriel* case quoted Ephesians 5: 21–33 in the Christian Bible: "Wives, be subject to your husbands, as you are to the Lord." It should be recalled that Justice Charles-Édouard Dorion, as chairman of the Commission on Women's Civil Rights, established in 1930, decided to uphold the legal incapacity of married women based on the fact that "our laws" [at that time] were "in conformity with unavoidable [facts of] nature and our Christian morals" (Quebec Council on the Status of Women 2007, 51).

Similarly, the 2004 decision in *Syndicat Northcrest v Amselem* would probably have had a different outcome in a fully secular state, when the Supreme Court of Canada, by a narrow five-to-four majority, allowed the installation of *succahs* on the balconies of the plaintiffs' apartments in the Sanctuaire du Mont-Royal complex, even though the declaration of co-ownership to which they had voluntarily adhered to clearly prohibited this type of construction for safety reasons and considering the nature of the building.[17] The dissenting judges emphasized the importance of the enforceability of the existing contract in reconciling competing rights, as they considered the Civil Code of Quebec to be the most important instrument for defining the principles governing public order and the general well-being of the citizens of Quebec. This reasoning applies *a fortiori* to the amendment to section 9.1 of the Quebec Charter, which adds the laicity of the state to the existing criteria for modulating the exercise of rights and freedoms and which now reads as follows: "In exercising his fundamental freedoms and rights, a person shall maintain a proper regard for democratic values, State laicity, public order and the general well-being of the citizens of Quebec ... In this respect, the scope of the freedoms and rights, and limits to their exercise, may be fixed by law."

From an Incomplete Status to the Full Recognition of Quebec Laicity

The Act Respecting the Laicity of the State is the fulfillment of a long-awaited exercise of parliamentary sovereignty. Indeed, it is the seventh bill on this issue to be introduced in the National Assembly of Quebec since 2008. It follows several bills that, for the most part, were ultimately not adopted for a variety of reasons: Bill 94 in 2010,[18] Bill 60 in 2013,[19] followed by the introduction, in 2013 and 2014, of Bills 398, 491, and 492,[20] and later by the adoption of Bill 62 in 2017.[21] This legislative history demonstrates the extent to which the driving forces of Quebec civil society have mobilized to resolve this important societal issue as well as the urgent need for legal clarity in this area. These bills were preceded by the report of the Bouchard-Taylor Commission, mandated by the then Liberal government in 2007–8, which conducted public hearings throughout Quebec and recommended the adoption of a white paper on secularism (laicity of the state) (Bouchard and Taylor 2008, 154–55, 261, 272). Despite the many ideological flip-flops of its eponymous commissioners since then, this recommendation remains in effect.

For historian of ideas Yvan Lamonde (2013, 347–48), the secularism project, particularly the deconfessionalization of schools, has been a fundamental although unfulfilled project since the time of the Quiet Revolution, and indeed this lack of fulfilment has weighed heavily on the Quebec collective unconscious (see also Lamonde 2010). The quest for a true secularism of the state takes its place alongside major historical milestones or disruptions in Quebec society – from the Great Depression in 1929 to the "Grande Noirceur" (a so-called dark period during which strongly conservative Quebec premier Maurice Duplessis ruled from 1936 to 1939 and from 1944 to 1959 along with the Catholic high clergy) and the Refus global (a powerful artistic manifesto from 1948, calling for emancipation from the Catholic Church and rejection of the inwardness of Quebec society at the time). These disruptions were accompanied by an appeal for "the life of the spirit," for freedom of thought, and for the advent of a new spiritual life, freed from any overbearing religious institutions, which led ultimately to the deconfessionalization of schools and culture (Lamonde 2013, 349–51).

The Genesis of Bill 21: Answering a Goal of Pressing and Substantial Importance

National Framework

The democratic philosophical ideal of secularism is grounded in the universal. But, as we have mentioned above, the embodiment of the laicity of the state varies according to different political and legal systems, based on the trajectory of each political community deploying it. A recent judgment of the Supreme Court of Canada sheds important light on this matter. *Reference re Supreme Court Act, ss. 5 and 6* concerns eligibility criteria for appointment to the highest court in the land for candidates from Quebec. In this landmark decision, the Supreme Court of Canada emphasized the importance of "not only civil law training and experience on the Court, but also to ensure that Quebec's *distinct legal traditions and social values* are represented on the Court, thereby enhancing the confidence of the people of Quebec in the Supreme Court as the final arbiter of their rights."[22] This objective protects "both the *functioning* and the *legitimacy* of the Supreme Court as a general court of appeal for Canada."[23] For the Supreme Court of Canada, thereby endorsing the words of Professor Peter H. Russell, "this broader purpose" is supported "by the historical record," considering that "Quebec's civil-law system was an essential ingredient of its distinctive culture."[24] The Act Respecting the Laicity of the State must be seen in the same light.

Quebec's Distinctive Character

Quebec attaches great importance to affirming the secular nature of the state, including in its public schools. And this stems both from its unique civil law tradition and from Quebec's distinct culture and social values that differentiate it from the other provinces of the Canadian federation. Civil law is based on a deductive and codified approach, which makes it more difficult to accept piecemeal, case-by-case law, such as the concept of reasonable accommodation,[25] which was initiated under the Canadian Charter and is closer to the common law legal system. Social solidarity, which underlies the goal of state laicity of ensuring equality between all citizens, is a collective value of great importance in Quebec. It is enshrined in several laws and social measures that Quebec has adopted over the years. Three examples include the introduction in 1997 of a family policy that created a significant network of publicly funded early childhood education and care centres (Roulot-Ganzmann 2017); the protection afforded to workers in Quebec, a jurisdiction with the highest rate of unionization in North America (Beaudoin 2016; Institut de la statistique du Québec 2019); and the fact that Quebec is the only province where married women retain their original surnames, which serves as a powerful symbol of equality between spouses.[26]

Quebec is now giving legal substance to this political and social goal of a comprehensive laicity of the state. This important aspiration has mobilized Quebec particularly since the Quiet Revolution. From 1961 to 1969, the Mouvement laïque de langue française (MLF) provided an impetus to this project, as illustrated by the MLF's archive, which is deposited at the Bibliothèque et Archives nationales du Quebec.

Education as a Vector for the Transmission of Culture and Values

The MLF focused its action on the advent of a true secular school system, with the aim of respecting the freedom of conscience of each individual in order to take account of the growing pluralism of Quebec society. The MLF presented its position to the Royal Commission on Education in the Province of Quebec (Parent Commission). However, it was not until almost three decades later, in 1998, that the first milestone in the deconfessionalization of school boards was reached. Deconfessionalization involved the outright renunciation of the legal guarantees for public education granted to Catholics and Protestants in Quebec at the time of the founding of Canada,[27] and this gesture by the "majority" was definitely significant. The process of school deconfessionalization was only completed in 2008 with the introduction of the Program on Ethics and Religious Culture, following the end of denominational religious instruction in 2005 (see Proulx 2010).

In this respect, Bill 21 constitutes the last milestone toward true secularism in Quebec public schools, by defining a more genuine duty of restraint for teachers and school administrators, resulting in their being prohibited from wearing religious symbols during the exercise of their functions. For sociologist and jurist Guy Rocher, a leading figure in the Quebec school reform process (through the Parent Commission), "this reform involved all of culture, namely the transmission of values" (quoted in Lamonde 2013, 342).

The Scope and Potential Limits of Rights Measured against Democracy

In a seminal article, the jurist Aharon Barak (2002, 44), president of the Supreme Court of Israel from 1995 to 2006, expresses the essence of the dialogue between individual rights and the needs of the community that characterizes a democracy: "Human rights are the rights of a human being as part of society. The rights of the individual must conform to the existence of society, the existence of a government, and the existence of national goals. The power of the state is essential to the existence of the state and the existence of human rights themselves" (Barak 2002, 43). And he adds the following about the inseparability of fundamental rights and their potential limits: "Both the needs of the state and human rights are part of one constitutional structure, which simultaneously provides for human rights and allows them to be limited. A unique feature of democracy is this fact that the breadth and limits of human rights derive from a common source" (44).

Since the advent of charters of rights, many people assume that constitutionalizing fundamental rights makes them absolute. Individual rights are often presented as untouchable, especially where religion is concerned. Individual claims become a screen for a one-way pluralism, where an alleged "openness to the other" is in fact invoked in order to better close in on oneself. To be convinced of this, one has only to consider the frequently vehement tone and content of grievances against Bill 21 as well as opposition to all Quebec's previous attempts to regulate the neutrality of the state in religious matters. This manner of treating individual rights as absolute is based on a series of premises – namely, that individual rights are superior to everything else, that freedom is acquired against the state, and that the majority is necessarily tyrannical toward minorities. However, these preconceived liberal thoughts do not apply to state laicity because the state is actually the primary institution providing the conditions for the exercise of freedom of conscience and religion, which have materialized through the notion of popular sovereignty and the pre-eminence of the political nation over religious orders. Moreover, since state laicity is the essential condition for religious and spiritual pluralism, it protects all citizens – first and foremost, those from religious minorities.

The circumference of the state's imparted duty to protect all citizens is broader in extent than the sum of individual claims combined, and it unfolds on a broad continuum, which is not static either for the individual or for the state itself. Religions have a great power of attraction, they are thousands of years old, and they are transnational in scope, whereas the rule of law only goes back a few centuries and is geographically restricted. In the absence of a fully circumscribed neutrality of the state, freedom of religion is in conflict with itself since it is caught between its claims for expansion and its intrinsic quest to take up a public stance within the state domain.

The Compatibility of the Act Respecting the Laicity of the State with the Existing Body of Case Law

Even before the advent of this fundamental piece of legislation, the principle of secularism and religious neutrality of the state already existed in Canadian constitutional law. From the landmark *Big M Drug Mart* decision of 1985,[28] to more recent cases such as *Mouvement laïque québécois v Ville de Saguenay* in 2015[29] and *Law Society of British Columbia v Trinity Western University* in 2018,[30] the courts have inferred this principle as an integral part of the right to freedom of conscience and religion set out in the charters, without which these freedoms are immediately impaired. The Act Respecting the Laicity of the State marks a decisive step in this process of evolutionary interpretation because it formalizes an essential dimension of freedom of conscience and religion – namely, its societal dimension, which had previously been carved out piecemeal without any overall well-directed plan or social consensus. By circumscribing the state's duty and giving it prospective clarity, the Quebec legislator is acting in full accordance with the rule of law.[31]

I had the opportunity to analyze the evolution of Canadian jurisprudence on freedom of conscience and religion and the flexibility granted to the state to legislate in the public interest in a 2013 in-depth article (Latour 2013) and in two subsequent submissions to parliamentary committees of the Quebec National Assembly in 2016 and 2019 respectively (Latour 2016, 2019). Given the format of this book, I will focus primarily on the impact of two recent court decisions.

The *Mouvement laïque québécois* Decision and the Advent of Real and Apparent State Neutrality

> Appearance serves the apparatus.
> – Jean-François Colosimo (2019, 87)

The Supreme Court of Canada's important decision in the *Mouvement Laïque Québécois* case on reciting prayers at meetings of the City of Saguenay municipal council has paved the way for Bill 21 for several reasons. First, Canada's highest court stated for the first time that "this neutrality requires that the State neither favour nor hinder any particular belief, and the same holds true for non-belief ... It *requires* that the State *abstain* from taking any position and thus avoid adhering to a particular belief."[32] Given this positive duty for the state to abstain from religious matters, true state neutrality presupposes the separation of the state and religions. And this position sounds the death knell for "open secularism," which is the main buoy of Bill 21's detractors. In its ruling, the Supreme Court also holds that the state is embodied by its representatives when they are in the exercise of their functions, and it therefore rejects the oft-repeated sophism that the state alone must be neutral but not the individuals acting on its behalf: "Obviously, the state itself cannot engage in a religious practice, so the practice would be one engaged in by one or more state officials, who would have to be acting in the performance of their functions."[33]

And the Supreme Court of Canada goes on to say, with respect to what is conveyed by appearance: "Where state officials, in the performance of their functions, *profess, adopt* or *favour* one belief to the exclusion of all others, the first two criteria for discrimination mentioned above, namely that there be an exclusion, distinction or preference and that it be based on religion, are met."[34] The least that can be said is that state officials manifesting their religious belief through a display of clothing simultaneously meet all three of these criteria because in so doing they profess, adopt, and visibly favour one religion to the exclusion of others. Finally, *a contrario,* the Supreme Court confirms that restrictions can be imposed on the freedom of conscience and religion of state representatives manifesting their religious beliefs: "On the other hand, it goes without saying that the same restrictions do not apply to the exercise by State officials of their own freedom of conscience and religion when *they are not acting* in an official capacity."[35]

The *Trinity Western University* Decision and Its Impact on the Educational Mission of Teachers

The importance and necessity for society of ensuring the real and perceived religious neutrality of teachers seem to be crucial, considering the role of the public school in the formation of citizenship and the development of autonomous thinking in students. In this regard, the recent *Trinity Western University* case has established that public authorities, in their role of protecting public interest and the equality of everyone, including the equality of opportunity, could not endorse, or give the perception that they were endorsing, discriminatory elements inherent to a religious dogma.[36] In this judgment, the Supreme Court of Canada upheld the decision of the Law Society of British Columbia (LSBC) that refused to approve Trinity Western University's proposed evangelical Christian law school, on the basis of the need to uphold and protect the public interest.

Indeed, Trinity Western had sought to make attendance at the proposed law school conditional upon students and faculty members signing a covenant prohibiting "sexual intimacy that violates the sacredness of marriage between a man and a woman," thereby creating barriers to entering the legal profession, particularly for lesbian, gay, bisexual, transgender, and queer (LGBTQ) students. By promoting equality to ensure equal access to the legal profession, supporting diversity within the bar, and preventing harm to LGBTQ law students, the LSBC "could pursue its overarching statutory duty: upholding and maintaining the public interest in the administration of justice, which necessarily includes upholding a positive public *perception* of the legal profession."[37]

Considering the moral and intellectual authority of teachers over their students, and based on this ruling that prescribes that equality must be exercised institutionally, one may wonder about the discriminatory effect on an LGBTQ student of a teacher who displays their adherence to a religion, knowing that all major religions outlaw or degrade homosexuality. For the Supreme Court of Canada in *Trinity Western University*, "being required by someone else's religious beliefs to behave contrary to one's sexual identity is degrading and disrespectful. Being required to do so offends the public perception that freedom of religion includes freedom from religion."[38]

This is just one example of the equality violations that may arise from the interference of religion with the civic educational mission of the state. For this reason, the state must preserve and protect the public interest in order to prevent, at the outset, any infringement of the rights of the students benefiting from this education. With respect to the infringement alleged by the prospective law students and the evangelical Christian university, the highest court in Canada held that the restriction on freedom of religion in this case was of minor importance: "Put otherwise, denying someone an option they would merely appreciate certainly falls short of 'forced apostasy.'"[39] By analogy, we submit that it is not absolutely necessary for a believer to wear religious symbols at all times and in all places, especially if they are to embody the mission of the state and thereby become, in the course of their duties, a state official representing in their person the aspiration to equality of all their fellow citizens, which is in itself a noble mission.

The Purpose of Bill 21: A Legitimate Goal and the Introduction of a New Paradigm

The societal objective of the Act Respecting the Laicity of the State must be considered as a whole, particularly in the sense that it increases the aspiration and treatment of all citizens in full equality. The Quebec state is involved in promoting this goal of equality since it is the state that is first and foremost obliged to offer secular institutions and services to all its citizens. This is very much to the state's credit rather than its discredit. The act is fully valid at the constitutional level because, while it is in line with existing law, it also carries with it the ferment of its own validity, both at the declarative and interpretative levels. First, the act introduces a new paradigm into the law in enunciating the rights it generates. The secular nature of the state, which has been given the status of a fundamental right, is intended to increase 1) the breadth and full exercise of freedom of conscience and religion and the safeguarding of related freedoms such as freedom of opinion; 2) the equal treatment of all citizens; and 3) the protection and promotion of the integrity of civil law.

Second, the Act Respecting the Laicity of the State reshapes the framework for balancing the fundamental rights and freedoms guaranteed and the criteria for setting out their potential limits. By significantly amending section 9.1 of the Quebec Charter, which has the status of a limitations provision, the principle of laicity of the state is now added to the existing criteria of respect for democratic values, public order, and the general well-being that the state can invoke to justify its legislative action in the event of an infringement of a freedom. Until now, the Supreme Court of Canada has held that section 9.1 of the Quebec Charter is the equivalent of section 1 of the Canadian Charter and subject to the general tests developed by the court in interpreting what constitutes a reasonable and justifiable limit on freedom in a free and democratic society.[40] The new wording of section 9.1 of the Quebec Charter should underpin jurisprudence that charts a new course, given the clear invitation to the courts to ensure the protection of the rights of Quebec citizens by balancing them with the rights of others as well as with other public values, including the secular nature of the state.

Proportionate Means

> The middle ground lies between too much and too little.
> – Aristotle, *Nicomachean Ethics*

Legislating is a delicate balancing act, especially when it comes to drafting a law that has such a vital objective for the future of a nation as establishing the laicity of the state. I believe that the content of Bill 21 is balanced and reflects a spirit of equilibrium and compromise that corresponds to the consensus of civil society and parliamentarians that has emerged in Quebec on this subject over the past fifteen years. It should be noted that the desire to affirm and define the laicity of the state in Quebec is generally well received and hardly arouses any resistance; it is rather its corollary – the prohibition of the wearing of religious symbols by certain representatives of the state in authority – that raises passions. In this regard, the Act Respecting the Laicity of the State does not seek to generalize this prohibition to all public servants, as it is the case in certain other democratic states and since the necessary lessons were drawn from the high-pitched reactions to Bill 60 in 2013.

Quebec has modulated the duty of neutrality according to functions where there is consensus and where the citizen is at the heart of the state's mission as a user of public services – notably, in the areas of justice and education – where impartiality and trust in the state and its mission are truly essential and should moreover be guaranteed by real and institutionalized neutrality. In order to allow for a smooth transition, Bill 21 contains a grandfather clause for religious symbols, linked to the position an individual held in an organization the day before the bill was introduced. In the opinion of many, the use of the notwithstanding clause is specifically intended to protect the validity of Bill 21 with respect to these grandfathered rights. I do not believe that this measure has a disproportionate impact on religious freedom as a whole given the objectives of the act and the fact that it only restricts a specific and limited element of a purportedly religious practice and only during the time at which the public function is exercised.

The Perspective of the European Court of Human Rights (EctHR)

Given the importance to the Supreme Court of Canada that "the [Canadian] Charter be presumed to provide at least as much protection as is found in Canada's international human rights obligations,"[41] the jurisprudence of the ECtHR is of great relevance here, given the common sources of the commitments made by the signatory states of the European Convention on Human Rights and the international obligations to which Canada is a party.[42] The ECtHR has made consistent rulings, as indicated in the recent *Ebrahimian* case, where the court "has already approved strict implementation of the principles of secularism (...) and neutrality, where this involved a fundamental principle of the

State," since it is "a corollary of the principle of equality" and promotes "respect for pluralism and diversity."[43] For the Strasbourg court, "the State's role as the neutral and impartial organiser of the exercise of various religions, faiths and beliefs ... is conducive to public order, religious harmony and tolerance in a democratic society."[44]

Conclusion

Establishing the laicity of the state as a founding principle of Quebec constitutes a major milestone in the architecture of fundamental rights that Quebec has built over generations. The Act Respecting the Laicity of the State is first and foremost a generator of rights. By enshrining the obligation of the state's religious neutrality already imposed by case law, the Quebec state gives full effect to the unrestricted exercise of freedom of conscience and religion, sets out the fundamental right to secular public institutions and services, and increases the equal treatment of all citizens. This impartiality of public authorities with regard to all religious or spiritual choices is in keeping with the respect of pluralism and diversity. By promoting autonomous thought and the emancipation of individuals and institutions, the principle of laicity also encourages the full development of freedom of thought, opinion, and expression, the combined effect of which allows for the exercise of a citizenship at a practical, concrete level.

As the cornerstone of individual civil and political rights, the Act Respecting the Laicity of the State has been given a leading role in the Quebec constitutional order, where it forms a triptych together with the Quebec Charter and the Civil Code of Quebec, whose integrity it protects. Representatives of the state personify the authority of that state; in fulfilling that role, they embody the state's mission; they must therefore support the requirement of neutrality of public services since they also act as custodians of the aspiration of their fellow citizens to equality. The state not only serves the individual: it also serves the common good and the community. Beyond the differences between citizens, we need to think in a common mode and one that does not stem from individual rights alone. "Mass individualism," to use Alessandro Baricco's (2019, 250) striking formula, does not replace the political community.

The strength of a democracy lies in its institutions, which must be able to stand the test of time.

The approach of the Quebec government is significant and rooted in its history. The Act Respecting the Laicity of the State is measured. It is an initiative responding to a democratic imperative for which many jurisdictions – particularly, civil law jurisdictions – have opted throughout the world to protect the greatest number: "The development of legislation on secularism can be compared to legislation developed on other subjects, such as, for example, the fight against sexual or sexist violence: new 'rights' call for new laws that intervene in questions on which the legislator had previously remained discreet or silent" (Raynaud 2019, 209).

Let me close by drawing on a linguistic metaphor, which flows naturally through the Quebec imagination but, perhaps, explains the initial gap on the topic of laicity of the state between it and the rest of Canada. In the confluence of existing fundamental rights and freedoms, the advent of a genuine state secularism (*laïcité*) is a nourishing river (*fleuve*) whose dynamic effect is to create a shared horizon for the future to combine pluralism and liberty and to irrigate the heritage of a common world. The symbol is all the stronger because the words "*fleuve*" and "*laïcité*" each express an untranslatable reality in English, the polysemy of their equivalent terms "river" and "secular" being powerless to express their full meaning and truth. This loss of meaning in translation somehow reflects Quebec's own path and its singularity in Canada, which are essential to grasp the teleological, social, and political scope of the Act Respecting the Laicity of the State. I sincerely hope that this reflection will enlighten my fellow citizens across Canada and trigger a fruitful dialogue on this important subject that reaches beyond the boundaries of the "two solitudes."

The Canadian Constitution is alive, and the societal dialogue continues between the judiciary and the political since the judge is the fiduciary of the social contract. This turns the task of judging into a social act that requires balancing various interests in society, so that justice itself also takes part in the realization of meaning through history, something to which every nation, including Quebec, aspires.

Notes

1 An Act Respecting the Laicity of the State, SQ 2019, c. 12.

2 An Act Respecting the Laicity of the State, ss. 3–6. We are here summarizing the persons listed in Schedule II of this Act.

3 *Mouvement laïque québécois v City of Saguenay*, [2015] 2 SCR 3, para. 75 (*Mouvement laïque québécois*).

4 Charter of Human Rights and Freedoms, RSQ 1977, c. C-12 (Quebec Charter).

5 An Act Respecting the Laicity of the State, ss. 18, 19 respectively, amending the Quebec Charter.

6 See, in particular, the anthology of founding texts on secularism selected and presented by the philosopher Henri Peña-Ruiz (2003).

7 An Act Respecting the Laicity of the State, s. 4, para. 2.

8 ECtHR, *Ebrahimian v France*, Application no. 64846/11, 2015, paras. 24, 67 (*Ebrahimian*).

9 For a representative overview of the different secular solutions developed by European states, see Portier 2017. Philippe Portier (2017, 211–21) identifies two major institutional polarities between, on the one hand, the states of northern Europe and the south-east, where the majority populations were respectively of Protestant or Orthodox traditions, where "a system of confessionality was affirmed" and, on the other hand, the states further south, with a Catholic majority, where "a separatist type of model was imposed," to which he adds "the mixed system that prevailed in the intermediate zone of Europe."

10 Translated from "le monde que nous avons perdu" in French.

11 See An Act Respecting the Laicity of the State, s. 11, para. 1, which gives substance to the primordial nature of the act in the Quebec legal system: "11. The provisions of this Act prevail over any contrary provisions of any subsequent Act, unless such an Act expressly states that it applies despite this Act."

12 Through the combined effect of the guiding principles set out in section 2 of the Act Respecting the Laicity of the State, which guarantee the right to equality of all citizens and the freedoms of conscience and religion and the advent of a new fundamental right to secular parliamentary, governmental, and judicial institutions as well as to secular public services, to which all citizens of Quebec are now entitled under section 4 of the act.

13 Canadian Charter of Rights and Freedoms, Part 1 of the Constitution Act, 1982, being Schedule B to the Canada Act 1982 (UK), 1982, c. 11 (Canadian Charter).

14 Civil Code of Quebec, SQ 1991, c. 64.

15 *Gabriel v Directeur de l'état civil*, 2005 CanLII 746 (QC CS).

16 An Act to Establish a New Civil Code and to Reform Family Law, SQ 1980, c. 39; see Civil Code of Quebec, s. 393 (Act to Establish a New Civil Code and to Reform Family Law).

17 *Syndicat Northcrest v Amselem*, [2004] 2 SCR 551.

18 Bill 94, An Act to Establish Guidelines for Requests for Accommodation within the Administration and Certain Institutions, 2010, which was introduced during the 39th Legislature, 1st Session and was reinstated during the 39th Legislature, 2nd Session on February 24, 2011 (Kathleen Weil, Minister of Justice).

19 Bill 60, Charter Affirming the Values of State Secularism and Religious Neutrality and of Equality between Women and Men, and Providing a Framework for Accommodation Requests, 2013, which was introduced during the 40th Legislature, 1st Session (Bernard Drainville, Minister responsible for Democratic Institutions and Active Citizenship).

20 Bill 398, Charter of Quebec State Secularism, 2013, which was introduced during the 40th Legislature, 1st Session (Francoise David); Bill 491, An Act Respecting the Religious Neutrality of the State and the Fight against Religious Fundamentalism and to Amend the Charter of Human Rights and Freedoms and the Act Respecting the Ministère du Conseil Exécutif, 2014, which was introduced during the 40th Legislature, 1st Session (Fatima Houda-Pépin); Bill 492, Charter of Secularism, 2013, which was introduced during the 40th Legislature, 1st Session (Nathalie Roy).

21 The Act to Promote Respect for the Religious Neutrality of the State and Aimed in Particular at Regulating Requests for Accommodation for Religious Reasons in Certain Organizations, SQ 2017, c. 19, which became An Act to Foster Adherence to State Religious Neutrality and, in particular, to Provide a Framework for Accommodations on Religious Grounds in Certain Bodies, c. R-26.2.01, https://www.legisquebec.gouv.qc.ca/en/document/cs/R-26.2.01.

22 *Reference re Supreme Court Act, ss. 5 and 6*, [2014] 1 SCR 433, para. 49 (emphasis added). This case was in response to a challenge to the appointment of Justice Marc Nadon from the Federal Court of Canada, who was not selected from among the judges of the Quebec Court of Appeal or the Quebec Superior Court or the lawyers who had been members of the Barreau du Québec for at least ten years.

23 *Reference re Supreme Court Act*, para. 49 (emphasis in the original).

24 *Reference re Supreme Court Act*, para. 49, citing Russell 1969, 8.

25 See, for example, *Ontario Human Rights Commission v Simpsons-Sears*, [1985] 2 SCR 536. It should be noted that the principle of accommodation originated in American law.

26 Act to Establish a New Civil Code and to Reform Family Law.

27 Constitution Act (UK), 1867, 30 & 31 Vict., c. 3, s. 93 (see new s. 93A) and the adoption of Bill 118 on the non-confessional status of Quebec schools on June 14, 2000.

28 *R. v Big M Drug Mart Ltd*, [1985] 1 SCR 295.

29 *Mouvement laïque québécois*.

30 *Law Society of British Columbia v Trinity Western University*, [2018] 2 SCR 293 (*Trinity Western University*).

31 The Supreme Court of Canada established in *Reference re Independence & Impartiality of Judges of the Provincial Court of PEI*, [1997] 3 SCR 3, that one aspect of the rule of law "is the constitutional principle that the exercise of all public power must find its ultimate source in a legal rule" (para. 10).
32 *Mouvement laïque québécois*, para. 72 (emphasis added).
33 *Mouvement laïque québécois*, para. 84.
34 *Mouvement laïque québécois*, para. 84 (emphasis added).
35 *Mouvement laïque québécois*, para. 119 (emphasis added).
36 *Trinity Western University*.
37 *Trinity Western University*, para. 40 (emphasis in the original).
38 *Trinity Western University*, para. 101.
39 *Trinity Western University*, para. 90.
40 *Ford v PG du Québec*, [1988] 2 SCR 790. The criteria for the justificatory analysis were set out in *R. v Oakes*, [1986] 1 SCR 103 and were then repeated in *Mouvement laïque québécois*, para. 90, summarizing *R. v Edwards Books and Art Ltd*, [1986] 2 SCR 713: "The impugned provision must therefore satisfy the justification test enunciated in *Oakes*, which requires the state to prove on a balance of probabilities (1) that the legislative objective is of sufficient importance, in the sense that it relates to pressing and substantial concerns, and (2) that the means chosen to achieve the objective are proportional. This second requirement has three components: (i) the means chosen must be rationally connected to the objective; (ii) they must impair the right in question as little as possible; and (iii) they must not so severely trench on individual or group rights that the objective is outweighed by the seriousness of the intrusion (*Edwards Books*, at pp. 768–69)."
41 *Ktunaxa Nation v British Columbia (Forests, Lands and Natural Resource Operations)*, [2017] 2 SCR 386, para. 65.
42 Convention for the Protection of Human Rights and Fundamental Freedoms 1950, 213 UNTS 222.
43 *Ebrahimian*, paras. 66, 67 (emphasis added).
44 *Ebrahimian*, para. 55, citing the 2005 case of Leyla Şahin also decided by the European Court of Human Rights.

References

Arendt, Hannah. 1998. *The Human Condition*. Introduction by Margaret Canovan. 2nd ed. Chicago: University of Chicago Press.

–. 2005. *The Life of the Mind*. Boston: Harcourt.

Barak, Aharon. 2002. "A Judge on Judging: The Role of a Supreme Court in a Democracy." *Harvard Law Review* 116 (1): 19–161. https://openyls.law.yale.edu/bitstream/handle/20.500.13051/3109/Foreword_A_Judge_on_Judging_The_Role_of_a_Supreme_Court_in_a_Democracy.pdf?sequence=2&isAllowed=y.

Baricco, Alessandro. 2019. *The Game*. Paris: Gallimard.

Beaudoin, Danielle. 2019. "Dans quel pays y a-t-il la plus forte présence syndicale? La réponse en carte." *Radio-Canada*, April 29. https://ici.radio-canada.ca/nouvelle/778821/taux-presence-syndicale-pays-monde-carte.

Bouchard, Gérard, and Charles Taylor. 2008. *Building the Future. A Time for Reconciliation*. Quebec City: Commission de consultation sur les pratiques d'accommodement reliées aux différences culturelles. https://numerique.banq.qc.ca/patrimoine/details/52327/1565995.

Colosimo, Jean-François. 2019. *La religion française*. Paris: Les Éditions du Cerf.

Dieckhoff, Alain, and Philippe Fortier, eds. *L'enjeu mondial: Religion et Politique*. Paris: Presses de Sciences Po, 2017.

Institut de la statistique du Québec. 2019. "Taux de présence syndicale, résultats selon le sexe pour diverses caractéristiques de la main-d'œuvre et de l'emploi, Québec, Ontario et Canada." In *CIRANO. Le Québec économique*, September 17. https://qe.cirano.qc.ca/theme/marche-travail/main-doeuvre/tableau-taux-syndicalisation-secteur-dactivite-2019.

Lamonde, Yvan. 2010. *L'heure de vérité. La laïcité québécoise à l'épreuve de l'Histoire*. Montreal: Del Busso Éditeur.

–.. 2013. *Trajectoires intellectuelles et politiques des XIXe et XXe siècles québécois*. Montreal: Del Busso Éditeur.

Latour, Julie. 2013. "Assurer la protection législative de la laïcité: une démarche essentielle pour la cohésion sociale et la fraternité citoyenne." In *Pour une reconnaissance de la laïcité au Québec*, edited by Daniel Baril and Yvan Lamonde, 111–36. Quebec City: Les Presses de l'Université Laval.

–. 2016. *Brief on Bill 62, Loi favorisant le respect de la neutralité religieuse de l'État et encadrant notamment les demandes d'accommodements pour motifs religieux dans certains organismes*. November 2.

–. 2019. *Brief on Bill 21: Tabled at the Commission des institutions of the National Assembly*. May 9. https://www.ledevoir.com/opinion/idees/571562/gerard-bouchard-et-la-denaturation-de-la-laicite.

–. 2020. "Gérard Bouchard et la dénaturation de la laïcité." *Le Devoir*, January 25.

Pena-Ruiz, Henri. 2003. *La laïcité*. Paris: Flammarion.

Portier, Philippe. 2017. "Les régimes de laïcité en Europe." In *L'enjeu mondial: Religion et Politique*, edited by Alain Dieckhoff and Philippe Fortier, 211–21. Paris: Presses de Sciences Po.

Proulx, Jean-Pierre. 2010. "De la confessionnalité à la laïcité scolaire. Il est un débat séculaire qui dure et perdure." *Le Devoir*, September 25, 2010. https://www.ledevoir.com/societe/education/296831/de-la-confessionnalite-a-la-laicite-scolaire-il-est-un-debat-seculaire-qui-dure-et-perdure.

Quebec Council on the Status of Women. 2007. *Droit à l'égalité entre les femmes et les hommes et liberté religieuse*. Quebec City: Conseil du statut de la femme. https://csf.gouv.qc.ca/wp-content/uploads/avis-droit-a-legalite-entre-les-femmes-et-les-hommes-et-liberte-religieuse.pdf.

Raynaud, Philippe. 2019. *La laïcité: Histoire d'une singularité française*. Paris: Gallimard.

Roulot-Ganzmann, Hélène. 2017. "La politique familiale du Québec a 20 ans: bilan." *Le Devoir*, May 27. https://www.ledevoir.com/societe/education/499507/la-politique-familiale-du-quebec-a-20-ans-bilan.

Russell, Peter H. 1969. *The Supreme Court of Canada: A Bilingual and Bicultural Institution*. Ottawa: Royal Commission on Bilingualism and Biculturalism.

Zuber, Valentine. 2017. "La défense de la liberté religieuse sur la scène internationale." In Dieckhoff and Fortier 2017, 187–96.

7

Arguments Relating to the Unconstitutionality of the Act Respecting the Laicity of the State

A Massive Rebuttal

DANIEL TURP

The Act Respecting the Laicity of the State was enacted and came into effect on June 16, 2019.[1] The act is without doubt the most widely attacked piece of legislation in Quebec's national history. Opponents are up in arms about this new fundamental law, which is quasi-constitutional in nature[2] and which states in Article 1 that "the State of Québec is a lay State." Opponents of the act are mounting a constitutional challenge of unprecedented scope. One of the four court challenges is seeking that the entire Act be declared unconstitutional, and close to half of its articles (fifteen out of a total of thirty-six articles) plus two paragraphs of two of its three schedules be invalidated, as shown by data in Table 7.1 in the Appendix at the end of this chapter.[3]

The day after the Act Respecting the Laicity of the State was adopted, an application for judicial review (declaration of invalidity) and an application for an interim stay were filed with the Superior Court of Quebec in the case of *Hak et al. v P.G. Québec*.[4] Three months later, on September 26, 2019, an application for declaratory judgment and damages was lodged with the same court in the case of *Lauzon et al. v A.G. Québec*.[5] This was followed on October 21, 2019 by another application for judicial review and for declaratory judgment in the case of *English-Montreal School Board et al. v A.G. Québec* (*EMSB et al.*).[6] Then, on

November 6, 2019, an application was lodged with the court seeking a permanent injunction, claiming that several articles of this law were unconstitutional, unenforceable, invalid, inoperative, and void, in the case of *Fédération autonome de l'enseignement v Jean-François Roberge, Simon Jolin-Barrette and Attorney-General of Québec* (*FAE* case).[7]

Four cases relating to the constitutionality of the Act Respecting the Laicity of the State are now pending before the Superior Court of Quebec. They have been joined under case management, and the joint hearing is scheduled to begin on November 2, 2020. Several requests to intervene have also been accepted by the court. The following organizations will be able to present their views before the tribunal: the Public Service Alliance of Canada, the Francophone Canada chapter of Amnesty International, the Lord Reading Law Association, the Mouvement laïque québécois, Pour les droits de femmes du Québec, and the World Sikh Organization. While it would be useful to examine the arguments of unconstitutionality put forward by these various intervening parties, this chapter will focus on the multiple and diverse arguments put forward by the plaintiffs. After examining the arguments aimed at setting aside the application of the notwithstanding provisions contained in the Act Respecting the Laicity of the State, we will analyze the arguments aimed at demonstrating that this Act infringes certain constitutional principles, the rights guaranteed in the Quebec Charter of Human Rights and Freedoms (Quebec Charter)[8] and the Canadian Charter of Rights and Freedoms (Canadian Charter),[9] and the division of legislative powers.

Arguments Relating to the Notwithstanding Provisions of the Act Respecting the Laicity of the State

One of the most controversial aspects of the Act Respecting the Laicity of the State is the use that the National Assembly in Quebec has made of its power under section 52 of the Quebec Charter and section 33 of the Canadian Charter to derogate from the rights contained in these two charters. Indeed, sections 33 and 34 of the Act Respecting the Laicity of the State provide that

> 33. This Act and the amendments made by it to the Act to foster adherence to State religious neutrality and, in particular, to provide

> a framework for requests for accommodations on religious grounds in certain bodies apply despite sections 1 to 38 of the *Charter of Human Rights and Freedoms* (chapter C-12).
>
> 34. This Act and the amendments made by Chapter V of this Act have effect notwithstanding sections 2 and 7 to 15 of the *Constitution Act, 1982* (Schedule B to the *Canada Act*, chapter 11 in the 1982 volume of the *Acts of the Parliament of the United Kingdom*).

Read together with the third recital of the preamble to the Act Respecting the Laicity of the State, which states that "in accordance with the principle of parliamentary sovereignty, it is incumbent on the Parliament of Québec to determine the principles according to which and manner in which relations between the State and religions are to be governed in Québec," these two notwithstanding provisions are clearly intended to prevent any declaration of unconstitutionality of the act by the courts that might be based on the sections of the Quebec Charter and the Canadian Charter referred to in sections 33 and 34. These rights correspond in every respect to those mentioned in section 52 of the Quebec Charter and section 33 of the Canadian Charter.

In the *FAE* case, the plaintiff stated that it wishes to demonstrate that "the use of notwithstanding clauses cannot be justified by mere technicalities and that the precedent set by *Ford v Quebec (Attorney General)* and *Devine v Quebec* three decades ago should be revisited in light of the current context to include substantive requirements."[10] It is doubtful that the courts will have any reason to require more from section 33 in 2020 than they did in 1988. In our view, the court would be more than reluctant to revisit its pronouncement in the first of the cases referred to by the plaintiff regarding the conditions that must be met to satisfy the requirements of section 33:

> The essential requirement of form laid down by s. 33 is that there must be an express declaration that an Act or a provision of an Act shall operate notwithstanding a provision included in s. 2 or ss. 7 to 15 of the *Canadian Charter*. A section 33 declaration is sufficiently express if it refers to the number of the section, subsection or paragraph of

> the *Charter* which contains the provision or provisions to be overridden. Of course, if a legislature intends to override only a part of a provision contained in a section, then there would have to be a sufficient reference in words to the part to be overridden ... In so far as requirements of the democratic process are relevant, this is the form of reference used in legislative drafting with respect to legislative provisions to be amended or repealed. There is no reason why more should be required under s. 33.[11]

Sections 33 and 34 fully satisfy the conditions set out in section 33 of the Canadian Charter and section 52 of the Quebec Charter. They should therefore render moot arguments based on the sections guaranteed by the Quebec Charter and the Canadian Charter that are intended to invalidate several sections of the Act Respecting the Laicity of the State. If the courts were to reach such a conclusion, the inclusion of such notwithstanding provisions would in principle neutralize arguments based on the rights and freedoms guaranteed in the two charters, whether it be the right to life, security, and liberty (Article 1 of the Quebec Charter and Article 7 of the Canadian Charter); the fundamental freedoms of conscience, religion, thought, belief, opinion, and expression (Article 3 of the Quebec Charter and Article 2 of Canadian Charter); the right to the preservation of dignity (Article 4 of the Quebec Charter) as well as the right to equality and non-discrimination (Article 10ff of the Quebec Charter and Article 15 of Canadian Charter).

The notwithstanding provision of section 34 of the Act Respecting the Laicity of the State, which is intended to give effect to its sections independently of sections 2 and 7–15 of the Canadian Charter, does not seem to make it possible to deprive of effect two sections of the Canadian Charter that are invoked in the arguments of some of the plaintiffs – namely, section 23, which relates to minority language education rights, and the general provision of section 28, which states that "notwithstanding anything in this [*Canadian*] *Charter*, the rights and freedoms referred to in it are guaranteed equally to male and female persons." In the case of section 23, it would therefore have to be shown that it had been violated, whereas, in the case of section 28, the burden of proof would be to show that it was more than an interpretive clause and that it guaranteed a right that could be infringed by the Act Respecting the Laicity of the State.

The Violation of Rights Guaranteed by the Canadian Charter and the Quebec Charter

Where violations of the Canadian Charter are concerned, the first question is whether the provisions of the Act Respecting the Laicity of the State could be declared unconstitutional on the basis of their incompatibility with sections 23 and 28 of the Canadian Charter, which are not referred to in the notwithstanding clause of section 33 of the Canadian Charter. In the *EMSB* case, the plaintiff asked the court to declare that sections 4, 6, 8, 9, 10, 13, 14, and 16 of the act were unjustified violations of section 23 of the Canadian Charter and were of no force and effect with respect to English-language school boards in Quebec and, more specifically, with respect to the English Montreal School Board. The plaintiffs argued that the provisions of the act, by regulating the wearing of religious symbols by the staff of English-language school boards, infringe the right of management and control recognized to linguistic minorities by section 23(3)(b) of the Canadian Charter, as interpreted by the Supreme Court of Canada in *Mahé v Alberta*.[12]

> In that case, the Court recognized that "minority language representatives should have exclusive authority to make decisions relating to the minority language instruction and facilities, including: ... (b) appointment and direction of those responsible for the administration of such instruction and facilities ... (d) recruitment and assignment of teachers and other personnel." The exercise of this power must, however, be understood as vital to ensuring "that [the] language and culture [of the linguistic minority] flourish" [and that] "what is essential, however, to satisfy that purpose is that the minority language group have control over those aspects of education which pertain to or have an effect upon their language and culture.[13]

Is it essential to the vitality of the language and culture of the English-speaking official minority in Quebec that its personnel, including its teachers, not be subject to rules of general application designed to ensure the implementation of the principle of laicity in Quebec's legal system and which also include a prohibition on the wearing of religious symbols in the performance of their duties? The courts should answer this question in the negative.

With respect to the argument concerning the violation of section 28 of the Canadian Charter in the *Lauzon et al.* and *EMSB* cases, the question is whether section 28 guarantees a right or freedom or whether it is rather an interpretive clause. Debates about the scope of the section will be interesting, but it is likely that the Supreme Court of Canada will refuse to give the section an independent normative scope. The Attorney General of Quebec may wish to cite the views of the Department of Justice Canada on "Section 28 – Gender Equality Rights":

> Section 28 requires that the rights and freedoms guaranteed in the *Charter* be implemented without discrimination between the sexes. Section 28 is often cited as a companion section with section 15 in cases alleged to raise gender discrimination issues (*Sawridge Band v. Canada*, 2000 CanLII 15449; *R. v. Park*, [1995] 2 S.C.R. 836, *Symes v. Canada*, [1993] 4 S.C.R. 695). It does not, however, create an equality rights regime separate and apart from that contained in section 15 of the *Charter*. Instead, it serves an interpretive, confirmatory, and adjunctive function.[14]

If the function of section 28 is therefore one of interpretation, confirmation, and supplementation, and if it does not create an equality rights regime separate from section 15 of the Canadian Charter, then section 28 has not created a right or freedom. Moreover, because the Act Respecting the Laicity of the State provides that it has effect independently of the Canadian Charter, section 28 cannot ultimately be relied on to perform its function of interpreting, confirming, and supplementing the derogated right.

With respect to the other sections of the Canadian and Quebec charters – namely, the right to life, security, and liberty, the fundamental freedoms of conscience, religion, thought, belief, opinion, and expression, the right to the preservation of dignity, and the right to equality and non-discrimination – it should be recalled, as stated above, that the inclusion of the overriding provisions in the Act Respecting the Laicity of the State should preclude any argument that they are, in the words of the *FAE* case, "unconstitutional, unenforceable, invalid, inoperative and void." If, however, the courts were to set aside the application of the notwithstanding provisions or find that the Act Respecting the Laicity of the State infringes sections 23 and 28 of the Canadian Charter, they would undoubtedly be asked to consider that such infringement constitutes a limitation on rights and freedoms that is not prohibited. The question will therefore be to determine whether the infringement constitutes, within the meaning of section 1 of the Canadian Charter, a restriction provided for by law, within reasonable limits and demonstrably justified in a free and democratic society or, to use the distinct terminology of section 9.1 of the Quebec Charter, whether the act has determined the scope of, and provided for the exercise of, fundamental rights and freedoms in a manner consistent with democratic values, state laicity, public order, and the general well-being of the citizens of Quebec.

For the purposes of applying these two limitation clauses, the Quebec courts and, ultimately, the Supreme Court of Canada will use the test that was articulated in the *R. v Oakes* ruling – known as the "Oakes test" – which requires that it be shown that the limitation on a fundamental right must be provided for by law, that it must serve a real and pressing purpose, and that the means chosen are proportional, in that they are rationally connected to the purpose, that they infringe the right as little as possible, and that there is a proportionality between the limitation and the purpose.[15] The application of the "Oakes test" will give rise to an analysis of the facts that led to the adoption of the Act Respecting the Laicity of the State and the choices made by the Quebec legislator to implement the principle of laicity in the Quebec legal order and having the effect of limiting fundamental rights. It will not be difficult to demonstrate that the restrictions imposed are provided for by legal rules – in this case, those found in the act itself. It is not impossible that the Attorney General of Quebec could also prove that the objectives, stated in the explanatory notes to the act, are real and urgent:

> To enshrine the paramountcy of State laicity ... in Québec's legal order ... to [establish] the equality of women and men; to [establish] a stricter duty of restraint regarding religious matters ... for persons exercising certain functions, resulting in their being prohibited from wearing religious symbols in the exercise of their functions; to [fulfill] the magistrature's duty of impartiality; to [ensure] a balance between the collective rights of the Québec nation and human rights and freedoms.

The application of the proportionality test will be particularly decisive when it comes to demonstrating that the limitations on fundamental rights provided for in the Act Respecting the Laicity of the State do not entail violations of either the Quebec Charter or the Canadian Charter. If a rational connection with the objectives can be demonstrated without too much difficulty, the satisfaction of the minimal impairment criterion can be based on the fact that the prohibition of the wearing of religious symbols has been limited to well-defined categories of persons, that it applies to these persons only in the context of the performance of their duties, and that a grandfather clause has been inserted into section 31 of the act. It will also be necessary to demonstrate that the minimal impairment test is met in its application to the rules on the provision and receipt of services with face uncovered, as set out in section 8 of the act and that this will be facilitated by the existence of the exceptions set out in section 9, which may be invoked on the grounds of health, disability, or the specific requirements of one's functions or the performance of certain tasks.

Moreover, two other arguments have been made in support of the claim that certain provisions of the Act Respecting the Laicity of the State violate fundamental human rights, and these arguments deserve brief comment. In the *FAE* case, the Quebec Superior Court was asked to declare numerous sections of the Act Respecting the Laicity of the State unconstitutional, unenforceable, invalid, inoperative, and void, as being in violation of Articles 2, 18, 19, 26, and 27 of the International Covenant on Civil and Political Rights (International Covenant).[16] Although Quebec declared itself bound by this treaty even before Canada deposited its instrument of accession,[17] and the texts of several sections of the Quebec Charter are inspired by the various provisions of the International Covenant (Morel 1987), the covenant itself has not been incorporated into Quebec law. On the consequences of the absence of such incorporation of this treaty, the Quebec Superior Court stated the following:

> [127] The Court is of the opinion that there can be no no-fault liability in this case based on the *International Covenant on Civil and Political Rights*. In this regard, the Court rejects AG Canada's contention that the mere accession of the *International Covenant* by the Executive Branch, as in this case, does not give the it the force of law or any binding effect in domestic law because the it has never been expressly incorporated into Canadian law, which has not prevented Canada from implementing certain obligations set out in the *Covenant* through various mechanisms, including legislation, regulation and the development of programs and policies.
>
> [128] The *Covenant* is not more applicable even if it can be referred to in interpreting a domestic obligation. This does not mean, as the plaintiffs contend, that sections 7 and 24(1) of the *Canadian Charter of Rights and Freedoms* must be interpreted under this *Covenant*. If domestic law is inconsistent with an international instrument that is not otherwise incorporated into domestic law, the domestic law must prevail. Moreover, no matter how international a cross-border instrument may be, it cannot impinge on provincial jurisdictions without the express consent of one or other of the affected provinces.[18]

In addition to this argument based on this international treaty binding on Quebec since 1976, which must be set aside for the reasons given above, there is an argument based on the Quebec Act of 1774![19] Thus, in the *Lauzon* case, an argument both original and unusual was presented by the plaintiffs who asked the court to declare that articles 4, 6, 8–10, 13, and 16 are invalid and inoperative because they contravene the free exercise of religion enshrined in Articles V and VII of the Quebec Act of 1774. Arguing that section 26 of the Constitution Act, 1982 expressly preserves pre-existing rights in Canada and that section 52 also recognizes by the use of the word "includes" in subsection 52(2) that the list of laws enumerated in that subsection is not an exhaustive definition of the constituent elements of the Constitution of Canada, counsel concluded their argument as follows: "In conclusion, the right to free exercise of religion recognized in Articles V and VII of the *Québec Act* is an integral part of the *Constitution* of Canada. Thus, the incompatibility of regular laws with this constitutional right renders them invalid under the principle of constitutional supremacy recognized in section 52 of the *Constitution Act, 1982*."[20]

This argument is obviously formulated to circumvent the obstacle posed by the notwithstanding provision of section 34 of the Act Respecting the Laicity of the State, which can only apply to the sections mentioned in section 33 of the Canadian Charter. However, it is difficult to see how a pre-existing right – in this case, the right to free exercise of religion mentioned in the Quebec Act of 1774 – could not be subject to derogation, whereas the same freedom of religion guaranteed in section 2(a) of the Canadian Charter can be subject to such derogation. It is doubtful that the courts would wish to nullify the exercise of parliamentary sovereignty embodied in the notwithstanding clause of section 33 of the Canadian Charter, the importance of which will be recalled when it comes to the application of the constitutional principles that are also invoked in arguments seeking to have the provisions of the Act Respecting the Laicity of the State declared unconstitutional.

Infringement of Constitutional Principles

Each of the plaintiffs also invokes constitutional principles, as each is presumably aware that sections 33 and 34 of the Act Respecting the Laicity of the State would prevent them from basing their claim of unconstitutionality of the sections of the act based on provisions of the Quebec Charter and the Canadian Charter. Thus, the principle of judicial independence, the existence of which has been affirmed and reaffirmed on several occasions by the Supreme Court of Canada, is invoked in *Hak et al.* (Attorney General), which seeks to have sections 5 and 6, on the requirements of laicity of the state and on the prohibition of wearing a religious symbol, declared invalid and inoperative in their application to judges.[21] In order to invalidate the provisions on the prohibition of wearing a religious symbol as well as the various provisions of the Act Respecting the Laicity of the State aimed at ensuring its implementation, the plaintiffs have also invoked, in turn, other constitutional principles set out by the Supreme Court of Canada in the *Reference re Secession of Québec,* whether it be the principle of the rule of law, the principle of democracy, or the principle of the protection of minorities (see also Pinard 2007; Tremblay 2012).[22]

While the nature of such principles and their place in the hierarchy of constitutional norms continues to be debated, the Supreme Court of Canada has delineated their scope. While these principles may have a role in filling gaps in the written Constitution and have been presented as "principles of interpretation," they must be applied as the Canadian court of last resort has stated that "they must be balanced against the principle of parliamentary sovereignty."[23] While the principle of rule of law may not infringe on parliamentary sovereignty,[24] the same must be said of the other principles of democracy and the protection of minorities. In this case, parliamentary sovereignty is clearly at stake since, as the Quebec legislator reminds us in the third recital of the Act Respecting the Laicity of the State, it is on this basis that the choice rests to resort to the power of derogation provided for in section 52 of the Quebec Charter and in section 33 of the Canadian Charter.

Accordingly, the constitutional principles to which the parties wish to appeal in order to have the judges deprive the rules contained in Quebec's new fundamental law of effect should be set aside by the judges called upon to take note of the clearly expressed intention of the Quebec Parliament to exercise its parliamentary sovereignty and to give effect to the provisions of the Act Respecting the Laicity of the State independently of the sections guaranteeing certain fundamental rights enshrined in the two charters. With respect to constitutional architecture, the attorneys for the plaintiffs in the *Hak et al.* have argued:

> Like the repeal of the right to vote for religious minorities, the transformation of public bodies into bodies accessible only to a (majority) subgroup is intended to alter the fundamentally inclusive nature of these institutions and, therefore, the Canadian constitutional structure,

> its "internal architecture." Neither Québec, nor any other province, nor Parliament has the jurisdiction to unilaterally alter this constitutional architecture, even in the exercise of any of its legislative powers. A province or Parliament could not, therefore, exclude religious persons from working for a public institution, just as it could not exclude women or racialized persons from such institutions. Such exclusion would transform the very nature of the public sphere in the province. Thus, Québec's attempt to unilaterally alter the architecture of the *Canadian Constitution* by enacting sections 6 and 8 of the Act is unconstitutional, and these sections must therefore be declared invalid.[25]

As articulated in the *Reference re Senate Reform,* the concept of constitutional architecture is akin to that of a constitutional principle in that, as the Supreme Court of Canada stated in the opinion in that reference, "the notion of architecture expresses the *principle* according to which 'the individual elements of the *Constitution* are linked to the others, and must be interpreted by reference to the structure of the *Constitution* as a whole'" (see also Karazivan 2015; Guénette 2017).[26] Thus, and as with constitutional principles, the concept of constitutional architecture cannot be successfully invoked to deprive the rules of the Act Respecting the Laicity of the State of effect and should also be set aside so as to ensure respect for the sovereignty of the Quebec Parliament and its right to give effect to its legislation independently of the articles guaranteeing certain fundamental rights enshrined in both charters.

Infringement of the Division of Legislative Powers

Hak et al. is the only case in which it has been argued that the adoption by the Quebec National Assembly of the Act Respecting the Laicity of the State violates the division of legislative powers provided for in sections 91 and 92 of the Constitution Act, 1867.[27] According to the plaintiffs in this application for judicial review and declaration of invalidity, Quebec's new fundamental law deals with criminal law, which is an exclusive jurisdiction of the Parliament of Canada under section 91(27) of the Constitution Act, 1867:

> The combination of the purpose of the act, the prohibitions it contains and the sanctions it creates clearly demonstrates that the true character of the act is the imposition of a moral conception of Quebec society which eliminates persons who wear religious symbols from public bodies. The Supreme Court has concluded in such cases as *Saumur v. City of Quebec*, [1953] 2 SCR 229; *Henry Birks & Sons (Montreal) Ltd. v. City of Montreal*, [1955] SCR 799; and, most recently, *R. v. Big M Drug Mart Ltd*, [1985] 1 SCR 295, that Parliament has exclusive jurisdiction to compel or prohibit religious observance in pursuit of a morality-related objective by virtue of its criminal law jurisdiction conferred by s. 91(27) of the *Constitution Act, 1867*.
>
> By virtue of its substantive nature, the act fetters the essential content of Parliament's legislative competence, rendering it *ultra vires*.[28]

Much could be said about this argument, and a review of the extensive case law will be required, including an analysis of the recent opinion of the Supreme Court of Canada in *Reference re Genetic Non-Discrimination Act*.[29] Suffice it to say that, of the criteria that have been set out for legislation to be characterized as criminal in nature, one is particularly critical – namely, that the conduct to be subjected must deserve the stigma of criminality. The sanctions in the Act Respecting the Laicity of the State seem far removed from addressing such conduct and are not intended to address a "public wrong" or an "evil." Are they not intended to ensure compliance with a law designed to implement a principle of laicity that seeks the separation of state and religion, the religious neutrality of the state, the equality of all citizens, and the freedom of conscience and religion?

Conclusion

The government of Quebec has adopted the Act Respecting the Laicity of the State and incorporated in it overriding provisions aimed at neutralizing the possibility for the courts to render inoperative the provisions implementing the principle of laicity. In so doing, the government may have had in mind a judgment of the Supreme Court of Canada in which it was stated that "a secular response that requires witnesses to park their religion at the courtroom door is inconsistent with the jurisprudence and Canadian tradition, and limits freedom of religion where no limit can be justified."[30] It was undoubtedly also a question of opting for a vision that distances itself from the concept of multiculturalism enshrined in the Canadian Charter and that could be an obstacle to the affirmation, found in the last recital of the preamble to the act, that a balance must be struck between the collective rights of the Quebec nation and the rights and freedoms of the individual. And perhaps the Quebec legislator and quasi-constituent wanted to adopt an Act that, as several Quebec citizens recently recalled, "allows laicity to be enshrined in law for the first time and to be recognized as an essential condition for the protection of freedom of conscience and the equality of all citizens" (Ben Anmar et al. 2020).

Appendix

Table 7.1 **A summary of the cases regarding the unconstitutionality of the Act Respecting the Laicity of the State (Bill 21) and the Act to Foster Adherence to State Religious Neutrality (Bill 62)**

Cases	*Hak et al. v A.G. Québec* File no. 500–17–108353–17 Application for Judicial Review (Declaration of Invalidity and Application for an Interim Stay June 17, 2019	*Lauzon et al. v A.G. Québec* File no. 500–17–109731–193 Application for a Declaratory Judgment and Damages September 26, 2019	*English-Montreal School Board et al. v A.G. Québec* File no. 500–17–109983–190 Application for Judicial Review and Declaratory Judgment October 21, 2019	*Fédération autonome de l'enseignement v Jean-François Roberge, Simon Jolin-Barrette and Attorney General of Québec* File no. 500–17–107204–193 Application for Permanent Injunction and for Unconstitutionality, Unenforceability, Invalidity, Inoperability, and Nullity November 6, 2019
Applications	To declare the Bill 21 invalid and inoperative To declare sections 5 and 6 of Bill 21 invalid and inoperative	To declare sections 4 and 6 of Bill 21 invalid and inoperative To declare sections 4, 6, 7–10, and 13–16 of Bill 21 invalid and of no force and effect	To declare that the amendment to section 1 of Bill 62 ... infringes on sections 2 and 15 of the Canadian Charter To declare that sections 4, 6, 7, 8, 9, 10, 13, 14, and 16 of Bill 21 violate the Canadian Charter and are of no force and effect	To declare unconstitutional claims of enumeration of religious symbols among teaching staff ... To declare unconstitutional, void, unenforceable, invalid, and inoperative sections 4, 6, 12, 13, 14, and paragraph 10 of Schedule II of Bill 21

Applications	To declare sections 6 and 8 of Bill 21 invalid and of no force and effect To declare section 8 (Schedule III, 1) of Bill 21 invalid and inoperative	To declare that the amendments to the preamble and section 9.1 of the Quebec Charter infringe sections 2 and 15 of the Canadian Charter To declare that the amendment to section 1 of Bill 62 ... infringes on sections 2 and 15 of the Canadian Charter To pay damages	To declare that sections 4, 6, 7, 8, 9, 10, 13, 14, and 16 of Bill 21 violate the Canadian Charter and are of no force and effect with respect to English language school boards in Quebec To declare that sections 4, 6, 7, 8, 9, 10, 13, 14, and 16 of Bill 21 violate the Canadian Charter and are of no force and effect with respect to the English-Montreal School Board	To declare unconstitutional, null, void, inapplicable, invalid, and inoperative section 16 of Bill 21 To declare the existence of a constitutional practice according to which the quasi-constitutional text of the Quebec Charter can only be modified by a unanimous decision of the Quebec National Assembly To declare that the Quebec legislator has not respected the constitutional practice according to which the quasi-constitutional text of the Quebec Charter can only be modified by a unanimous decision of the Quebec National Assembly, when adopting sections 18 and 19 of Bill 21 To declare sections 18 and 19 of Bill 21 unconstitutional, null, inapplicable, invalid, and inoperative To declare unconstitutional, null and void, inapplicable, invalid, and inoperative section 31 of Bill 21 To declare sections 33 and 34 of Bill 21 unconstitutional, void, unenforceable, invalid, and inoperative

Argument 1	Infringement of the principle of judicial independence Infringement of the division of powers (Constitution Act, 1867, section 91(27)) (Criminal Law) Unjustified infringement of section 3 of the Canadian Charter	Infringement of the principle of the rule of law Infringement of the right to free exercise of religion (Québec Act, 1774, Articles V and VII) Unjustified infringement of sections 2 and 15 of the Canadian Charter Unjustified infringement of sections 2 and 15 of the Canadian Charter Section 24 of the Canadian Charter ($500.00)	Unjustified infringement of sections 2 (a) and (b) and 15 of the Canadian Charter Unjustified infringement of section 23 of the Canadian Charter Unjustified infringement of section 23 of the Canadian Charter	To declare unconstitutional claims of enumeration of religious symbols among teaching staff ... To declare unconstitutional, void, unenforceable, invalid, and inoperative sections 4, 6, 12, 13, 14, and paragraph 10 of Schedule II of Bill 21 To declare unconstitutional, null, void, inapplicable, invalid, and inoperative section 16 of Bill 21 To declare the existence of a constitutional practice according to which the quasi-constitutional text of the Quebec Charter can only be modified by a unanimous decision of the Quebec National Assembly To declare that the Quebec legislator has not respected the constitutional practice according to which the quasi-constitutional text of the Quebec Charter can only be modified by a unanimous decision of the Quebec National Assembly, when adopting sections 18 and 19 of Bill 21 To declare sections 18 and 19 of Bill 21 unconstitutional, null, inapplicable, invalid, and inoperative

Argument 1				To declare unconstitutional, null and void, inapplicable, invalid, and inoperative section 31 of Bill 21 To declare sections 33 and 34 of Bill 21 unconstitutional, void, unenforceable, invalid, and inoperative
Argument 2	Infringement of security of tenure of judges (Constitution Act, 1867, section 100) Violation on grounds of vagueness	Infringement of division of powers (Constitution Act, 1867, section 91(27)) (Criminal Law)	Unjustified infringement of section 23 of the Canadian Charter	Infringement of the right not to be discriminated against on the basis of religion Infringement of sections 1, 3, 4, 10, 10.1, 11, 12, 13, 16, 17, 18, 18.1, 20, 49, 52, and 54 of the Quebec Charter Infringement of the constitutional principle of the protection of minorities
Argument 3	Infringement of the rule of law	Unjustified infringement of section 28 of the Canadian Charter	Unjustified infringement of section 28 of the Canadian Charter	Infringement of the right to equality and protection against discrimination based on sex and religious affiliation Infringement of Articles 2, 18, 26, and 27 of the International Covenant on Civil and Political Rights (ICCPR) Infringement of Articles 2, 18, 19, 26, and 27 of the ICCPR Infringement of sections 1, 3, 4, 10, 10.1, 11, 12, 13, 16, 17, 18, 18.1, 20, 49, 52, and 54 of the Quebec Charter

Argument 4	Alteration of the constitutional architecture	Unjustified infringement of sections 3 and 10 of the Quebec Charter		Infringement of the constitutional principle of the protection of minorities Infringement of Articles 2, 18, 19, 26, and 27 of the ICCPR
Argument 5	Violation of constitutional principles (democracy and protection of minorities)	Unjustified infringement of sections 2 and 15 of the Canadian Charter		

Notes

1 Act Respecting the Laicity of the State, SQ 2019, c. 12.

2 This quasi-constitutional character is conferred on the Act Respecting the Laicity of the State by Article 11, which reads as follows: "11. The provisions of this Act prevail over any contrary provisions of any subsequent Act, unless such an Act expressly states that it applies despite this Act. The provisions of sections 1 to 3 do not prevail over any contrary provisions of any previous Act."

3 Thus, the articles of the Act Respecting the Laicity of the State for which a declaration of unconstitutionality is sought are Articles 4, 5, 6, 7, 8, 9, 10, 13, 14, 16, 18, 19, 31, 33, and 34 as well as paragraph 10 of Schedule II and paragraph 1 of Schedule III.

4 Quebec Superior Court, *Hak et al. v P.G. Québec*, Application for Judicial Review (Declaration of Invalidity and Application for an Interim Stay), File no. 500–17–108353–17, June 17, 2019 (*Hak et al.*). In this chapter, we will not analyze the debates surrounding the application for a stay that was rejected by both the Quebec Superior Court in *Hak et al. v Attorney General of Québec*, 2019 QCCS 2989 (July 18, 2019) and the Quebec Court of Appeal in *Hak et al. v Attorney General of Québec*, 2019 QCCA 2145 (December 12, 2019), with the Supreme Court of Canada having also rejected the application for leave to appeal the latter decision on April 9, 2020.

5 Quebec Superior Court, *Lauzon et al. v A.G. Québec*, Application for Declaratory Judgment and Damages, File no. 500–17–109731, September 26, 2019 (*Lauzon et al.*).

6 Quebec Superior Court, *English-Montreal School Board et al. v A.G. Québec*, Application for Judicial Review and Declaratory Judgment, File no. 500–17–109983–190, October 21, 2019 (*EMSB et al.*).

7 Quebec Superior Court, *Fédération autonome de l'enseignement v Jean-François Roberge, Simon Jolin-Barrette and Attorney-General of Québec*, Application Seeking a Permanent Injunction, File no. 500–17–107204–193, November 6, 2019 (*FAE* case).

8 Charter of Human Rights and Freedoms, RSQ 1977, c. C-12 (Quebec Charter). It is interesting to note that sections 18 and 19 of the Act Respecting the Laicity of the State make two amendments to the Quebec Charter by inserting, after the third paragraph of the preamble, a new recital according to which "the Québec nation considers State laicity to be of fundamental importance," and by mentioning "State laicity" in the first paragraph of the limitation clause in section 9.1.

9 Canadian Charter of Rights and Freedoms, Part 1 of the Constitution Act, 1982, being Schedule B to the Canada Act 1982 (UK), 1982, c. 11 (Canadian Charter).

10 *FAE* case, para. 19.10; *Ford v Quebec (Attorney General)*, [1988] 2 SCR 712 (*Ford*); *Devine v Quebec*, [1988] 2 SCR 790.

11 See *Ford*, 37.

12 *Mahé v Alberta*, [1990] 1 SCR 342 (*Mahé*); see also *Arseneau-Cameron v Prince Edward Island*, [2000] 1 SCR 3 which is also cited by the applicants. Since the filing of the application, the Supreme Court of Canada has rendered another decision dealing

with the issue of the scope of control and management in *Conseil scolaire francophone de la Colombie-Britannique v British Columbia,* 2020 SCC 13.

13 *Mahé,* 275–76.

14 See Department of Justice Canada, *Canadian Charter of Rights and Freedoms: Section 28- Gender Equality Rights,* https://www.justice.gc.ca/eng/csj-sjc/rfc-dlc/ccrf-ccdl/check/art28.html.

15 *R. v Oakes,* [1986] 1 SCR 103.

16 International Covenant on Civil and Political Rights, 1966, 999 UNTS 171 (ICCPR).

17 Order in Council no. 1438–76 Concerning the Ratification of the International Covenant on Economic, Social and Cultural Rights, the International Covenant on Civil and Political Rights, the Optional Protocol to the International Covenant on Civil and Political Rights, and the Signing of an Agreement between Ottawa and the Provinces Respecting the Terms and Conditions and the Machinery for Provincial Participation in the Implementation of These International Instruments, April 21, 1976, reprinted in *Recueil des ententes internationales du Québec* (1984–89), 818. Canada acceded to the ICCPR on May 19, 1976, and the treaty came into force for both Quebec and Canada on August 19, 1976.

18 See *Dumont v Québec (Attorney General),* 2009 QCCS 3213 (footnotes omitted; author's translation).

19 Quebec Act 1774, 14 Geo. III, c. 83.

20 *Lauzon et al.,* 18. para.121.

21 In the application of *Hak et al.,* paras. 151–53, an additional argument in support of a declaration of unconstitutionality of sections 5 and 6 was based on section 100 of the Constitution Act, 1867 (UK), 30 & 31 Vict., c. 3, on the security of tenure of judges. There is no indication, however, that a sanction for a violation by judges to whom the State Secularism Act applies could result in the removal of a judge by the National Assembly and thus a violation of judicial independence in its individual dimension of security of tenure. This issue of judicial independence and security of tenure could also be addressed under section 11(f) of the Canadian Charter as the Supreme Court of Canada did in *Reference re Remuneration of Judges of the Provincial Court (P.E.I.),* [1997] 3 SCR 3.

22 *Reference re Secession of Québec,* [1998] 2 SCR 217.

23 See *Babcock v Canada (Attorney General),* [2002] 3 SCR 3, para. 29.

24 As noted by constitutional scholars Henri Brun, Guy Tremblay, and Eugénie Brouillet (2014), three Supreme Court of Canada decisions point in this direction: *British Columbia v Imperial Tobacco Canada Ltd.,* [2005] 2 SCR 473, 497–505; *Charkaoui v Canada (Citizenship and Immigration),* [2007] 1 SCR 350, 417–18; *British Columbia (Attorney General) v Christie,* [2007] 1 SCR 873, 882–85.

25 *Hak et al.,* 142–44.

26 *Reference re Senate Reform,* [2014] 1 SCR 704, para. 26 (emphasis added).

27 Constitution Act, 1867, s. 93.

28 See *FAE* case, 107–8.

29 *Reference re Genetic Non-Discrimination Act,* 2020 SCC 17.

30 See *R. v N.S.*, [2012] 3 SCR 726, para. 2. See also the words of Justice Louis Lebel in that case, which also refers to multiculturalism: "Today, we may rightly say that, in s. 27 of the Charter, Canada accepts the importance of multiculturalism in its social life. In s. 27, Canada signals its acceptance that it's changing through every day of its history. At the same time, however, the recognition of multiculturalism takes place in the environment of the Constitution itself, and is rooted in its political and legal traditions. The Constitution requires an openness to new differences that appear within Canada, but also an acceptance of the principle that it remains connected with the roots of our contemporary democratic society" (761, para. 72).

References

Ben Anmar, Amani, et al. 2020. "Droits des femmes. Choisir une société laïque." *Le Devoir,* September 15. https://www.ledevoir.com/opinion/idees/585949/choisir-une-societe-laique.

Brun, Henri, Guy Tremblay, and Eugénie Brouillet. 2014. *Droit constitutionnel.* 6th ed. Cowansville, QB: Éditions Yvon Blais.

Guénette, Dave. 2017. "L'architecture constitutionnelle. Dimension artistique d'une construction juridique." *Les Cahiers de droit* 58 (1–2): 33–65.

Karazivan, Noura. 2015. "De la structure constitutionnelle dans le Renvoi relatif au Sénat: vers une gestalt constitutionnelle?" *McGill Law Review* 60 (4): 793–838.

Morel, André. 1987. "La Charte québécoise: un document unique dans l'histoire législative canadienne." *Revue juridique Thémis* 21 (1): 4–7.

Pinard, Danielle. 2007. "Certaines utilisations de principes constitutionnels implicites par la Cour suprême du Canada." *Jahrbuch des öffentlichen Rechts* 55: 625–62. https://www.mohrsiebeck.com/artikel/certaines-utilisations-de-principes-constitutionnels-implicites-par-la-cour-supreme-du-canada-101628joer-2007-0032?no_cache=1.

Tremblay, Luc. B. 2012. "Les principes constitutionnels non écrits." *Review of Constitutional Studies/Revue d'études constitutionnelles* 15 (1): 15–51.

8

Rights Guaranteed Equally to Both Sexes, the Notwithstanding Clause, and the Act Respecting the Laicity of the State

Overview and Contribution to the Debate from a Quebec Perspective

GUILLAUME ROUSSEAU

The Act Respecting the Laicity of the State includes a reference to the notwithstanding clause of section 33 of the Canadian Charter of Rights and Freedoms (Canadian Charter).[1] Since the adoption of the act, there has been a debate on the relationship between section 33 and section 28 of the Canadian Charter, which deals with rights guaranteed equally to both sexes. Since this debate is essentially taking place in English from a pan-Canadian perspective, the main points will be summarized here, and we will add our contribution from a Quebec perspective.

State of the Debate on Sections 28 and 33 of the Canadian Charter and the Act Respecting the Laicity of the State: An Imaginative Solution or Defence of Positive Law

In providing an overview of the situation, we need to analyze the positions of two authors who, in the context of the debate on the Act Respecting the Laicity of the State, argue that section 28 could be used to circumvent section 33 and then look at two authors who defend the opposite position.

The Thesis of Section 28 as a Means of Circumventing Section 33

This thesis is defended by University of New Brunswick professor Kerri

Froc and, to a lesser extent, by McGill University Dean of Law Robert Leckey.

Robert Leckey: Section 28 in the Service of a New Imaginary Paradigm

In late 2019, Robert Leckey (2019, 1) published a short article in *Constitutional Forum constitutionnel* entitled "Advocacy Notwithstanding the Notwithstanding Clause." Leckey's premise is that there has been a paradigm shift with respect to the notwithstanding clause. According to this view, the old paradigm was one of respect for rights, advocating the exceptional use of the notwithstanding clause and only after a judgment had declared a law contrary to a charter. This view holds that the new paradigm consists in denigrating the constitutional review by judges and demonstrating a majoritarian willingness to override rights without justification or demonstration of proportionality between the harms and benefits of a measure and, to do so, by invoking the notwithstanding clause on a pre-emptive basis. Leckey gives two examples to support his view that such a paradigm shift has taken place. The first example is the intention expressed by the Doug Ford government, although never fulfilled, to use section 33 to counter a ruling suspending the application of the 2018 Better Local Government Act, a law reforming municipal governance in Toronto.[2] His second example is the Act Respecting the Laicity of the State.

On the face of it, these two examples alone provide little evidence of a major paradigm shift, especially because there is much more solid evidence to strongly qualify, if not contradict, Leckey's (2019) thesis, at least as far as Quebec is concerned. Contrary to what he suggests, even before 2018, the use of the notwithstanding clause in Quebec was relatively frequent and almost always pre-emptive – that is, it was invoked prior to a judgment declaring that a statute contravened a charter. Between 1982 and 2017, Quebec used section 33 of the Canadian Charter on sixty-one occasions[3] and all but once in a preventive fashion (Rousseau and Côté 2017). Moreover, during the parliamentary debates prior to adoption of the Act Respecting the Laicity of the State, the minister responsible for this law justified resorting to this provision on the grounds that Quebec traditionally resorted to the notwithstanding clause on a frequent basis.[4] Rather than demonstrating a paradigm shift, this recourse was in line with a long-standing tradition and, therefore, with an already-existing paradigm. This is especially true since the act aims not to show a majoritarian desire to override rights without justification or demonstration of proportionality but, rather, to protect the freedom of conscience of recipients of public services and to create a right to secular public services by public officials interfering to the least extent possible with the free exercise of religion.[5] This last element is implicitly conceded by Leckey (2019, 2), when he mentions that the government insisted on the freedom of religion that state employees in positions of authority would continue to enjoy outside of work hours and in private spaces.

Leckey (2019) is therefore clearly overstating the case in claiming that there has been a paradigm shift. At most, we can concede that in the years immediately prior to 2018 there were more instances of renewals of the notwithstanding clause than first-time use of such a provision. In this limited sense, the Act Respecting the Laicity of the State provides something somewhat new. But it is not a paradigm shift from respect for rights to a majoritarian willingness to override rights without justification or, to use the language of political science, from liberalism to populism. Rather, the act represents a shift from a more elitist conception of law[6] to one seeking to distance itself from both elitism and populism. The parliamentary committee found that there were as many groups wanting the government to do more in secularizing the state as there were groups that wanted it to do less. Although public opinion sided with the groups that wanted more secularization, the government opted to bring about a compromise rather than allowing popular will to triumph (Crop 2018).

In short, Leckey (2019) starts from a historical misreading of the use of the notwithstanding clause to conclude a supposed paradigm shift and thus justify in the rest of his article a judicial hyper-activism that would counter the Act Respecting the Laicity of the State. Indeed, he implicitly concedes that this law and its use of the notwithstanding clause are perfectly valid in the current state of the law. For this reason, he invites lawyers to be bold, ambitious, and imaginative, to reread the constitutional text and case law with fresh eyes, to consider the important role played by the Canadian Charter in the lawyerly imagination, to take a healthy distance from orthodoxy and prevailing wisdom, and to play an altered role (2, 6). It is in this imagined context of an alternative future law that his unargued proposal to use section 28 to circumvent section 33 becomes possible.

We will now turn to another author, for whom circumventing section 33 becomes possible thanks to a mythologized past.

Kerri A. Froc: Originalism and Section 28 as the Origins of a Possible Constitutional "Big Bang"

In the same issue of *Constitutional Forum constitutionnel* that contained Leckey's article, Kerri A. Froc (2019, 19) published a short article in which she argues that section 28 allows for the circumvention of section 33 in the context of the Act Respecting the Laicity of the State. She then expresses perplexity and annoyance that this claim was initially ignored during the judicial debate on the constitutionality and suspendability of this law. Nonetheless, as this reading is the subject of her doctoral dissertation, she takes advantage of the debate around this law to expound it again and present its three main arguments (Froc 2015). She refers to the text of Article 28 and especially its first words, which read: "Notwithstanding anything in this Charter, the rights and freedoms referred to in it are guaranteed equally to male and female persons." She points to the history of this section since a draft wording during the debates leading up to the adoption of the Canadian Charter would have stated, "Notwithstanding anything in this Charter except section 33" was abandoned.

Similarly, earlier language was dropped that would have added to section 33 – after the words "Parliament or the legislature of a province may expressly declare in an Act of Parliament or of the legislature, as the case may be, that the act or a provision thereof shall operate notwithstanding a provision included in section 2 or sections 7 to 15 of this Charter," the following words were to have appeared: "or section 28 of this Charter in its application to discrimination based on sex referred to in section 15." Froc (2019) insists that these words were abandoned thanks to lobbying by feminist pressure groups. What she does not emphasize is that, beyond this lobbying, the first of these verbal formulations was problematic because of its wording. It appeared to allow section 33 to have the effect of neutralizing the impact of section 28 on sections 3– 6 and 16–23 of the Canadian Charter, sections that the framers intended to exclude from the scope of section 33.[7] As for the second draft, it confirms that the Constitution did not create a substantive right that could stand alone but, rather, an interpretative provision that could be applied in conjunction with other provisions of the Canadian Charter.

Finally, Froc (2019) cites the Quebec Superior Court in *Syndicat de la fonction publique v Quebec (Attorney General),* where the court states that "because of the historical context of its adoption and the objectives sought to be achieved, section 28 would protect the right to sex equality in a particular way" and that "the legislator could not derogate from it by applying section 33."[8] Moreover, according to Froc, section 6 of the Act Respecting the Laicity of the State, which prohibits the wearing of religious symbols by persons in authority, is contrary to sections 2(a) and 15 of the Canadian Charter because it affects women more than men. She draws this conclusion from what she calls a preliminary analysis of the data, which consists of pointing out that in Quebec there are more Muslims, and, therefore, more Muslim women wearing the veil, than Jews and Sikhs, and, therefore, Jewish or Sikh men wearing a yarmulke or turban. She adds that this law would target Muslim women because the minister responsible for the status of women has stated that she perceives the hijab as a sign of oppression (Froc 2019, 20).

Froc (2019) forgets to point out, however, that this statement was in response to a journalist's question about the hijab, which was not a question about the raison d'être of the Act Respecting the Laicity of the State (Gagnon 2019), and that this minister was not responsible for the law and that she also specified that any symbol dictated by a religion is a sign of oppression (Messier 2019). Actually, Froc neglected to mention many other elements contradicting her thesis in her article. Fortunately, other authors draw attention to these other elements, and they help to explain why Froc herself admits that if the courts were to allow section 33 to be circumvented by section 28 in the context of the Act Respecting the Laicity of the State, it would be a "big bang" in Canadian constitutional law (21).

The Thesis that Section 28 Does Not Allow for the Circumvention of Section 33

This thesis is defended by the lawyer Asher Honickman and Maxime St-Hilaire, a professor in the Faculty of Law at the Université de Sherbrooke.

Asher Honickman: Section 28 Interpreted in Context

Asher Honickman (2019) notes that interpreting the opening words of section 28 ("notwithstanding anything in this Charter") in the manner suggested by Froc (2019) means that this section circumvents not only section 33 but also section 1, and, therefore, section 28 creates an absolute right. This remark is all the more relevant since Froc relies on the history of claims made by feminist groups during the debates prior to the adoption of the Canadian Charter to support her interpretation that section 28 allows section 33 to be circumvented. However, it is known that these claims were also, and even primarily, intended to counter section 1 (Canadian Advisory Council on the Status of Women 1980).

Honickman also insists that, even if section 28 were to prevail over section 33 in the event of a conflict, there would still have to be a conflict between these sections. But there cannot be since the two sections deal with completely different subjects: the interpretation of rights, on the one hand, and the application of rights, on the other. For Honickman, it is clear that section 28 is an interpretive provision, not a right, particularly in light of the fact that it is located in a section of the Canadian Charter that is devoted to "General Provisions," which includes such provisions, rather than in the section entitled "Equality Rights." Accordingly, the words "Notwithstanding anything in this Charter" refer not to section 33, but to sections 25 and 27, which are interpretive provisions concerning the rights of Aboriginal peoples and the multicultural heritage of Canadians that might have encouraged interpretations less favourable to women, had it not been for section 28.

Honickman (2019) also points out that the word "guaranteed" in section 28 is related to the word "guarantees" in section 1. Therefore, if section 1 were to be interpreted in the same way as section 28, and thus give a broad meaning to the words "guaranteed" and "guarantees," the result would be contrary to the intention of the constituents since section 1 would allow section 33 to be circumvented (since section 1 prohibits the restriction of rights "subject only to such reasonable limits prescribed by law as can be demonstrably justified in a free and democratic society," whereas section 33 allows such restriction without such justification). For Honickman, therefore, these words must be interpreted more strictly, and it must be understood that these two sections deal with two different things: section 1 deals with the possession of rights and section 33 with their application. Finally, with respect to the abandonment of earlier language that would have made it clear that section 28 cannot be used to circumvent section 33, Honickman points out that such legislative history is relevant, but far from determinative – unless, we may add, one adopts an originalist approach.

Maxime St-Hilaire: Section 28 Interpreted in an Evolutionary Manner

In addition to reiterating Honickman's (2019) main arguments, Professor Maxine St-Hilaire (2019) develops several others. He points out that Froc's (2019) interpretation of section 28 is based on an originalist argument, in the sense of being based on the historical origins of this provision. This is obviously true, as Froc (2015, 22–102) relies on the legislative history of section 28 and assumes reliance on a kind of originalism. And, in our view, it is particularly ironic that she offers such an argument considering that originalism has often worked against women's rights. Even those women's groups she cites so frequently, who were in the early 1980s proposing what would become section 28, were suspicious of originalism (Eberts 1980). One of the reasons for this distrust was the famous "Persons" case in which the Supreme Court of Canada ruled that women were not persons within the meaning of the section of the Constitution allowing for the appointment of persons to the Senate because the Fathers of Confederation in 1867 did not imagine that persons appointed to the Senate could be women.[9]

St-Hilaire (2019) calls for a more progressive interpretation in that he proposes to take greater account of the case law relating to section 28 – case law that was therefore subsequent to its adoption. With regard to Froc's (2015, 257–374) dissertation, he points out that she "seems to admit that the current case law cannot support, at least not positively, her interpretation of section 28 of the *Canadian Charter*." In this regard, he notes that the position that section 28 is related to section 15, subject to section 33, and is not the creator of a separate equality rights regime "is supported by the case law," while the position that section 28 could be used to circumvent section 33 "is more speculative." While St-Hilaire's reasoning on this point may be qualified by the decision in the *Syndicat de la fonction publique* case, his reasoning remains valid.[10] The decision in the *Syndicat* case was rendered by a trial court, whose discussion of the possibility that section 28 might allow section 33 to be circumvented was merely *obiter* – that is, an incidental expression of opinion that has no impact on the answer to the legal question posed by the case before the court. In fact, this judgment was only subsequently repeated on just one occasion in Quebec's jurisprudence, which came after St-Hilaire's analysis was published.

In a judgment dealing with an application to suspend the application of sections of the Act Respecting the Laicity of the State, a dissenting judge of the Quebec Court of Appeal cited this case, adding that the interaction between sections 28 and 33 had never been analyzed by a court of appeal, and then characterized the question raised by this issue, and thus the possibility that section 28 could allow section 33 to be circumvented, as serious.[11] On the other hand, in the same judgment, a majority judge described the possibility as "uncertain," concluded that "the new arguments ... based on section 28 of the *Canadian Charter* cannot be accepted at this stage of the judicial proceedings," and more broadly described the reasoning for invalidating the Act Respecting the Laicity of the State by invoking section 28 as "not obvious at first sight."[12] It should be noted that, rather than citing the *Syndicat de la fonction publique* case, this judge referred to the BC Court of Appeal in the *McIvor* case,[13] which stated that "section 28 is a provision dealing with the interpretation of the Charter. It does not, by itself, purport to confer any rights, and therefore cannot be 'contravened.'"[14] Finally, we may note in the Quebec Court of Appeal decision on an application to suspend the application of sections of the *Act Respecting the laicity of the State;* a second judge from the majority concluded that "[t]he Attorney General [of Québec] is also correct in stating that it is not clear that section 28 of the Charter prevents the Québec legislature from invoking the notwithstanding clause."[15] That leads us to a specifically Quebec perspective on this issue.

Contribution to the Debate on Sections 28 and 33 of the Canadian Charter and the Act Respecting the Laicity of the State: A Specifically Quebec Perspective

In this contribution to the debate from a specifically Quebec perspective, I would like to examine the relationship between Quebec and sections 28 and 33.

Quebec and Section 28

In her analysis of section 28 and the Act Respecting the Laicity of the State, Froc (2019, 19) argues that this section and the removal of language in an earlier draft of the Canadian Charter explicitly confirming section 33 could not be circumvented and are the combined result of the work of "angry women from across the country." She also concludes that this justifies a finding that such circumvention is possible. Her argument overlooks the special place occupied by Quebec women in the history of the development of the Canadian Charter and the fact that this section is a compromise far short of what women's groups in English Canada originally wanted but close to Quebec's position on one key point.

Another History of Section 28

If Quebec did not sign the 1982 Constitution and its Canadian Charter, it is not because René Lévesque and Pierre Trudeau could not agree on technicalities during the 1980–82 negotiations. It is because they held very different positions. The Lévesque government, in particular, was wary of a charter of rights that would be placed above the sovereignty of the Quebec Parliament. And this government position was supported by a broad consensus within Quebec society at the time. For this reason, when Quebec found itself isolated from an agreement between the federal government and the English-speaking provinces, it was as much the result of a contest between politicians as a conflict between two societies. Quebec's isolation in this regard was also reflected in various pan-Canadian civil society organizations involved in the constitutional debate.

In her dissertation, Froc (2015, 110) herself admits that the feminist movement that pushed for a sex equality provision in the Canadian Charter was led by English-speaking women (Gotell 1990; Gill 2010). The major events organized by this movement to mobilize and consult with Canadian women were often marked by an under-representation of French-speaking Quebec women, in part because organizations representing the latter were unwilling to participate in events that might appear to support the Trudeau government and its proposed Charter (Froc 2015, 160). There is every indication that the views of the few Quebec women present at these events, and more broadly in this movement, did not carry much weight. At least one proposal concerning the national rights of Quebec and its people was excluded on the grounds that it was out of order (168, 185).

As a result, at the same time that it was advocating for a sex equality provision in the Canadian Charter, the women's movement in Canada was weakened by numerous divisions, primarily between English-speaking and French-speaking women (Froc 2015, 152). In addition, women were generally not very influential in politics at the time in English Canada, whereas, in Quebec, they had played a key role in the 1980 referendum (130). The women's movement was therefore not in a position to impose its views on the elected officials, almost all of whom were men, and they adopted the Canadian Charter, which explains why section 28, far from perfectly reflecting these views, was in fact the result of a compromise.

The Compromise of Section 28

What Froc's (2019) article on section 28 and the Act Respecting the Laicity of the State fails to mention, but what her doctoral dissertation does demonstrate, is that the women's movement pushing for what became section 28 originally wanted much more than that. The movement was pushing for a provision in the Canadian Charter that specified that women and men have equal status, rights, and privileges under the law, which would have gone far beyond the mere guarantee of rights eventually mentioned in section 28 (Froc 2015, 135). As the objective of such a provision was to counter section 1, a motion was even tabled by a parliamentarian so that a provision on the equal guarantee of the rights and freedoms of the Canadian Charter to women and men would replace section 1. But it was rejected (138). The women's movement was also advocating for such a provision or guarantee to counter the possible effects of what would become section 27 – namely, that "this Charter shall be interpreted in a manner consistent with the preservation and enhancement of the multicultural heritage of Canadians."

André Lamoureux (2019), a political scientist at Université du Québec à Montréal, has studied the history of the women's movement and negotiations leading to the Canadian Charter, and he notes:

> On the one hand, the legislator committed to recognizing the rights enumerated in the *Charter* for both sexes. On the other hand, the legislator also allowed himself to limit these rights, including rights with respect to women, thanks to the notwithstanding clause, which is central to this exercise of restriction. That is the 1982 compromise ... In 1981, the women's movement initially aspired to have a chapter of recognized rights and freedoms for women, superseding the other provisions of the *Charter* and protected from the notwithstanding clause. However, this aspiration was frustrated by the government of Pierre Elliott Trudeau. It never came to be.

Considering the above, we can conclude that section 28 is not intended to circumvent sections 1 and 33 but, rather, to counter section 27. We can also conclude that this is the meaning of the words "notwithstanding anything in this Charter" that are contained in section 28. Such an interpretation has the advantage of being consistent with Quebec's positions, which are unfavourable to this multiculturalism provision in the Constitution and favourable to section 33 (Froc 2015, 145).

Quebec and Section 33

To understand the relationship between Quebec and section 33, we first need to discuss federalism, Quebec's distinct character, and sex equality as it is understood in Quebec.

Section 33, Federalism, and Quebec's Distinct Character

As early as 1968, when the federal government began proposing the adoption of a charter of rights, Quebec immediately expressed reservations in the name of its distinct character and federalism:

> In a unitary country with a homogeneous society, declarations of rights can be seen as summations of the moral philosophy accepted by the entire population, and the rights of citizens can be derived therefrom. The result is to entrench in the Constitution a certain homogeneity of ethical concepts whose application is the responsibility of the courts. We feel that in a federal system and particularly in the case of Canada, it would be a serious political mistake to proceed in that way. Québec's civil law tradition and the way in which it recognizes and protects fundamental rights are in fact significantly different from the approach in *common law* courts.[16]

During the negotiations leading to adoption of the Canadian Charter, Quebec favoured the idea of a notwithstanding clause since, logically, a notwithstanding clause was a way to circumvent a conception of certain rights enshrined in a charter – in this case, in order to preserve Quebec's civil law tradition within the framework of the Canadian federation where the common law is dominant (Brunelle 1989).[17]

Although Quebec did not subsequently sign the 1982 Constitution, this idea was taken up by other provinces as a condition of their consent to the adoption of the Canadian Charter, which is why legal experts Marc-André Roy and Laurence Brosseau (2018, 4), authors of an official federal publication about the notwithstanding clause, state that "acceptance (reluctant in some cases) of the clause by all the participants in the November 1981 First Ministers' Conference, except Quebec, allowed the impasse to be broken and the *Charter of Rights*, among other constitutional changes, to become reality." Gil Rémillard (2007, 69–70), professor, lawyer, and former minister of intergovernmental affairs even refers to section 33 as the "fruit of one of the most significant compromises in the history of Canadian federal-provincial relations."

The importance of section 33 for the 1982 Constitution can be compared to that of section 133 for the 1867 Constitution, which enshrines a certain legislative, parliamentary, and judicial bilingualism at both the Quebec and federal levels. This comparison is relevant and useful because section 133 was deemed not to be circumvented by section 92(1) of the 1867 Constitution, even though the latter section stated that "in each Province the Legislature may exclusively make Laws in relation to Matters coming within the Classes of Subjects next hereinafter enumerated, that is to say: 1. The Amendment from Time to Time, *notwithstanding anything in this Act,* of the Constitution of the Province, except as regards the Office of Lieutenant Governor" (emphasis added). The words "notwithstanding anything in this Act" in this section are very similar to the words "notwithstanding anything in this Charter" in section 28 of the Canadian Charter. The fact that the jurisprudence determined that the words in section 92(1) did not have the effect of circumventing section 133, particularly given the historical importance of the compromise embodied in the latter section,[18] argues for the proposition that similar words in section 28 should not permit circumvention of section 33, given that it also embodies a historically significant compromise.

Although Quebec did not sign the 1982 Constitution, this compromise is particularly important for it. For with the advent of the Canadian Charter, Quebec has made frequent use of section 33. Counting only the three instances of use in the Act Respecting Constitution Act, 1982, rather than the systematic use of section 33 in all Quebec legislation between 1982 and 1985, Quebec has used this section sixty-seven times between 1982 and 2019, and six sections referring to it are still in force.[19] Almost every time, it has done so in the name of an objective related to Quebec's identity or to social progress – for example, in the area of sex equality (Rousseau and Côté 2017)[20] – which is normal in a state with a civil law tradition where the legislative, rather than the judicial, branch is at the heart of the evolution of law. As can be seen from the quotation above, it is understandable why the minister responsible for the Act Respecting the Laicity of the State has claimed to be in favour of the practice of using section 33 for purposes of national identity or social progress, considering that the preamble to this Act refers to the Quebec nation and its specific characteristics, including civil law, as well as to equality between men and women.

Section 33 and Sex Equality in Quebec

From the outset in 1981, Allan Blakeney, the premier of Saskatchewan, who refused to allow section 28 to circumvent section 33 (Lavoie 1981), was concerned that the equal guarantee of rights to both sexes under the Canadian Charter would prevent measures specifically favouring women at the expense of men (Froc 2015, 254). This concern is relevant today since, if the words "notwithstanding anything in this Charter" contained in section 28 mean that this section allows for the circumvention of sections 1 and 33, they also mean that the Canadian Charter allows for the circumvention of section 15(2). After section 15(1) specifies that "every individual is equal before and under the law and has the right to the equal protection and equal benefit of the law without discrimination and, in particular, without discrimination based on ... sex," section 15(2) adds that "subsection (1) does not preclude any law, program or activity that has as its object the amelioration of conditions of disadvantaged individuals or groups including those that are disadvantaged because of ... sex." In other words, if it was not for section 15(2), measures that favour women over men could be found unconstitutional under section 15(1) unless they are protected by section 33.

This is of particular concern given that there are currently at least three statutes in Quebec that provide for more favourable treatment of women than men that are protected by section 33. Section 32 of the Act Respecting the Teachers Pension Plan states:

> 32. Any teacher who ceases to participate in the plan is entitled to a pension if the teacher
>
> (1) has attained normal retirement age, that is, 65 years of age;
> (2) has at least 33 years of service;
> (3) has, in the case of a female teacher, attained 60 years of age;
> (4) has at least 10 years of service and is not under 62 years of age;
> (5) has at least 32 years of service and is not under 55 years of age;
>
> ...
>
> (6.1) in the case of *a female teacher*, has at least 10 years of service and is not under 58 years of age;

> (7) has at least 22 years of service and is not under 55 years of age or, in the case of *a female teacher,* 50 years of age.

Section 51 of the same Act provides as follows:

> 51. The deferred pension is payable, as the case may be,
>
> (1) from 65 years of age;
> (2) from 60 years of age, in the case of *a female teacher;*[21]

And the second paragraph of section 78.1 states that "sections 28, 32 and 51 have effect despite section 15 of the *Constitution Act, 1982* (Schedule B to the *Canada Act,* chapter 11 in the 1982 volume of the *Acts of the Parliament of the United Kingdom*)."

The Act Respecting the Civil Service Superannuation Plan provides in sections 56, 84, and 114.1, paragraph 2:

> 56. An officer who ceases to participate in the plan is entitled to a pension if he
>
> (1) has at least 35 years of service;
> (2) has 10 or more years of service and has reached 62 years of age or, in the case of *a female officer,* 60 years of age or over; ...
>
> A pension is also granted to an officer who has at least 22 years of service and has reached 55 years of age or, in the case of *a female officer,* 50 years of age ...
>
> 84. A deferred pension is payable, as the case may be,
>
> (1) from 65 years of age;
> (2) from 60 years of age, in the case of *a female officer*
>
> 114.1 ... Sections 56 and 84 have effect despite section 15 of the *Constitution Act, 1982* (Schedule B to the *Canada Act,* chapter 11 in the 1982 volume of the *Acts of the Parliament of the United Kingdom*).[22]

The Act Respecting the Pension Plan of Certain Teachers contains a Schedule II under which the premium amounts per ten dollars of annual pension are higher for women than for men. For example, at ages eighteen, sixty-five, and eighty, this schedule provides for amounts of $3,141, $40,782, and $22,591 for men and $3,537, $45,922, and $28,661 for women.[23] And section 62 states that "the provisions of this Act have effect despite section 15 of the *Constitution Act, 1982* (Schedule B to the *Canada Act,* chapter 11 in the 1982 volume of the *Acts of the Parliament of the United Kingdom*)."

If section 28 provides a way around sections 1, 15(2), and 33, it certainly provides a way to challenge these statutory provisions. The courts are very strict about inadmissibility and will only dismiss a challenge at an early stage in cases of "clearly unsuccessful applications" because "where there is doubt, caution should be exercised and a premature end to litigation should be avoided and the applicant should be given a chance to be heard on the merits."[24] Thus, under this assumption of the primacy of section 28, these statutory provisions could be challenged, and, if this were the case, the challenge would most likely not be dismissed quickly by a court. In practical terms, this means that such a challenge would be heard on the merits months or years after it was launched and would therefore have the effect, meanwhile, of throwing thousands of retired women into legal uncertainty with respect to their pensions, even though the challenge itself might ultimately fail.

Of course, similar laws that benefit women at the expense of men and that invoke section 33 in order to provide this benefit do not exist in other provinces or at the federal level. There are several reasons for this situation. Generally speaking, Quebec uses this section far more often than the other provinces and the federal Parliament. More specifically, the use of section 33 in relation to pensions is explained by the particular historical context in Quebec. Prior to the 1960s, a very large number of people, many of them women, lived in religious and generally Catholic communities, where they devoted their lives to serving the Catholic Church and its works, particularly in the field of education, without receiving remuneration, which would have enabled them to prepare for a comfortable retirement. With the Quiet Revolution of the 1960s, many of these people left their communities and pursued careers within public organizations. Then, in 1978, the Act Respecting the Pension Coverage of Certain Teachers was passed to provide retirement protection for religious teachers secularized after June 30, 1965.[25] This law ceased to have effect in 1986, except for some of its provisions, which are still in effect through section 52 of the Act Respecting the Pension Plan of Certain Teachers, which is protected by section 33.

In other words, Quebec's historical trajectory, which distinguishes it from other provinces, explains its use of this section. As a result, allowing section 33 to be circumvented would limit Quebec's ability to implement measures that meet its specific needs. By analogy, what is true for these pension laws would also be true for the Act Respecting the Laicity of the State, an Act that, in the words of its first and fifth recitals, is based on the existence of a Quebec nation, which "has its own ... specific history that have led it to develop a particular attachment to State laicity" and the importance it attaches to "equality of women and men." Just as it would be unfair to allow section 33 to be circumvented by section 28 and thus open the door to challenging laws on pension plans that benefit women, so it would be unfair to allow this circumvention and thus open the door to challenging this law aimed at reinforcing sex equality.

Even though many feminists in English Canada, like Froc, claim that the Act Respecting the Laicity of the State is detrimental to equality between men and women, a large majority of women in Quebec think the opposite and support the prohibition of the wearing of religious symbols by civil servants in authority, including teachers. At least, that is what two opinion polls indicate. Indeed, a Nanos survey reveals that 57 percent of women in Canada, including Quebec, oppose this ban, while, according to a Crop survey in Quebec, barely 29 percent of women oppose it (*Globe and Mail* 2019, 3). The earlier-mentioned Crop survey on laicity and immigration of November 2018 goes in the same direction. Therefore, to use section 28 to invalidate this law would not mean the triumph of sex equality. Instead, it would mean the triumph of a certain conception of this equality, which is more widely held in English Canada, at the expense of another conception of this equality, which is held by a vast majority of women in Quebec.

Conclusion

Leckey and Froc are both opposed to the Act Respecting the Laicity of the State. And for this reason, they call for an imaginative solution that is far removed from positive law and that would constitute a constitutional "big bang": an interpretation that would have the effect of allowing section 33 to be circumvented by section 28. But the imaginative solution they promote is supported neither by the text of the Canadian Charter nor by its history or jurisprudence. All three sources confirm that section 28 is an interpretive provision, not a free-standing substantive right. And that is a good thing too because, otherwise, it would be easier to challenge a number of Quebec laws promoting sex equality, starting with the Act Respecting the Laicity of the State.

Notes

1 Act Respecting the Laicity of the State, SQ 2019, c. 12; Canadian Charter of Rights and Freedoms, Part 1 of the Constitution Act, 1982, being Schedule B to the Canada Act 1982 (UK), 1982, c. 11 (Canadian Charter).

2 *City of Toronto et al. v Ontario (AG)*, 2018 ONSC 5151, reversed by *Toronto (City) v Ontario*, 2018 ONCA 761; Better Local Government Act, 2018, SO 2018, c. 11.

3 Counting only the three cases in the Act Respecting the Constitution Act, 1982, SQ 1982, c. 21, rather than the hundreds of cases of use of section 33 of the Canadian Charter made in all Quebec statutes between 1982 and 1985.

4 "This is why notwithstanding provisions are introduced in the Bill. This approach is legitimate; it is provided for in our legislation; and it has frequently been used by the Québec government. Québec has used these provisions on more than 100 occasions since 1975. It has almost always done so in order to promote its distinct character or to achieve social progress. With Bill 21, we are following in this tradition – a tradition to which we are completely committed." Committee on Institutions, Quebec National Assembly, *Journal des débats. Commissions parlementaires*, 42nd Legislation, 1st Session, June 4, 2019 (Simon Jolin-Barette).

5 On this subject, see Act Respecting the Laicity of the State, ss. 2(4), 4, para. 2, and the words of the minister responsible for this Act: "Up till now, what jurisprudence protects and takes solely into account, is the freedom of conscience and religion ... of State employees who are on duty. From now on, the laicity of the State will also take into account the freedom of conscience and religion of citizens. When citizens seek a public service, they will also be able to benefit from this legal guarantee ... which moreover generates rights for all citizens of Québec." Committee on Institutions, *Journal des débats*.

6 On the elitist conception of the law, which is reflected, in particular, in the analysis of constitutionality based on fundamental rights, see Mathieu 2017; Taillon 2019.

7 In fact, by virtue of its own wording, section 33 refers only to the rights contained in sections 2 and 7–15 of the Canadian Charter and therefore excludes from its scope the rights in sections 3–6 and 16–23 of the Charter (the other sections of the

Charter – sections 1 and 24–34 – do not confer any rights). However, thanks to section 28, these rights in sections 3–6 and 16–23 are guaranteed equally to both sexes. If section 28 were to read "notwithstanding any other provision of this Charter except section 33, the rights and freedoms referred to in this Charter are guaranteed equally to male and female persons" – that is, with the words "except section 33," this would mean that section 33 could be applied against section 28 even when the latter is used to guarantee the rights in sections 3–6 and 16–23 to both sexes, even though the wording of section 33 is clearly intended to exclude sections 3–6 and 16– 23 from the scope of the latter section.

8 *Syndicat de la fonction publique v Quebec (Attorney General)*, [2004] RJQ 524, para. 1422 (*Syndicat de la fonction publique*).

9 *Reference as to the Meaning of the Word "Persons" in Section 24 of the British North America Act, 1867*, [1928] SCR 276, reversed by the Privy Council in *Edwards v A.G. Canada*, [1930] AC 124.

10 *Syndicat de la fonction publique.*

11 *Ichrak Nourel Hak v Québec (Attorney General)*, 2019 QCCA 2145, paras. 39–64 (*Ichrak Nourel Hak*).

12 *Ichrak Nourel Hak*, paras. 124, 127, 139.

13 *McIvor v Canada (Registrar, Indian and Northern Affairs)*, 2009 BCCA 153, para. 64.

14 *Ichrak Nourel Hak*, para. 130.

15 *Ichrak Nourel Hak*, para. 93.

16 First reactions of the Government of Quebec to the white paper tabled in the House of Commons by Pierre Elliot Trudeau, federal minister of justice on February 1, 1968, as cited in Secrétariat aux affaires intergouvernementales canadiennes 1991 and quoted in Tremblay 1995, 119.

17 "On September 11 and 12, the Government of Quebec distributed a discussion paper entitled *Proposed Common Provincial Position* to representatives of the other provinces. This discussion paper sought to identify commonalities in the positions of each province on a number of issues. With respect to a *Bill of Rights*, it proposed that fundamental and democratic rights be protected and that legal rights and anti-discrimination rights be subject to a notwithstanding clause. This proposal, dubbed the 'Château Consensus,' never obtained the unanimous support of the provinces, however, and Québec eventually abandoned it" (Roy and Brosseau 2018, 3, referring to Sheppard and Valpy 1982, 60–62).

18 On this subject, see *Attorney General of Quebec v Blaikie et al.*, [1979] 2 SCR 1016, 1023–1027; *Blaikie et al. v Quebec (Attorney General)*, [1978] CA 351; *Blaikie et al v Quebec (Attorney General)*, [1978] SC 37, 72–73; Côté and Rousseau 2019, 67; see also *Attorney General of Ontario v OPSEU*, [1987] 2 SCR 2, para. 89 ("other provisions of the Constitution Act, 1867 may similarly have been intangible and considered to fall outside s. 92(1), not because they were essential to the implementation of the federal principle, but because, for historical reasons, they were a fundamental

condition of the union formed in 1867. Thus, in *Blaikie, supra,* it was concluded that s. 133 of the *Constitution Act, 1867* was such a provision").

19 Constitution Act, 1982, Schedule B to the Canada Act 1982 (UK), 1982, c. 11.

20 The latter section lists sixty-two cases of the use of section 33, and five more have since been added. An Act Amending Certain Acts Establishing Public Sector Pension Plans, SQ 2019, c. 20, ss. 1, 2, 3, 4, 9.

21 Act Respecting the Teachers' Pension Plan, RSQ, c. R-11 (emphasis added).

22 Act Respecting the Civil Service Superannuation Plan, RSQ, c. R-12 (emphasis added).

23 Act Respecting the Pension Plan of Certain Teachers, RSQ, c. R-9.1.

24 *Pharmesspoir inc. v Groupe Jean Coutu (PJC) Inc.*, 2015 QCCA 1154, para. 3. This judgment is cited in other more recent judgments dealing with the new Code of Civil Procedure, RLRQ, c. C-25.01. See, for example, *Desgagné v Beaulieu*, 2019 QCCS 5462; *Parisien v Hôtel du Lac Tremblant Inc.*, 2018 QCCA 2217.

25 Act Respecting the Pension Coverage of Certain Teachers, RSQ, c. P-32.1 (repealed).

References

Brunelle, Dorval. 1989. "Les droits et libertés à l'heure de la dérogation." *Cahiers de recherches sociologiques* 13: 105–7, 116.

Canadian Advisory Council on the Status of Women. 1980. *Women, Human Rights and the Constitution*. Ottawa: Special Joint Committee on the Constitution.

Côté, François, and Guillaume Rousseau. 2019. *Restaurer le français langue officielle*. Montreal: Institut de recherche sur le Québec.

Crop. 2018. *Questions sur la laïcité et l'immigration Foto – novembre 2018*. Report prepared for Radio-Canada. November. https://www.crop.ca/docs/quebecois-_faveur-laicite-19-9413-2018-RadioCanada.pdf.

Eberts, Mary. 1980. *Women and Constitutional Renewal*. Ottawa: Canadian Advisory Council on the Status of Women.

Froc, Kerri Anne. 2015. "The Untapped Power of Section 28 of the Canadian Charter of Rights and Freedoms." PhD diss., Queen's University.

–. 2019. "Shouting into the Constitutional Void: Section 28 and Bill 21." *Constitutional Forum constitutionnel* 28 (4): 19–22. https://journals.library.ualberta.ca/constitutional_forum/index.php/constitutional_forum/article/view/29391/21390.

Gagnon, Marc-André. 2019. "Le hijab incarne 'l'oppression des femmes' selon Isabelle Charest." *Journal de Québec*, February 5.

Gill, Amy. 2010. "In Their Finest Hour: Deciphering the Role of the Canadian Women's Movement in the Formulation of the Charter of Rights and Freedom." MA thesis, University of Ottawa.

Globe and Mail. 2019. "Canadians Split on Support for Québec Religious Ban – More Likely to Oppose Legal Action, National Survey Released." Nanos survey, July.

Gotell, Lise. 1990. *The Canadian Women's Movement, Equality Rights and the Charter*. Ottawa: Canadian Research Institute for the Advancement of Women.

Honickman, Asher, 2019. "Deconstructing Section 28." *Advocates for the Rule of Law,* June 29. http://www.ruleoflaw.ca/deconstructing-section-28/.

Lamoureux, André. 2019. "La leçon de 1982." *La Presse,* December 11.

Lavoie, Gilbert. 1981. "Les droits des femmes demeureront soumis à l'arbitraire des provinces." *La Presse,* November 19.

Leckey, Robert. 2019. "Advocacy Notwithstanding the Notwithstanding Clause." *Constitutional Forum constitutionnel* 28 (4): 1–8. https://journals.library.ualberta.ca/constitutional_forum/index.php/constitutional_forum/article/view/29389/21388.

Mathieu, Bertrand. 2017. *Le droit contre la démocratie?* Paris: Librairie générale de droit et de jurisprudence.

Messier, François. 2019. "Tout symbole 'dicté" par une religion est un 'signe d'oppression,' dit le ministre Charest." *Radio-Canada,* February 6.

Rémillard, Gil. 2007. "Petite histoire de la clause 'nonobstant.'" *Policy Options,* February. https://policyoptions.irpp.org/wp-content/uploads/sites/2/assets/po/the-charter-25/remillard.pdf.

Rousseau, Guillaume, and François Côté. 2017. "A Distinctive Québec Theory and Practice of the Notwithstanding Clause: When Collective Interests Outweigh Individual Rights." *Revue Générale de Droit* 47 (2): 391, 424–31.

Roy, Marc-André, and Laurence Brosseau. 2018. *La disposition de dérogation de la Charte*. Ottawa: Library of Parliament.

Secrétariat aux affaires intergouvernementales canadiennes. 1991. *Les positions traditionnelles du Québec en matière constitutionnelle, 1936–1990,* Quebec City: Ministère du Conseil exécutif.

St-Hilaire, Maxime. 2019. "L'article 28 de la Charte Canadienne des droits et libertés: des dispositions interprétatives sujettes à interprétation." *Doubleaspect.blog,* February 4. https://doubleaspect.blog/2020/02/04/25293/.

Sheppard, Robert, and Michael Valpy. 1982. *The National Deal: The Fight for a Canadian Constitution*. Toronto: Fleet Books.

Taillon, Patrick. 2019. *Une loi nécessaire et pondérée pour corriger les excès de la jurisprudence canadienne*. Brief presented to the Committee on Institutions, National Assembly, May 15.

Tremblay, André. 1995. *La réforme de la Constitution au Canada*. Montreal: Thémis.

Laicity in the Light of Institutional Dialogue in Canada

9

PATRICK TAILLON

Over the last twenty-five years, Quebec has been using all the legal instruments at its disposal to assert a specific model of the relationship between the state and religions – from the 1997 constitutional amendment on the deconfessionalization of school boards[1] to the adoption in 2019 of the Act Respecting the Laicity of the State (Bill 21)[2] as well as the amendments made in 2005 and 2019 to the Quebec Charter of Human Rights and Freedoms (Quebec Charter).[3] By incorporating this secular model into the relevant constitutional and quasi-constitutional instruments, Quebec is competing with Canadian jurisprudence regarding the individual freedom to display religious beliefs that developed at the beginning of the 2000s, notably in *Multani v Commission scolaire Marguerite-Bourgeoys*[4] and in *Syndicat Northcrest v Amselem*.[5]

Of course, over the short term, we will not face the question of the compatibility of this Quebec model of secularism with a "maximalist" interpretation of the individual freedom to display religious beliefs for several years. Invoking the notwithstanding clauses in section 33 of the Canadian Charter of Rights and Freedoms (Canadian Charter)[6] and in section 52 of the Quebec Charter,[7] provided for in sections 11 and 34 of the Act Respecting the Laicity of the State, considerably limits the ability of judges to give precedence to their interpretation and balance of rights over those adopted by the Quebec legislator. Nonetheless, sooner or later, the temporary effect of section 33 of the Canadian Charter may subside. And that will be a moment of truth for Canadian federalism and constitutionalism. To what extent can Canadian federalism, predicated on a wide margin of appreciation for the provinces and territories, be reconciled with the frequently uniform interpretation of rights and freedoms as advocated by the courts? And where the guarantee of rights is concerned, is it the expression of a single, pan-Canadian jurisprudential solution or, on the contrary, does it value a plurality of approaches taken by the various legislators of the federation?

While awaiting the moment of truth, we can already gain a better understanding by applying "dialogue theory" to examine the evolution of jurisprudence and legislative interventions over the past two decades on the theme of religious freedom and neutrality. This theory of institutional dialogue is advocated by the Supreme Court of Canada.[8] It considers that the legitimacy of control of the constitutionality of laws stems from the possibility, for the political powers, to respond or reply to interpretations developed by the courts. This theory of dialogue is based on a deliberative conception of legitimacy and sees in the back and forth between judges and legislators a means of exchanging and improving rules, which in turn favours conciliating points of view and valuing the contribution of each party in the process of defining, interpreting, and reconciling fundamental rights. This dialogue is embodied in a variety of procedures: judicial restraint, the choice of remedies (for example, suspending declarations of invalidity and reading down, reading in, or reading out), parliamentary and ministerial analysis of the constitutionality of bills, and so on.

There are many processes for encouraging deliberative dialogue between judges and legislators. But the ability of policy makers to "respond" to interpretations advocated by the courts rests primarily on three processes. These three "cards" in the "deck" of elected officials are well known and form a kind of hierarchy. First, section 1 of the Canadian Charter provides legislators with the option of pursuing a public policy objective through a range of reasonable means. Second, the notwithstanding clause in section 33 of the Canadian Charter gives legislators a final say, an ability to impose their balance of rights and interests and to temporarily escape the interpretation of rights guaranteed by the courts, at least those that fall within the scope of section 33. Third, there is also the process of amending the Constitution. This latter process is more frequently adopted in Europe,[9] and while, *a priori*, this process may seem purely hypothetical in Canada, it should nonetheless not be completely ruled out in the case of issues subject to more flexible review procedures, such as the language and confessional rights covered by section 43 of the Constitution Act, 1982.[10]

The issue of laicity in Quebec is probably the most complete example in Canadian history of the progressive use of these three processes of institutional dialogue. If this theory really means something to the Supreme Court of Canada – if it is anything more than a mere rhetorical device – legal challenges to the use of the notwithstanding clause following adoption of the Act Respecting the Laicity of the State should provide an opportunity to reconfirm the foundations of this theory as well as its terms and relevance. After all, the Supreme Court would be ill-advised to use this theory to justify correcting ordinary legislation, while rejecting the same theory when political authorities in turn attempt to correct certain excesses of case law by means of the quasi-constitutional and constitutional instruments available to them.

The rise of the judiciary following the adoption of the Canadian Charter in 1982 came like a thunderclap into the institutional landscape of the Canadian federation. The courts' substantive or material control of the power of derogation, as well as their refusal to incorporate the constitutional affirmation of the principle of secularism, would mark an unprecedented loosening of the constraints and limits that were, until now, binding on the judiciary. In this sense, the case *Hak v Attorney General of Quebec*[11] goes far beyond the debate on reconciling two fundamental rights, which, moreover, are by no means absolute: the right of civil servants in positions of authority to display their religious convictions in the exercise of their duties, on the one hand, and the right of citizens to receive public services from a neutral and secular state, on the other. These rights, like all other guaranteed rights, must constantly be balanced, limited, and reconciled. The question raised by the first wave of challenges to the Act Respecting the Laicity of the State is not what limitations, reconciliations, and balances fall within a "reasonable range" of possible solutions. The question is whether elected officials still have the power to participate in this process of balancing rights. What power, what room for manoeuvre, do sections 1 and 33 of the Canadian Charter and the explicit amendment of quasi-constitutional and constitutional texts give them? We will try to answer this question here by first reviewing the most recent statements by judges and politicians, before comparing the Canadian case with the standard objectively presented by comparative law with regard to the margin of appreciation of elected officials in institutional dialogue.

The Words of Judges: The Origin of the Law; Jurisprudence to Be Corrected

This observation may seem brutal. It certainly involves a certain amount of subjectivity, but it is better to state things clearly: for several decades, the case law of the Supreme Court of Canada on religious freedom and neutrality has given rise to a problem of social acceptability in Quebec. The excessive or, at the very least, "maximalist" interpretation of freedom of religion is in no way immutable or intangible. It is the result of an evolutionary process of balancing rights – a process in which both the judiciary and political powers participate. When excesses occur, this process follows, in many ways, the laws of physics. Isaac Newton's action/reaction principle states that "for every action, there is an equal and opposite reaction." Thus, the stronger or more vigorous the action, the greater will be the reaction in the opposite direction. It is in this light that dialogue theory and the deliberative ideal underlying it rely not so much on confidence in the legitimacy of the judges' or legislators' decision as on a continuous process of refinement through a succession of judicial and political corrections.

Supreme Court of Canada jurisprudence on the freedom to express religious convictions bears witness to this process of perfecting and adjusting the words of judges. In the first stage of the dialogue, the Supreme Court established the existence of a "maximalist" freedom. Following the principle of action/reaction, this jurisprudence gave rise in Quebec to a response in which there was a mixture of incomprehension and disapproval. The "crisis" over religious accommodation and the wide-ranging consultations preceding the Bouchard-Taylor

Commission's report both reflect this problem of social acceptability concerning the Supreme Court's jurisprudence and the sometimes exemplary, sometimes clumsy implementation of this jurisprudence by the authorities (Bouchard and Taylor 2008). Of course, the issue here is not whether the maximalist approach advocated by the courts in the early 2000s is either "good" or "bad." There are several indications that it has been generally well received in the rest of Canada. Nevertheless, it has been strongly criticized in Quebec, where it has fuelled a strong polarization of opinion that has, at times, itself contributed to a deterioration in public debate.

The report of the Bouchard-Taylor Commission set down in black and white, several times, this problem of social acceptability. The report highlights the vigour with which Canadian multiculturalism was criticized during the commission's hearings (Bouchard and Taylor 2008, 19, 21, 39, 117–19, 205, 214). The commissioners wrote, "Canadian multiculturalism, inasmuch as it emphasizes diversity at the expense of continuity, is not properly adapted to Québec's situation" (121). For many people in Quebec, the Canadian model of multiculturalism is too individualistic and libertarian and not concerned enough with the common good: moreover, the multiculturalism model creates more than justifiable distrust of the majority society, which sees itself as a fragile political community, preoccupied with its capacity for integration and its social cohesion.

Quebec was long dominated by religious authorities, and the onset of modernity at the time of the Quiet Revolution was largely associated with an accelerated secularization of its institutions. Yet many Quebeckers responded with criticism to decisions of the Supreme Court of Canada in the early 2000s – decisions that cultivated the (in many ways mistaken) feeling that the individual right to express religious beliefs is unlimited. Other observers, including Louis-Philippe Lampron (2011), deplore a form of implicit hierarchization of rights that tends to favour the individual freedom to express religious beliefs (see also Lampron and Brouillet 2011; Gaudreault-Desbiens 2011). Once again, the point here is not to establish whether this criticism of the court's jurisprudence by a great many Quebeckers is accurate but, rather, to note that this criticism exists and has occupied, through the theme of the "crisis" over religious accommodation, a prominent place in the public debate over the last two decades.

Since then, the Quebec legislator, on the one hand, and the judiciary, on the other hand, have been trying to correct the decisions of the courts, notably in the *Multani* and *Amselem* decisions. It must be said that the scope of the right to express religious beliefs was affirmed in particularly broad terms. Under the criteria developed by the Supreme Court of Canada at the time, constitutionally protected religious practices include all "sincerely held religious beliefs." This concept includes anything that an individual "sincerely believes or is sincerely undertaking in order to connect with the divine or as a function of his or her spiritual faith."[12] Therefore, the right to express religious beliefs is protected, even if the practice in question is optional in the eyes of the religious authorities or experts on that religion,[13] even if the practice is inconsistent in the individual, and even against a contractual waiver of rights.[14] It is difficult to define the scope of constitutionally protected spiritual beliefs and activities more broadly than that. Moreover, in accordance with the requirements of "reasonable accommodation" (section 15 of the Canadian Charter) and "minimal impairment" (section 1 of the Canadian Charter), the state must adapt its practices to provide for exceptions or accommodations, on a case-by-case basis, to reconcile the expression of religious beliefs with other public policy imperatives. By granting the same protection to all religious practices, whether they are objectively obligatory within the religion concerned, and by leaving legislators very little room for manoeuvre in imposing general and impersonal rules (in favour of the logic of case-by-case accommodation), the court has committed itself to the most maximalist interpretation of religious freedom possible.

This first phase of the Supreme Court of Canada's jurisprudence was followed by a second phase, in which the court seemed to have undertaken a shift in its interpretation of religious freedom. Since the late 2000s, the court has frequently recognized limitations on religious freedom. On a case-by-case basis, these limitations on the freedom to express religious beliefs are not widely debated, but they are nonetheless very real. Several authors have taken note of this phenomenon, which has not, until now, been explicitly assumed or claimed by the Supreme

Court (Brun, Tremblay, and Brouillet 2014). The extent of this shift is also difficult to assess. The more time passes, the more the shift seems to be confirmed, but a great deal of continuity remains. In practice, the shift lies, for the most part, in a tightening of evaluation criteria. Officially, however, the Supreme Court maintains that it is keeping these evaluation criteria. It refrains from making explicit any shift along these lines. The decisions of the Supreme Court suddenly became less favourable to religious claims, although the court has not explained its reasoning behind this tightening of criteria.

The first change not explicitly articulated by the Supreme Court of Canada now takes account of the objective assessment of the belief – in other words, its optional or compulsory character.[15] In this respect, the Supreme Court is taking a position similar to that taken by the European Court of Human Rights (ECtHR).[16] This is an important about-face that largely contradicts the definition of subjective belief set out in *Amselem*. However, the court mobilizes an objective belief solely at the stage of its analysis of proportionality. In so doing, it retains a subjective definition of belief at the beginning of its reasoning, while ultimately incorporating the objective dimension of the analysis at the justification stage. Similarly, a careful reading of *Ktuxana Nation v British Columbia* shows that the court limits freedom of religion based on a criterion that has not been part of the analytical framework since *Amselem*.[17] On this occasion, it refused to protect the "object" of devotion. Freedom of religion thus includes the right to believe, the right to express a belief, but it does not include the very object of devotion – in this case, the spirit of the mountain for the Ktunaxa people. In other words, the right to publicly display a belief in state or communal institutions appears to be better protected than the movable or immovable objects – tangible or intangible – to which believers are devoted (churches, temples, sacred places, and so on). Certainly, the court does not openly articulate the novelty of this approach. Perhaps this is only an isolated decision, but it is certainly part of the shift that has characterized the more restrictive decisions of the last decade.

The extent of this shift is difficult to measure, often because the Supreme Court of Canada's own reasoning is unclear. In addition to *Ktunaxa Nation, R. v N.S.* is part of this sudden tendency for the court to cultivate ambiguity on religious freedom.[18] When faced with the issue of a witness wearing a niqab in a criminal case, the court was sharply divided, and its majority ultimately left it to another court – in this case, the trial court – to decide whether, in the circumstances before it, the freedom to express religious beliefs through the wearing of a niqab during an interrogation could override the rights of the accused to a full answer and defence as well as the public interest imperative of assessing the credibility and truthfulness of the testimony. In fact, *N.S.* is in many respects unclassifiable: in keeping with the maximalist approach, the court did not rule out the possibility of face-to-face testimony, but, by placing the burden of deciding the particular case before the trial judge, it shows that the right to face-to-face testimony is not absolute and that there may be a justification for its being restricted.

Beyond the ambiguity that remains, *Multani* seems to have been overturned for two reasons. On the one hand, the framework of analysis, the method, and the criteria of justification applied by the Supreme Court of Canada to an administrative decision of the school authorities have, since *Doré v Barreau du Québec*[19] and *Loyola High School v Quebec (Attorney General)*,[20] been based on a different, more flexible method, as evidenced, among other things, by the reasoning of the Supreme Court in the two *Trinity Western University* decisions of 2018.[21]

On the other hand, the most recent appellate court decisions, including *Singh v Montreal Gateway Terminals Partnership*,[22] *Trinity Western University*, *Ktunaxa Nation*, *Mouvement laïque québécois v Saguenay (City of)*,[23] *S.L. v Commission scolaire des Chênes*,[24] and *Alberta v Hutterian Brethren of Wilson Colony*[25] are sufficiently numerous and convergent to support this thesis of a change in the attitude of appellate courts in reconciling religious freedom with other legitimate rights and interests. For example, *Saguenay* placed limits on the ability of city council officials to display their beliefs; *Singh* and *Hutterian* put security and identification imperatives ahead of personal liberty; and, most importantly, both *Trinity Western University* and *Commission scolaire des Chênes* have given precedence to a certain idea of "living together" and the importance of other shared values, including respect for sexual minorities.

These more recent judgments reiterate an obvious point that was lost in the decisions of the 2000s – namely, that the freedom to express religious beliefs is not absolute: it is no less and no more important than other rights and must be balanced and reconciled with the public interest. These rulings are an attempt to correct the balance of rights and legitimate interests. Again, the question is not to determine whether the maximalist approach of the early 2000s was wrong but, rather, to point out that the appellate courts of the 2010s, through *Singh*, *Trinity Western University*, *Ktunaxa Nation*, *Saguenay*, *Commission scolaire des Chênes*, and *Hutterian*, suddenly tilted against the individual freedom to display religious beliefs.

The Words of Elected Officials: The Constitutional Affirmation of the Principle of Laicity

We have noted case law developments that indicate a form of "judicial dialogue" whereby the Supreme Court of Canada of the 2010s corrected the Supreme Court of the previous decade. But we have also seen an evolution from actions taken by the Quebec Legislature to affirm the principle of laicity. Indeed, prior to the adoption of the Act Respecting the Laicity of the State, Canadian jurisprudence had developed in a constitutional and legislative environment that did not provide for the principle of secularism or prohibitions with a legal basis that was as clear, explicit, and intelligible as we find in Bill 21. As the Quebec Court of Appeal wrote in the *Saguenay* case:

> [64] There is no such thing in Québec as a *Charter of Secularism*. In the absence of a formal statement of principle as to the values which the State intends to protect in the context of its obligation to maintain neutrality, we must adhere to the liberal rule that a religiously neutral State essentially means that no religious views are imposed on its citizens, that its governmental action in all its forms remains free from such influence, and that this is indeed the case.[26]

With the advent of Bill 21, which enshrines the principle of laicity in Quebec, there is reason to believe that jurisprudential adaptations are required. The interpretive and discretionary room for manoeuvre of the courts varies according to the legislative and constitutional environment: decisions rendered in a context where all the provinces seem to adhere to the same model of organization of the relationship between the state and religions must necessarily be adapted when one of the members of the federation chooses to opt for a different model.

In order to understand the extent to which the principle of laicity has been affirmed in Quebec's legal system, it is necessary not only to look at the content of the 2019 law but also to consider the historical development of Quebec and the diversity of legal instruments that it has used to give its model a privileged place in the hierarchy of norms. In order to emphasize the importance of Quebec's "voice" in institutional dialogue, it has used all the instruments at its disposal: section 1 of the Canadian Charter, the addition of an interpretive provision to the Quebec Charter (section 50.1) on the equality of women and men, the notwithstanding clause, the adoption of quasi-constitutional norms, and even a constitutional amendment through section 43 of the Constitution Act, 1982. From 1997 to 2019, these legal instruments have been progressively deployed to exercise Quebec's legitimate right to correct the Supreme Court's maximalist approach.

The secularization movement in Quebec that began with the Quiet Revolution has too often been underestimated. In 1997, this movement led to a constitutional amendment with the agreement of the federal authorities. Quebec then consolidated the secularization of its education system by transforming Quebec's denominational Catholic and Protestant school boards into linguistic French and English school boards. Although the term "laicity" is not explicitly used in the 1997 amendment, it is nonetheless present in the intention of the constituent power. In addition to inscribing this strong desire for the secularization of educational institutions in the Canadian Constitution, several quasi-constitutional amendments have been made in Quebec's legal system that have a supra-legislative character. First, in 2005, the right of parents to have their children receive religious instruction in public schools in accordance with their convictions, which was enshrined in the Quebec Charter, was repealed. From that point onwards, in accordance with the ideal of secularism, a compulsory course in ethics and religious culture would be taught to all students, providing a common instrument of culture and citizenship.

The courts' response to these legislative and supra-legislative changes has been mixed. The choice of an ethics and religious culture course was respected,[27] but it was subject to exceptions or religious accommodations.[28] Unfortunately, this took place without the Supreme Court giving due consideration to the supra-legislative aspect of this reform, at least its extension in the amendment of the Quebec Charter and in the Constitution Amendment, 1997.[29] Subsequently, in the wake of the Bouchard-Taylor Commission's report, Quebec sought to legislate using the leeway and space for dialogue that section 1 of the Canadian Charter could provide (Bouchard and Taylor 2008).[30] In 2008, the adoption of an interpretive provision on the importance of the equality of women and men in the interpretation of freedoms (section 50.1 of the Quebec Charter) was a clear signal to the courts of the need to balance rights and protect against community pressures in favour of harmful religious practices.

In 2011, the Liberal government of Jean Charest introduced Bill 94.[31] However, the bill was never passed by the Quebec National Assembly, partly due to criticism from the opposition. Similarly, in November 2013, the Parti Québécois government (a minority government) tabled the draft Charter Affirming the Values of State Secularism and Religious Neutrality and of Equality between Women and Men and Providing a Framework for Accommodation Requests.[32] This proposed charter sought to strengthen secularism and would have prohibited the wearing of conspicuous religious symbols by all government employees. Once the Quebec Liberal Party won the April 2014 general election, this proposed charter died on the order paper.

In 2017, the Quebec National Assembly adopted Bill 62, tabled by the Liberal government of Philippe Couillard and entitled An Act to Promote Respect for the Religious Neutrality of the State and Aimed in Particular at Regulating Requests for Accommodation for Religious Reasons in Certain Organizations.[33] Shortly after its adoption, section 10 of Bill 62 (the obligation to give and receive government services with a face uncovered) was challenged in court, and Justice Babak Barin of the Quebec Superior Court suspended this provision.[34] Much of the content of Bill 62 was eventually incorporated into the Act Respecting the Laicity of the State. This provisional suspension of the law, taking place even before the act could take effect, is to the detriment of the presumption of the constitutionality of laws. In many respects, it represents a departure from the theory of institutional dialogue, which is nevertheless valued by the Supreme Court of Canada. The Act Respecting the Laicity of the State is a moderate piece of legislation, whose content is carefully aligned with the case law it sought to slightly influence slightly. Nonetheless, it was suspended – without evidence, without debate on the merits, and without deference to that attempt at dialogue. While Quebec was seeking to act reasonably within the leeway that legislators are supposed to have under section 1 of the Canadian Charter, the Superior Court cavalierly proceeded with the suspension and thereby reduced the space for dialogue.

This is the context in which Quebec developed the Act Respecting the Laicity of the State. Indeed, Quebec was aware of the risks of judicial intransigence at the provisional stage and also anxious that its voice in the inter-institutional dialogue should have some effect and show its reasonableness in practice and in use. Quebec was forced to resort to stronger legal instruments and procedural avenues to grant the Act Respecting the Laicity of the State a special place in the hierarchy of norms, after receiving signals from the courts that section 1 of the Canadian Charter no longer offered the necessary space for dialogue, at least at the stage of the interim analysis of the law. The precedent set in 2017 by the suspension of Bill 62 led the Quebec National Assembly to use all legal means at its disposal to give the law a pre-eminent or "quasi-constitutional" character and to exempt it from the jurisprudential interpretation of religious freedom advocated by Canadian courts.

In anticipation of a potential court challenge to the law, Quebec relied on the features of the Commonwealth model of constitutionality review and specifically on three processes (Gardbaum 2013). First, section 11 of the Act Respecting the Laicity of the State affirms that "the provisions of this Act prevail over any contrary provisions of any subsequent Act," unless the legislator explicitly manifests his or her desire to derogate from it. Like section 52 of the Quebec Charter, this aspect of section 11 has the effect of giving the law "quasi-constitutional" status. The term "quasi" reflects the special situation of a supra-legislative, but sub-constitutional, statute whose content is substantially fundamental and which can be amended through the ordinary legislative process, although such amendments rarely occur provided that the will to derogate is expressly stated.

Second, the act amends the Quebec Charter in its preamble and section 9.1 to explicitly enshrine the principle of laicity and to ensure that it is taken into account in the adjudicative process of reconciling the various rights and interests protected by this quasi-constitutional charter. The fourth and eighth recitals of the preamble of the act read as follows: "AS it is important that the paramountcy of State laicity be enshrined in Québec's legal order; ... AS State laicity should be affirmed in a manner that ensures a balance between the collective rights of the Québec nation and human rights and freedoms." The term "paramountcy" is here synonymous with "quasi-constitutional" (Issalys and Lemieux 2009, 93, para. 2.10; Samson 2015, para. 14). Then, sections 18 and 19 of the Act Respecting the Laicity of the State modify the preamble and section 9.1 of the Quebec Charter, which now read as follows:

> Whereas respect for the dignity of human beings, equality of women and men, and recognition of their rights and freedoms constitute the foundation of justice, liberty and peace; Whereas the Québec nation considers State laicity to be of fundamental importance;
>
> ...
>
> 9.1. In exercising his fundamental freedoms and rights, a person shall maintain a proper regard for democratic values, State laicity, public order and the general well-being of the citizens of Québec.

The law may, in this respect, determine the scope of these rights and freedoms and regulate their exercise.

The inclusion of the laicity of the state in section 9.1 of the Quebec Charter is particularly important since this provision is the one that frames the process of justifying the reasonable limits that can be placed on rights and freedoms. It is the equivalent of section 1 of the Canadian Charter or the analysis of legitimate aims and proportionality under the European Convention on Human Rights.[35] By including laicity in the catalogue of fundamental rights, values, and principles that must be reconciled by the courts, Quebec has demonstrated its clear intention to establish a model that is different from the rest of Canada and to uphold laicity and the rights it entails, particularly those in sections 2, 3, and 4 of the act,[36] as supra-legislative norms that are quasi-constitutional and on a par with the other rights and freedoms guaranteed by section 52 of the Quebec Charter.

Third, and this is probably the most controversial aspect of the law, the Quebec National Assembly exercises its right to "derogate" from most of the rights guaranteed by the Canadian Charter[37] and by the Quebec Charter, through sections 33 and 34 of the Act Respecting the Laicity of the State.[38] In so doing, in the short term and in the event of an eventual constitutional challenge, the act must be interpreted "notwithstanding" or without regard to the definition of freedom of religion advocated by Canadian courts.[39] In other words, this derogation gives precedence, at least for a five-year renewable period, to "parliamentary sovereignty" and to the balance of rights advocated by Parliament over the interpretation of key rights and freedoms by judges. The judiciary thus loses for a time its "last word" in what is commonly called, in Canada, the dialogue between judges and legislators (Brouillet and Michaud 2011; Taillon and Binette 2017).

In terms of inter-institutional dialogue, this recourse to the notwithstanding clause is certainly a response to the limited leeway given to legislators by the courts in the analysis of section 1 of the Canadian Charter and to the temporary suspension in 2017 of an Act to Promote Respect for the Religious Neutrality of the State and Aimed in Particular at Regulating Requests for Accommodation for Religious Reasons in Certain Organizations, which was intended to regulate requests for religious accommodation in certain organizations. But, above all, the use of the notwithstanding clause is part of a process of constitutional affirmation of the principle of secularism or what others call the "autonomization" of the Quebec Charter (Lampron 2010). Indeed, the quasi-constitutional norms contained in the Act Respecting the Laicity of the State and in the Quebec Charter are supra-legislative within Quebec's legal order: they are part of the Quebec Constitution. On the other hand, as a result of the courts' inclination to standardize the interpretation of instruments protecting rights and freedoms, these quasi-constitutional rules are considered by the case law to be not only supra-legislative but also sub-constitutional.[40] However, by resorting to the notwithstanding clause, Quebec is making a strong constitutional gesture that transforms the hierarchy of norms for the duration of the notwithstanding clause. The quasi-constitutional affirmation of the principle of laicity is thus able to rise to the top of the hierarchy of norms – on a par with the 1997 constitutional amendment with respect to deconfessionalization – by giving the word of elected officials priority over that of the courts, at least in the interpretation of sections 2 and 7–15 of the Canadian Charter.

Quebec is the only province with a tradition of civil law and a French-speaking majority. The Act Respecting the Laicity of the State, like the Charter of the French Language,[41] is therefore an Act that seeks in many respects to mark the existence in Quebec of an original social project that is different from the rest of Canada. As in the case of language, Quebec has chosen to use the exceptions provided for in the instruments protecting rights and freedoms in order to avoid the – often very uniform – control of rights by Canadian courts. This desire to assert the specific character of Quebec is, in a way, the backdrop to the act, and it is especially evident in several recitals of the preamble:

> AS the Québec nation has its own characteristics, one of which is its civil law tradition, distinct social values and a specific history that have led it to develop a particular attachment to State laicity;
>
> AS the Québec State stands on constitutional foundations that have been enriched over the years by the passage of a number of fundamental laws;
>
> AS, in accordance with the principle of parliamentary sovereignty, it is incumbent on the Parliament of Québec to determine the principles according to which and manner in which relations between the State and religions are to be governed in Québec;
>
> AS it is important that the paramountcy of State laicity be enshrined in Québec's legal order;
>
> AS the Québec nation attaches importance to the equality of women and men;
>
> ...

> AS State laicity should be *affirmed* in a manner that ensures a balance between *the collective rights of the Québec nation* and human rights and freedoms. (Emphasis added)

The reference in the first recital to "distinct social values" is an explicit reference to the case law of the Supreme Court of Canada. Dealing with the composition of the Supreme Court,[42] the justices had made these "distinct social values" an essential legal consideration that should condition the interpretation of the Constitution. In addition to the civil law tradition, which is the foundation of Canadian bijuralism and a defining feature of Quebec law, there was now a recognition of "social values," the specificity of which, like language, history, and culture, was suddenly recognized and valued by Canada's highest court. In addition to the preamble, the choice to use the notwithstanding clause in the case of the rights guaranteed by the Canadian Charter is also a way of emphasizing the importance that the Quebec legislator places on affirming this originality or specificity of Quebec within the Canadian constitutional framework. Thus, beyond questions about the scope of religious freedom, the challenge to Bill 21 raises the question of whether Canadian federalism imposes a single model of state-religion relations – a model defined exclusively by the courts – or whether it is flexible enough to accept a variety of arrangements.

Diversity of Approaches and Discretion of Elected Officials: The Search for a New Standard

Reconciling the principle of federalism with the principle of the primacy of fundamental rights requires the existence of a constitutional review of laws that leaves the legislators of the member states of the federation a significant margin of appreciation. Articles 1, 33, and 38 and following of the 1982 Constitution are expressions of this necessary margin of appreciation of elected representatives, which, in accordance with the principle of federalism, must be manifested in the entire institutional dialogue. In other words, in a system comprising several entities, the protection of rights must be allowed to adjust to the context and societal choices that differ from one state to the next.

In Europe, the protection systems of ECtHR and federations such as Switzerland[43] and Germany[44] provide examples of a guarantee that can be adapted to member states that choose secularism, whereas this guarantee is not imposed on other member states that prefer cooperation with recognized churches or an established church. With the adoption of the Act Respecting the Laicity of the State, the Supreme Court of Canada now finds itself in a situation quite similar to jurisdictions with multi-level systems: one example is Switzerland, which must take account of the secular character of the cantons of Geneva[45] and Neuchâtel;[46] a second example is the ECtHR, which must take account of the specific approaches of France and Turkey to secularism. In Germany, the Basic Law leaves all unallocated jurisdictions to the federated entities (the Länder), including that of regulating the common law with respect to religious communities.[47] Therefore, subject to the other obligations imposed by the Constitution,[48] it is up to the Länder to develop their own legal regime for the relationship between the state and religion.

This coexistence of a variety of approaches to the relationship between federated entities and religions is fully consistent with the theory of federalism. Like the European system, these federations manage to guarantee rights and freedoms without imposing uniform laws on the member states. Finally, even in a unitary state like France, variations and asymmetries exist within the national territory in the relationship between the state and religions. The regime of Alsace-Lorraine, a territory annexed to Germany from the Franco-Prussian war of 1870 to the end of the First World War, still has consequences for the positive law of the present departments of Bas-Rhin, Haut-Rhin, and Moselle.

From these different models that coexist within multilevel governance, a significant amount of litigation has emerged in Europe, marked by the recognition of a margin of appreciation for the states. To date, twenty-seven cases from seven different member states have resulted in supranational decisions of the ECtHR. Of these decisions, twenty-three cases (except for one that was, in effect, a split decision),[49] have been found to be in compliance with the European Convention on Human Rights (see Figure 9.1 in the Appendix at the end of this chapter).

Primary and secondary schools, as well as post-secondary educational institutions, were among the most litigated locations before the ECtHR.

In particular, fourteen of the twenty-seven cases concerned public educational institutions. In all of these cases, the limitation on the right to express religious beliefs was found by the court to be in conformity with previous decisions of the national courts of the four European states involved in the cases (France in five decisions, Italy in one decision, Switzerland in one decision, and Turkey in six decisions).

Several jurisdictions, including the German Federal Constitutional Court,[50] the Geneva Council of State,[51] and the ECtHR,[52] emphasize that the school is an institution like no other, due to compulsory attendance and continuous, hierarchical relationships, which are intended, by definition, to influence students. Teachers maintain continual influence; they offer themselves as models that students may or may not choose to follow, and the persuasive effect that they exert on students takes many forms. In addition to the special role acknowledged for educational institutions, the European system for the protection of rights and freedoms is distinguished by a broader range of considerations in the analysis of the balance of rights and the proportionality of a restriction on the right to express religious beliefs. By taking into account the necessary protection of the rights of others, state institutions are able to balance the freedom to express religious beliefs in those institutions with the situation of other vulnerable persons – in particular, women believers who also belong to minorities but who do not wish to wear religious symbols, to be judged for this choice, or to be exposed to social pressure within state institutions whose representatives enjoy a considerable power relationship. Thus, under the regime of the ECtHR, the protection of the rights of others and the promotion of equality between men and women take different forms. After all, there are many ways to promote equality and human rights. The ECtHR does not fall into the trap of making its preferences prevail at the expense of the inevitable margin of appreciation of states. On the contrary, in most of the decisions on the regulation of religious symbols and clothing, the judges recall precisely the broad or particular character of the national margin of appreciation.[53]

In Europe, an important dimension of this margin of appreciation is aimed at preserving the capacity of states to make "societal choices" by ensuring that a balance between rights and legitimate interests remains within each of these models of coexistence of religious beliefs. In the view of the ECtHR, this lack of uniformity between states with respect to the regulation of the wearing of religious symbols is not the result of chance but, rather, the consequence of the different approaches and models that are followed.

While the members of the ECtHR have had several reservations about the general ban on concealing the face in the public space as recently as the 2017 cases of *Belcacemi and Oussar v Belgium*[54] and *Dakir v Belgium*,[55] the court has insisted that there was still no European consensus on the matter and that "the question whether or not it should be permitted to wear the full-face veil in public places in Belgium constituted a choice of society."[56] Similarly, it resorts to "living together" to justify certain restrictions on the right to externalize religious convictions through the wearing of the full-face veil.[57] Most importantly, although secularism is not included in the text of the European Convention on Human Rights, case law consistently refers to it as a "principle underlying the Convention."[58] The "safeguarding of the constitutional principle of secularism" is mentioned as a legitimate aim in itself within the meaning of the European Convention on Human Rights, while being formally linked to that of the protection of the rights of others.[59] The fact remains that the court, while favouring this principle, does not go so far as to impose it on the member states in the absence of a European consensus in this area.

Of course, the point here is not to claim that the balance of rights that emerges from the case law of the ECtHR is better or worse than that advocated by the Supreme Court of Canada. What is essential is to understand that, in these matters, there is no uniform, standardized, natural, or universal norm and that each state and each society has the duty to seek a point of balance that is reasonably adapted to its context and its particular historical experience. If Quebec is a society with "distinct social values" from the rest of Canada, as the Supreme Court of Canada recognized in 2014, then it is normal for its model and balance of rights to be different from that of the rest of the federation, and this is what the use of sections 1, 33, and 43 of the Constitution Act, 1982 should allow. This is what the ECtHR has incorporated into its jurisprudence by recognizing a "margin of national appreciation" for member states of the Council of Europe.

In addition to the European model, the Commonwealth model is even more concerned with ensuring that elected representatives have the final say, due to the influence of the British model of parliamentary sovereignty. This constitutionalism is aptly described in the work of Stephen Gardbaum (2013) and brings together states that share a concern for preserving the ability of elected officials to respond to the judicial review of their actions. First and foremost, as the United Kingdom and New Zealand do not have formal constitutions, the right of Parliament to participate in defining the balance of rights is respected in these states more than anywhere else. While Australia practices constitutional review as a result of federalism and division of powers, it does not yet have a constitutional catalogue to explicitly identify rights and freedoms. Although unique, Canada is no exception to this tradition, as the passage of the Constitution Act, 1982 was only possible by means of a fundamental historical compromise, now enshrined in section 33 of the Canadian Charter. This historic compromise was an essential condition for the majority of provinces – with the exception of Quebec – to adopt the Canadian Charter. It reconciled the British tradition of parliamentary sovereignty with the primacy of fundamental rights.

Conclusion

A fruitful dialogue between the judiciary and the political power cannot be a one-way street: the definition of the balance of rights is not, and must not be, the monopoly of the judiciary alone. It is up to each member state of the federation to find a balance. Having amended the Canadian Constitution in 1997 and the Quebec Charter in 2005, 2008, and 2019, then explicitly enshrined laicity in supra-legislative texts in 2019 and backed up this affirmation of the principle of laicity by invoking the notwithstanding clause in 2019, Quebec cannot do much more to demonstrate its willingness to participate in the balancing and definition of rights. Of course, recourse to the notwithstanding clause in the case of the charters is not an end in itself: it should neither be valued nor condemned. It is simply a necessary and legitimate choice that makes it possible to give legislative solutions enough time to produce their effects and to demonstrate – in practice – that they are reasonable and grounded in social acceptability.

Through the review of constitutionality, the judge weighs the excesses of the legislator, and, conversely, through the use of the notwithstanding clause, the legislator can, in turn, occasionally correct the shortcomings of case law. As Prime Minister Jean Chrétien said, derogation is necessary because the courts – like legislators – can make mistakes. This was the essence of his remarks in 1992 to his party's youth delegates who wanted to repeal the mechanism of section 33 of the Canadian Charter: "The notwithstanding clause is not as bad as you think ... Without it, you leave all the decisions in the hands of the court. If you have a good court, no problem. But the Supreme Court can make errors. They are judges. They are appointed. It's not a perfect system" (Spector 2003).

The Act Respecting the Laicity of the State was enacted to clarify and correct some of the case law on the wearing of full-face veils in the provision and receipt of public services. The Quebec legislator was justified in invoking the notwithstanding clause after decades of leaving it up to the courts to find reasonable solutions and after seeing Bill 62 suspended in 2017 without debate on the merits and in defiance of the presumption of constitutionality. The Act Respecting the Laicity of the State provides legal certainty, and a stable application of the law will show, in practice, its reasonable effects and will thus encourage over time an evolution of the jurisprudence of the courts on these issues. In these circumstances, only the use of the notwithstanding clause makes it possible to strike a new balance and promote a model of laicity specific to Quebec on conceptual bases that are reasonable but different from those to be found in the Canadian model.

Therefore, the review by the courts of a law that is intended to complement and correct jurisprudence is, in many respects, a fundamental debate about the respective roles of elected officials and the courts. It raises the question of who gets to participate in the discussion, who gets to decide, and who gets to have the final say. The truth is that the protection of fundamental rights through reconciling and balancing of interests is the product of a process and an ongoing dialogue, in which the courts, in the first instance, as well as the political authorities, must participate, especially when the solutions advocated by case law seem to be failing, as we have seen for several decades now in Quebec. Clearly, elected officials have a legitimate role to play: democratic deliberation about rights is possible, and it must be conducted in a way that allows citizens to take ownership of rights and to recognize themselves in those rights. In our view, by accepting political debate about the content of rights, we will better anchor these rights in the heart of each citizen, which will in turn prove to be the best way to ensure their long-term protection. On the other hand, when the judiciary arrogates to itself a monopoly on these issues by refusing any political and democratic debate on fundamental rights, it risks undermining over time the social acceptability of rights and increasing the polarization of the debate. The judiciary also risks calling into question its own legitimacy, which until now has been based on the inter-institutional dialogue that the notwithstanding clause allows.

Appendix

Figure 9.1 Geographical distribution of the twenty-seven cases that led to decisions of the European Court of Human Rights

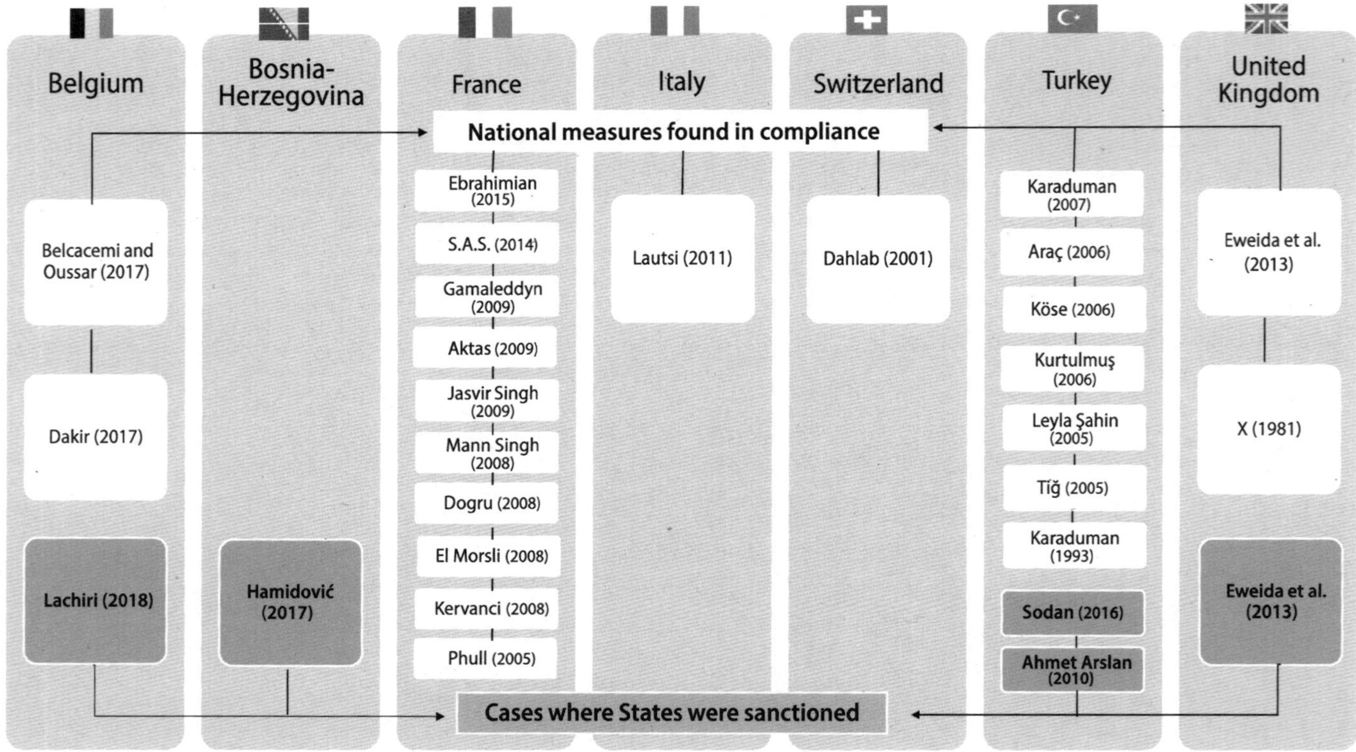

Notes

Acknowledgment: The author would like to thank Amélie Binette for her help in preparing this chapter.

1 Constitutional Amendment (Quebec), SI/97–141, 1997.

2 Act Respecting the Laicity of the State, SQ 2019, c. 12, ss. 11, 34.

3 Act to Amend Various Legislative Provisions of a Denominational Nature in the Education Field, SQ 2005, c. 20; Charter of Human Rights and Freedoms, RSQ 1977, c. C-12 (Quebec Charter).

4 *Multani v Commission scolaire Marguerite-Bourgeoys*, [2006] 1 SCR 256 (*Multani*).

5 *Syndicat Northcrest v Amselem*, [2004] 2 SCR 551 (*Amselem*).

6 Canadian Charter of Rights and Freedoms, Part 1 of the Constitution Act, 1982, being Schedule B to the Canada Act 1982 (UK), 1982, c. 11 (Canadian Charter).

7 Quebec Charter.

8 *Harper v Canada*, [2004] 1 SCR 827; *Doucet-Boudreau v Nova Scotia*, [2003] 3 SCR 3; *Sauvé v Canada (Chief Electoral Officer)*, [2002] 3 SCR 519; *R. v Hall*, [2002] 3 SCR 309; *Bell Express Vu Limited Partnership v Rex*, [2002] 2 SCR 559; *Little Sisters Book & Art Emporium Ltd. v Canada*, [2000] 2 SCR 1120; *R. v Mills*, [1999] 3 SCR 668; *Corbière v Canada (Minister of Indian Affairs and Northern Development)*, [1999] 2 SCR 203; *M. v H.*, [1999] 2 SCR 3; *Vriend v Alberta*, [1998] 1 SCR 493 (*Vriend*).

9 In France, on the issue of parity between men and women, see, for example, Constitutional Act no. 99–569 of July 8, 1999, on Equality between Women and Men, JORF no. 157, July 9, 1999; Act no. 2008–724 of July 23, 2008, JORF no. 171, July 24, 2008.

10 Constitution Act, 1982, Schedule B to the Canada Act 1982 (UK), 1982, c. 11.

11 *Hak v Attorney General of Quebec*, 2019 QCCA 2145.

12 *Amselem*, para. 46.

13 In *Amselem*, para. 54, Justice Frank Iacobucci, for the majority, had this to say about sincerely held beliefs: "An 'expert' or an authority on religious law is not the surrogate for an individual's affirmation of what his or her religious beliefs are. Religious belief is intensely personal and can easily vary from one individual to another. Requiring proof of the established practices of a religion to gauge the sincerity of belief diminishes the very freedom we seek to protect."

14 *Amselem*, paras. 71, 172, 176. These are the dissenting reasons of Justices Louise Lebel, Marie Deschamps, and Michel Bastarache as written by the latter.

15 See, *inter alia*, ECtHR, *Hamidović v Bosnia and Herzegovina*, Application no. 57792/15, December 5, 2017, para. 30; ECtHR, *Johnston and Others v Ireland*, Application no. 9697/82, December 18, 1986.

16 *Singh v Montréal Gateway Terminals Partnership*, 2019 QCCA 1494 (*Singh*); *Trinity Western University v Law Society of Upper Canada*, [2018] 2 SCR 453 (*Trinity Western University* 1); *Law Society of British Columbia v Trinity Western University*, [2018] 2 SCR 293 (*Trinity Western University* 2).

17 *Ktuxana Nation v British Columbia (Forests, Lands and Natural Resources Operations*, [2017] 2 SCR 386.
18 *R. v N.S.*, [2012] 3 SCR 726 (*N.S.*).
19 *Doré v Barreau du Québec*, [2012] 1 SCR 395.
20 *Loyola High School v Quebec (Attorney General)*, [2015] 1 SCR 613 (*Loyola High School*).
21 *Trinity Western University*, 1; *Trinity Western University*, 2.
22 *Singh*.
23 *Mouvement laïque québécois v Saguenay (City of)*, [2015] 2 SCR 3.
24 *S.L. v Commission scolaire des Chênes*, [2012] 1 SCR 235 (*Commission scolaire des Chênes*).
25 *Alberta v Hutterian Brethren of Wilson Colony*, [2009] 2 SCR 567.
26 *Saguenay (City of) v Mouvement laïque québécois*, 2013 QCCA 936, para. 64.
27 *Commission scolaire des Chênes*.
28 *Loyola High School*.
29 Constitutional Amendment (Quebec), SI/97–141, 1997.
30 It should also be noted that Gérard Bouchard and Charles Taylor, the two commissioners and main architects of this report, as well as Jocelyn Maclure, were all opposed to the Act Respecting the Laicity of the State. The former denounced the fact that the act was too restrictive, while the latter two more generally disavowed the content of the compromise proposed in their own report (Lecomte 2019; Maclure 2019; Pilon-Larose 2019).
31 Bill 94, An Act to Establish Guidelines for Requests for Accommodation within the Administration and Certain Institutions, 2010, which was introduced in a detailed study during the 39th Legislature, 1st Session and was reinstated during the 39th Legislature, 2nd Session on February 24, 2011 (Kathleen Weil, Minister of Justice). The latter Act prohibited, among other things, the provision and reception of services with the face covered.
32 Bill 60, Charter Affirming the Values of State Secularism and Religious Neutrality and of Equality between Women and Men, and Providing a Framework for Accommodation Requests, November 7, 2013, which was introduced during the 40th Legislature, 1st Session (Bernard Drainville, Minister responsible for Democratic Institutions and Active Citizenship).
33 Bill 62, Act to Promote Respect for the Religious Neutrality of the State and Aimed in Particular at Regulating Requests for Accommodation for Religious Reasons in Certain Organizations, SQ 2017, c. 19.
34 *National Council of Canadian Muslims (NCCM) v Attorney General of Québec*, 2017 QCCS 5459.
35 Convention for the Protection of Human Rights and Fundamental Freedoms 1950, 213 UNTS 222.
36 Among the consequences of the principle of laicity, section 3 of the Act Respecting the Laicity of the State endeavours to establish a requirement, or even a right, to neutral services for citizens who interact with the state:

3. State laicity requires parliamentary, government and judicial institutions to comply with all the principles listed in section 2, in fact and in appearance, in pursuing their missions.

For the purposes of this chapter,

(1) "parliamentary institutions" means the National Assembly and the persons appointed or designated by it to an office under its authority;
(2) "government institutions" means the bodies listed in paragraphs 1 to 10 of Schedule I;
(3) "judicial institutions" means the Court of Appeal, the Superior Court, the Court of Québec, the Human Rights Tribunal, the Professions Tribunal and the municipal courts.

This provision has the great merit of formulating the consequences of laicity by setting out the rights that laicity is intended to protect. Seen in this way, laicity enshrines and adds a right to State services that are offered in as reasonable or neutral manner as possible. Similarly, section 4(2) completes this provision by explicitly providing for "the right to lay parliamentary, government and judicial institutions, and to lay public services, to the extent provided for in this Act."

37 In the case of the Canadian Charter, which has the status of a constitutional text, the effect of the notwithstanding clause is to weaken the protection of rights. It is a compromise enabling elected officials to regain a form of final say. The notwithstanding clause can be invoked temporarily, for a period of five years, a term that can then be renewed. With the exception of political rights (the right to vote and to run for office), freedom of movement, and language rights, the notwithstanding clause can apply to all other Canadian Charter rights, including freedom of religion and the right to equality and non-discrimination. The notwithstanding clause is provided for in section 33 as a preventive mechanism (where it is incorporated at the time of enactment) or as a remedial mechanism (where it is adopted after a declaration of invalidity). Moreover, it should not be confused with the process of justifying a reasonable limit on rights, which is enshrined in section 1 and is akin to a functional equivalent of the legitimate aims and proportionality analysis under the European Convention on Human Rights.

38 In the case of the Quebec Charter, the notwithstanding clause plays a much more complex role. In accordance with the British principle of parliamentary sovereignty, the Quebec Charter is an "ordinary" statute, given that it can be amended through the normal legislative process. However, through the notwithstanding clause in section 52 of the Quebec Charter, the legislature has imposed an additional procedural requirement: the will to derogate must be expressly stated. This requirement is considered to be a formal condition (the British doctrine of manner and form), which, in substance, preserves the freedom of choice or sovereignty of Parliament, while adding a specific procedural framework. This leads to a strengthening of the protection of rights since the rights guaranteed by the Quebec Charter are then

given precedence over previous and subsequent legislation. Thus, in contrast to the notwithstanding clause in section 33 of the Canadian Charter, which has the effect of weakening the protection of rights that would otherwise prevail over ordinary laws in all circumstances, the notwithstanding clause in the Quebec Charter allows the rights guaranteed therein to prevail over ordinary laws, unless an express statement to the contrary is made.

39 See, *inter alia, Amselem; Multani; N.S.*

40 *Vriend v Alberta,* [1998] 1 SCR 493.

41 Charter of the French Language, SQ 1977, c. 5.

42 *Reference re Supreme Court Act, ss. 5 and 6,* [2014] 1 SCR 433, paras. 18, 49, 56–57, 59, 69, 104 (per Chief Justice Beverley McLachlin) and para. 145 (per Justice Michael Moldaver, dissenting).

43 *Decision of the Council of State of Geneva,* 2P.419/1996, November 12, 1997 (Switzerland) (*State of Geneva*).

44 BVerfGE 108, 282, *Headscarf Ban (Kopftuchurteil),* 2003 (German Federal Constitutional Court) (*Headscarf Ban*); BVerfG, *Order of the First Senate of 27 January 2015 – 1 BvR 471/10* (German Federal Constitutional Court) (*Order of the First Senate*).

45 The Constitution of the Republic and Canton of Geneva, October 14, 2012, c. A200, specifies in section 3, entitled "Laicity," that "the State is secular. It observes religious neutrality. It shall neither pay for nor subsidize any religious activity." The Public Education Act of September 17, 2015, c. 1 10, further provides for respect for the political and religious convictions of students and parents (s. 11) as well as the obligation for teaching staff to respect secularism (s. 123, para. 3), to be secular and not to exercise an ecclesiastical function or a preponderant religious role within a religion or religious movement (s. 123, para. 3).

46 Section 1 of the Constitution of the Republic and Canton of Neuchâtel, September 24, 2000, states that "the canton of Neuchâtel is a democratic, secular, social republic and guarantor of fundamental rights." See also section 97.

47 Basic Law for the Federal Republic of Germany, May 23, 1949, *Federal Law Gazette,* 1 (BGBl. III 100–1), s. 70, abs. 1 (German Basic Law).

48 In particular, the obligations under section 140 of the German Basic Law.

49 One of these twenty-three decisions was a half-victory for the United Kingdom, insofar as the judgment on two joined applications resulted in a finding of a violation of the European Convention on Human Rights with respect to the first application, but no violation with respect to the second. ECtHR, *Eweida and Others v United Kingdom,* Application nos. 48420/10, 59842/10, 51671/10, and 36516/10, January 15, 2013.

50 *Headscarf Ban; Order of the First Senate.*

51 *State of Geneva.*

52 ECtHR, *Kervanci v France,* Application no. 31645/04, December 4, 2008; ECtHR, *Dahlab v Switzerland* (admissibility), Application no. 42393/98, February 15, 2001 (*Dahlab*).

53 ECtHR, *S.A.S. v France* [GC], Application no. 43835/11, July 1, 2014 (*S.A.S.*); ECtHR, *Aktas v France* (admissibility), Application no. 43563/08, May 25, 2010 (*Aktas*); ECtHR, *Gamaleddyn v France* (admissibility), Application no. 18527/08, June 30, 2009 (*Gamaleddyn*); ECtHR, *Jasvir Singh v France* (admissibility), Application no. 25463/08, June 30, 2009 (*Jasvir Singh*); ECtHR, *Ranjit Singh v France* (admissibility), Application no. 27561/08, June 30, 2009 (*Ranjit Singh*); ECtHR, *Dogru v France*, Application no. 27058/05, December 4, 2008 (*Dogru*); ECtHR, *Kervanci v France*, Application no. 31645/04, December 4, 2008 (*Kervanci*); ECtHR, *Araç v Turkey* (admissibility), Application no. 9907/02, September 19, 2006; ECtHR, *Leyla Şahin v Turkey* [GC], Application no. 44774/98, November 10, 2005 (*Leyla Şahin*); *Dahlab*.

54 ECtHR, *Belcacemi and Oussar v Belgium*, Application no. 37798/13, July 11, 2017.

55 ECtHR, *Dakir v Belgium*, Application no. 4619/12, July 11, 2017 (*Dakir*).

56 *Dakir*, para. 53.

57 *S.A.S.*, para. 141.

58 *Gamaleddyn; Jasvir Singh; Ranjit Singh*, para. 114; *Dogru; Kervanci*, paras. 17–22.

59 ECtHR, *Ebrahimian v France*, Application no. 64846/11, October 12, 2015, para. 53; *Aktas; Gamaleddyn; Jasvir Singh; Dogru; Kervanci*, paras. 17–22; *Leyla Şahin*, para. 114.

References

Bouchard, Gérard, and Charles Taylor. 2008. *Building the Future. A Time for Reconciliation*. Quebec City: Commission de consultation sur les pratiques d'accommodement reliées aux différences culturelles. https://numerique.banq.qc.ca/patrimoine/details/52327/1565995.

Brouillet, Eugénie, and Félix-Antoine Michaud. 2011. "Les rapports entre les pouvoirs politiques et judiciaires en droit constitutionnel canadien: dialogue ou monologue?" In *Actes de la XIXe Conférence des juristes de l'État*, 3–35. Cowansville, QB: Éditions Yvon Blais. https://docplayer.fr/57305607-Les-rapports-entre-les-pouvoirs-politique-et-judiciaire-en-droit-constitutionnel-canadien-dialogue-ou-monologue.html.

Brun, Henri, Guy Tremblay, and Eugénie Brouillet. 2014. *Droit constitutionnel*. 6th ed. Cowansville, QB: Éditions Yvon Blais.

Gardbaum, Stephen. 2013. *The New Commonwealth Model of Constitutionalism*. Cambridge, UK: Cambridge University Press.

Gaudreault-Desbiens, Jean-François. 2011. "Les hiérarchies passagères, ou de la contingence dans l'équilibrage entre droits fondamentaux." *Revue québécoise de droit constitutionnel* 4: 7–41.

Issalys, Pierre, and Denis Lemieux. 2009. *L'Action gouvernementale*. 3rd ed. Cowansville, QB: Éditions Yvon Blais.

Lampron, Louis-Philippe. 2010. "La gestion du pluralisme religieux au Québec – Comment déroger à la Charte canadienne sans déroger à la liberté de religion."

Le Devoir, March 8. https://www.ledevoir.com/opinion/idees/284502/la-gestion-du-pluralisme-religieux-au-quebec-comment-deroger-a-la-charte-canadienne-sans-deroger-a-la-liberte-de-religion.

–. 2011. "Hiérarchie des droits fondamentaux et protection des convictions religieuses en droit constitutionnel québécois et canadien." *Revue québécoise de droit constitutionnel* 4: 43–60.

Lampron, Louis-Philippe, and Eugénie Brouillet. 2011. "Le principe de non-hiérarchie entre droits et libertés fondamentaux: l'inaccessible étoile?" *Revue générale de droit* 41: 93–141.

Lecomte, Anne-Marie. 2019. "Projet de loi sur laïcité: il manque un 'motif supérieur,' estime Gérard Bouchard." *Ici Radio-Canada Info*, May 8. https://ici.radio-canada.ca/nouvelle/1168659/gerard-bouchard-jolin-barrette-commission-parlementaire-laicite-signe-religieux-quebec-projet-loi.

Maclure, Jocelyn. 2019. "La laïcité véritable contre le populisme." *Le Monde*, May 3.

Pilon-Larose, Hugo. 2019. "Guy Rocher craint une 'reconfessionnalisation' de l'école publique.'" *La Presse*, May 15. https://plus.lapresse.ca/screens/d809db04-eefe-4773-94f9-9bbdd2eda4f8__7C___0.html.

Samson, Mélanie. 2015. "L'interprétation harmonieuse de la Charte québécoise et du *Code civil du Québec:* un sujet de discorde pour le tribunal des droits de la personne et les tribunaux du droit commun?" *La Revue des droits de l'homme* 14: n.p. https://journals.openedition.org/revdh/1481.

Spector, Norman. 2003. "Apples, Oranges and Equality." *Globe and Mail*, August 14.

Taillon, Patrick, and Amélie Binette. 2017. "Canada: une théorie 'vivante' de l'interpénétration pour un cadre constitutionnel désuet." In *Annuaire international de justice constitutionnelle*, 201–23. Marseille, France: Economica / Presses universitaires d'Aix-Marseille. https://www.persee.fr/doc/aijc_0995-3817_2018_num_33_2017_2580.

Part 4
Educational Perspectives

The Medium Is the Message 10

There's No Point Cluttering Educational Communication

CHARLES-ÉTIENNE GILL

"The medium is the message." I start some of my communications courses with Marshall McLuhan's ([1964] 2013) celebrated formulation, which helps us appreciate that a teacher in the classroom is not just transmitting a message. They are that very message. A teacher wearing a conspicuous religious sign is therefore sending a double message: a message of their faith and that of the subject matter taught in the course. But the religious sign may offend the student. The teacher is in a position of authority in the classroom and should respect the student's freedom of conscience, while refraining from creating interference or noise in educational communication.

Communication and Signs

When we discuss current events in the classroom, I notice something as a teacher, even about students opposed to the ban on teachers wearing religious signs: they see a big gap between plans to implement state laicity in Quebec and the way in which the media represent and even demonize these plans. I get students in my courses to support their observations with evidence drawn from serious documented sources – for example, briefs tabled before parliamentary committees. These students note that media coverage has polarized public perceptions by caricaturing positions in favour of laicity: in so doing, the media have done a disservice to Quebec society, if only because this prevents a substantive debate from taking place.

In undertaking press reviews of pieces of legislation on laicity (Bill 60, Quebec's proposed Charter of Values, and Bills 21 and 62), many of my students have noticed that the words "religious signs" are widely used, whereas very little attention has been given to the role of the sign itself in communication. We need to focus closely on this role. In my classes, students learn to mobilize the different functions of language, as theorized by the linguist Roman Jakobson (1960). He identifies three primary functions aiming to inform, influence, and express – namely the referential function, the conative function, and the emotive function, respectively. Jakobson also notes that language has secondary functions, including the metalingual function, the phatic function, and the poetic function – all three of which participate in communication and are just as important as the primary functions.

The poetic function is well illustrated by the sketch of the humourist André Sauvé, who recites a poem by Émile Nelligan and then makes changes to it by removing vowels and using *joual,* a popular Quebec French idiom known for its unique phonetic and lexical character and frequent use of borrowed English words. We communicate for the sake of communicating. We communicate simply because we enjoy it and not so much for the information we derive from it. The metalingual function relates to the code we use – for example, in explaining the Quebec verb "*tataouiner*" (wasting time) to someone who speaks continental European French. The phatic function relates to the contact – in other words, the communication channel itself – that we do not notice as long as it operates smoothly. We appreciate the importance of "good contact" when music gets too loud at a wedding, and it prevents us from hearing a good joke that someone makes at our table (Shannon and Weaver 1963).

These six functions (referential, conative, emotive, metalingual, phatic, and poetic) are useful theoretical tools in describing a communication situation. Contrary to the linear model of communication, which is overly simplistic and represents a message as passing between sender and receiver, these six functions help us understand that "participation in communication takes place at different levels according to multiple verbal and non-verbal modalities," while "intentionality does not determine communication since the act carried out in the here-and-now of the interaction is just one moment of a larger process" (Winkin, n.d.). Paul Watzlawick, another prominent communications theorist and one of the founders of the Palo Alto School, and his coauthors Janet Beavin-Bavelas and Don D. Jackson emphasize the important role of context: "You can't not communicate" (Watzlawick, Beavin-Bavelas, and Jackson [1967] 2011).

A teacher wearing a religious sign in the classroom is therefore not simply making a "passive" profession of faith: that teacher is actively sending a message that mobilizes at least three of Jakobson's functions: the phatic, the referential, and the emotive. This message may also include poetic elements – for example, if the sign is beautiful. Depending on the context, conative elements may also come into play – for example, if a Catholic teacher wearing a crucifix, or a Muslim teacher wearing a veil, seems weaker or more cheerful during Lent or Ramadan. As a result, when a sign representing the teacher's faith is not needed for communicating the subject matter of a source or for conditions favouring such communication, that sign constitutes interference – noise – in both the communication itself and the pedagogical relationship.

We can consider a useful sign in the classroom. The teacher may put on earmuffs – a sign agreed on in advance with the students. This sign indicates that the class is noisy and that students should quiet down so teaching and learning can continue. In this example, the teacher does not really intend to cut herself off from the rest of the class: she uses a (phatic) means of drawing attention to her perception of the level of noise in the classroom (emotive function), calling on students to quiet down (conative function) by pointing out that the class is objectively too noisy (referential function). Clearly, what a teacher intends to communicate is meaningful and means something. Opponents of the Act Respecting the Laicity of the State (Bill 21) want us to believe religious signs are not meaningful.[1] But this view contradicts the very purpose of religious signs themselves, which is to speak out, to challenge, and this is why I say that signs that have no function in the learning relationship constitute noise that unnecessarily clutters the communication channel.

Political Signs

To better illustrate my point, I will deal briefly now with political signs. They are often referred to, but it is rarely explained why teachers are not allowed to wear political signs in the classroom – for example, wearing a red baseball cap with the slogan "Make America Great Again." For some people, this message simply indicates the wearer's adherence to Donald Trump's main line of communication during the 2016 US election campaign: America is in decline, and Trump can set things right. In terms of communication, this is an authentic slogan, a rallying cry that enables a community to come together around this value. At the same time, by using the verb "make," this slogan implies reaching out to other people: if "you" share the view that America is in decline or if "your" situation is difficult, then you have a responsibility through your vote or activism to help set things right in America. "Make America Great Again" or "MAGA" is a conative statement, which is why it generates both support and opposition. This sign calls on all six functions of language.

What would happen if a teacher wore a MAGA cap in the classroom? The principal would not wait for a parent to lodge a complaint. Instead, the principal would summon the teacher and demand in no uncertain terms that the cap be removed. A MAGA cap in the classroom would be a political sign generating noise in pedagogical communication. Likewise, if the message were "I am a communist," "Black Lives Matter," "the market is the answer," or "there are only two genders," one suspects the result would be the same. Teachers are in positions of authority. They embody the school, and, at the same time, parents entrusting their sons and daughters to the teachers' charge. And this is not merely a symbolic statement: it is a concrete reality in the context of the classroom. When needed, the teacher can call for silence, organize compulsory activities, decide who gets to speak next, and separate students from one another. Obviously, during a normal day in the classroom, the freedom of association and expression of students is suspended or at least severely limited. Hence, the importance of a framework of rules, so that the students' freedom of conscience is always respected in a situation where they are more vulnerable.

The teacher who wears a visible political sign is given a platform. The students have no choice but to look at the teacher, whose sign constitutes a message to be decoded in a context of a captive audience, even though what that sign represents may be lost on them. And what should students do in the event of a message with which some of them disagree? Should these students pretend not to see the MAGA cap? Should they report their discomfort, express their disagreement? Why should students have to resort to one or the other of these solutions, thereby changing the pedagogical relationship, when the political message conveyed by the teacher has nothing to do with the learning situation, the teaching itself?

It is inappropriate to expose young people to a political sign in the classroom since they are not in a position of equality to discuss, argue, and make known their own reaction to the sign. It is normal to think that the desire to be accepted, even liked, by one's teacher translates into modesty or at least discomfort. Conflicts of loyalty may arise when parents have a political position opposed to the one conveyed by the teacher's political sign, even to the point of undermining part of the knowledge that the teacher is responsible for transmitting. Whether the person wearing a sign likes it or not, that sign projects an identification and constitutes a challenge to the environment. On the conative level, it is as if the person wearing the sign were asking other people to "decode" the sign by playing on the phatic function. Moreover, in the context of the classroom, we could add "and don't say anything about it." A teacher wearing a visible political sign in the classroom imposes this relationship on the class. There is nothing "passive" about the relationship. And it is natural to consider that teachers who persist in wearing the sign are also indicating that they do not understand why anybody could have any reservations about wearing political signs. This would be considered professional misconduct. For this reason, disciplinary action may be necessary.

Finally, if wearing a political sign in the classroom were permitted, then teachers would have to accept criticism (both positive and negative) of the political movement associated with the sign on an ongoing basis.

Understandably, this would disrupt learning. If the class were to maintain silence instead and end up accepting the presence of this sign as if it had no meaning, it would give an undue advantage to the political or ideological movement associated with the sign in question. Clearly, this situation would be highly undemocratic. Besides, nobody gets upset when teachers temporarily lose their right to political expression during the school day since they regain this right at the end of the day. Everyone understands that teachers must show restraint in expressing their political preferences.

Religious Signs

Opponents of Bill 21 say that the ban on wearing religious signs restricts their right to religious expression. There is some truth to this, although the restriction is very limited. However, teachers must show the same restraint in expressing religious preferences as they do when it comes to political preferences. According to the main argument of people claiming that Bill 21 unduly restricts religious rights, religion is different from politics, and an individual's religious "identity" is an indissociable part of their uniqueness as a human being. Whether signs are political or religious, they are irrelevant to the pedagogical relationship: they constitute noise that interferes with the transmission of knowledge. The debate can therefore be brought down to a single question, at least in the school setting: should the right of certain teachers to generate noise prevail over the right of students (a captive audience) to receive knowledge without interference?

There is no need to refer here to situations where teachers have sought to convert students (Buzzetti 2020). Situations like this are intolerable, but they have proven rare until now. It is enough to recall that religion is a sensitive subject for many Quebec families, whether they belong to a particular denomination or profess no faith. Religions not only provide meaning, comfort, and community solidarity, but they also sometimes give rise to wounds, conflicts, and opposition between some of their values and those favoured by families. We can imagine that a mother who has undergone an abortion will not want her children to be confronted with a teacher who shows their evangelical faith by wearing a pro-life message on their sweater. We can imagine that a Jehovah's

Witness father who asks his child not to draw Christmas cards will not appreciate a teacher wearing a large crucifix around their neck. We can imagine that a family that left its native country partly to give its daughters an equal chance at an education will not appreciate that the teacher in the classroom, who is of the same faith, is completely veiled. In cases like these, young people who learn other values at home are faced with multiple situations of teachers wearing religious signs, and this disrupts pedagogical communication. And let it not be said that "the school must be like the real world": the unique and specific pedagogical relationship between a teacher and students in the classroom must be free of any interference that could compromise optimal communication between everyone in the classroom.

It is often argued that a sign may have meaning solely for the person displaying it but not for other people. McLuhan's celebrated maxim "the medium is the message" helps us understand how irrelevant this argument really is: the meaning itself matters less than the communication imposed by the sign, the fact we are obliged to take it into account, even if, in the end, we choose to ignore it. The sign adds a layer to the exchange, a layer of communication (even if one pretends not to see the sign), which is not necessarily desired by all partners in the exchange. In the classroom setting, where young people are in a vulnerable position and the teacher is in a position of authority, forcing students to look at a religious sign goes against their right not to have to deal with this additional layer of exchange. In terms of communication, wearing a sign represents a challenge to others. Now, if the religious sign worn by teachers has a personal meaning for them alone, a meaning both intimate and private, why should teachers benefit from such an important platform during an entire school year?

Combining the teachers' status (with their signs) and religious signs worn in class results in a paradoxical injunction: notice my sign but do not talk to me about it; notice it, pretend it does not exist and too bad if it bothers you.

Conclusion: There is No Rift between Sign and Signifier

"The medium is the message," the obvious characteristic of teachers presenting themselves with a sign is the meaning of this sign itself, even if this meaning is equivocal and polysemous. Some people may disregard it, others may dispute it, but people cannot help but notice it, as if it were a flashing neon billboard: a message to be noticed and interpreted that is presented to them. The fact is that a captive receiver cannot do otherwise than interpret the sign when the situation requires him or her to notice it. The question of rights should not be considered only in relation to the sender but also in relation to the community of people receiving the message. People object to authority figures such as teachers wearing religious signs during their working hours – not because of some "visual allergy," as Quebec Court of Appeal Chief Justice Nicole Duval Hesler expressed, but, rather, because citizens do not want their children to be permanently exposed to noise superimposed on pedagogical communication between teachers and students (quoted in Pipro 2019).

Note

1 Act Respecting the Laicity of the State, SQ 2019, c. 12.

References

Buzzetti, Hélène. 2020. "Des exemples de prosylétisme à la CSDM." *Le Devoir*, March 3. https://www.ledevoir.com/politique/quebec/574072/loi-sur-la-laicite-de-l-etat-des-educatrices-voilees-ont-fait-du-proselytisme.

Jakobson, Roman. 1960. "Closing Statement: Linguistics and Poetics." In *Style in Language*, edited by Thomas A. Sebeok, 350–77. Cambridge, MA: MIT Press.

McLuhan, Marshall. (1964) 2013. *Understanding Media: The Extensions of a Man*. Berkeley, CA: Gingko Press.

Pipro, Raphael, and Audrey Ruel Manseau. 2019. "Loi sur la laïcité de l'État: une plainte contre la juge en chef de la Cour d'appel." *La Presse*, December 2. https://www.lapresse.ca/actualites/2019-12-02/loi-sur-la-laicite-de-l-etat-une-plainte-contre-la-juge-en-chef-de-la-cour-d-appel.

Shannon, Claude, and Warren Weaver. 1963. *A Mathematical Theory of Communication*. Chicago: University of Illinois Press.

Watzlawick, Paul, Janet Beavin-Bavelas, and Don D. Jackson. (1967) 2011. "Some Tentative Axioms of Communication." In *Pragmatics of Human Communication: A Study of Interactional Patterns, Pathologies and Paradoxes*, 29–52. New York: W.W. Norton.

Winkin, Yves. N.d. "Communication." In *Encyclopædia Universalis*. https://www.universalis.fr/encyclopedie/communication/.

11

Thinking About Laicity Today with Ferdinand Buisson

NORMAND BAILLARGEON

In recent years, Quebec society has taken part collectively in debates and discussions about laicity – from the Bouchard-Taylor Commission (2007–8), to Quebec's proposed Charter of Values (Bill 60), promoted by the Parti Québécois (2013–14), and the Act Respecting the Laicity of the State (Bill 21), adopted by the Coalition Avenir Québec government on June 16, 2019.[1] I do not think I am alone in feeling distress about these debates and discussions in more than one respect. How can this distress be explained? The problem is not so much a lack of information or the poverty of arguments put forward. Secularism is, after all, a vast and complex subject that, until recent years, had not been the subject of much discussion in the public sphere: it had received even less attention from the perspective of developing public policy. My distress stems instead from observing the virulence and even the violence of much public commentary, whether it be for or against state laicity.

I submit that few people will disagree with me on this score. I hope people will agree with the second observation I am making, which concerns another aspect of these debates and discussions that I have found astonishing, to say the least. I think we have collectively been the witnesses of, and, in some cases, the actors in, what I would simply call very peculiar and unexpected ideological reversals, and we have done this perhaps without having been fully aware of its extent or of its significance. Let us judge from the following examples, and I imagine everyone will be able to come up with examples of their own, if only based on their own personal experience. We have in fact collectively seen the idea of laicity – an idea traditionally identified with the Left (with reason, given its history and various incarnations) – suddenly, in many cases, borne along by ideological and political currents that we do not normally associate with it and that were even formerly opposed to it. And the idea of laicity has ended up being adopted by certain forms of nationalism and conservatism.

At the same time, the current Left, in at least some of its manifestations and particularly the most pronounced or radical ones, has opposed secularism, even in the moderate form it has taken in Quebec. The Left has done this by invoking arguments, such as banning any limits on the freedom of individuals – in this case, to express their religious convictions. This position was formerly promoted by the Right, whereas the Left had usually tended to respond by invoking the common good in one way or another. As a result, the Act Respecting the Laicity of the State was tabled by the Coalition Avenir Québec, a party that can fairly be considered centre-right, whereas Québec solidaire, a left-wing party, fought it, alongside the Quebec Liberal Party and the Conseil du patronat (the Quebec Council of Employers).

And the public discussions surrounding laicity have been accompanied by an outpouring of insults, heart-wrenching fractures, and repudiations. I have always been an anarcho-syndicalist, yet now I find myself (like many others) fighting alongside my former political adversaries, and I have been called all sorts of names, including "fascist," by some of my former political allies. I have long been interested in the issue of secularism, particularly because of its importance in education, and I have been quite active on the subject in Quebec, notably by editing a special issue of the magazine *À Bâbord!* in 2009–10; by organizing, with other contributors to this magazine, a colloquium held at the Université du Québec à Montréal to which were invited representatives of the various models of secularism then defended in the academic or activist literature (notably, republican secularism and so-called open secularism);

and, finally, by co-directing and publishing, along with Jean-Marc Piotte, a collective work on the subject (Baillargeon and Piotte 2012) and by contributing to another collective work (Baillargeon 2015). In the context of this work, I have made a careful study of the history of secularism in France, a study that has familiarized me with the important figure of Ferdinand Buisson (1841–1932), who remains, unfortunately and unjustly, very little known even in his native France.

In the following pages, I propose to portray his career and to try to use his example to cast light on the ideological reversals mentioned above. I will proceed in three steps. To begin with, I will briefly recall Buisson's career, situating him in the context of the evolution of the idea of secularism in France, which came to fruition with the Law on the Separation of the Church and State of 1905.[2] Then, starting from Buisson's ideas and his vision of secularism, I will try to show how his example can shed light on the discussions and debates in Quebec, which I think are important. And, finally, I propose to suggest how more recent, but troubling, developments in Western thought have contributed to, and partly explain, these strange ideological reversals mentioned earlier. I will also raise once again the violence and virulence of the debates and discussions we have had.

Some History: Ferdinand Buisson and Republican Secularism

Ferdinand Buisson was born in Paris in December 1841 into a Protestant family belonging to a lesser-known and austere current of this religion, the pietism of the French-speaking Protestant Revival (Brunet-Giry 2014). His father died when he was sixteen years old. In the face of adversity ("while supporting my family, I prepared my baccalaureate and bachelor's exams on my own" [quoted by Cadier-Rey 2015]), he pursued brilliant studies, completing his baccalaureate in literature in 1859 and then, four years later, a bachelor's degree in the same discipline in 1863. In 1868, he received both a bachelor's degree in science and an *agrégé* (the highest teaching degree in France) in philosophy. In 1866, he had already proved such a convinced republican that he refused to take the oath to Napoleon III, which was a prerequisite for obtaining a teaching post at the imperial university. Like the author Victor Hugo and the political figure Edgar Quinet, Buisson went into exile – in his case, in Switzerland – where he obtained a position as a professor of philosophy at the Nouvelle Académie de Neuchâtel.

It is worth taking a moment here to focus on the question of secularism as it has historically arisen in France (Baubérot 2017). This means going back to the French Revolution and the overthrowing of the Ancien Régime, which had long enabled the monarchy and the Catholic Church to wield not only immense political and economic power but also ideological power. Indeed, Article 10 of the 1791 Declaration of the Rights of Man and of the Citizen encouraged people to rise up against this power: "No one should be bothered on account of his opinions, even religious, provided their presentation does not upset the public order established by law." In striving to institute a civic "cult" of reason, a period of dechristianization began, and it was sometimes accompanied by violence.

In signing the Concordat with the Catholic Church in 1801, Napoleon put a temporary end to this episode of dechristianization. But the following years would see the accentuation of a conflict, and even a war, between those promoting and those opposing the secularization of society and its institutions. To simplify things without resorting to caricature, we can say that the promoters of secularism were typically left-wing, whereas opponents of secularism, including members of the clergy, were conservative and right wing. This conflict became more pronounced during the early years of the Third Republic (1870–1940) and led to the Law on the Separation of Church and State of December 9, 1905. According to the first article of this law, "the Republic ensures freedom of conscience. It guarantees freedom of worship limited only by the following rules in the interest of public order." And, according to the second article, "the Republic neither acknowledges, nor pays for nor subsidizes any form of worship."

But let us return to the Swiss period of Buisson's life. He would remain in a French-speaking and Protestant environment for the next four years, and this would prove important for the rest of his life for at least two reasons. First, Buisson adhered to a kind of liberal religious sentiment, a faith that can probably be best described today as a rationalist spirituality: this system of values did not have dogma, miracles, or clergy. He then broadened his political horizons by attending a congress in Geneva in 1867 organized by the International League for Peace and Freedom and presided over by Giuseppe Garibaldi and a congress in Lausanne in 1869 organized by Victor Hugo and, especially, by meeting many progressives, particularly through the First International, which was made up of socialist militants and thinkers as well as many anarchists, who, at that time, were still participating in the International. Among these latter figures, we may note the brothers Élie Reclus (1827–1904) and Élisée Reclus (1830–1905) as well as James Guillaume (1844–1916).

I would like to insist on this point because Buisson's secularism – I will return to this theme – is closely related to progressive, universalist, liberal values, is firmly grounded in the Left and even in anarchism, and is intimately associated with the idea of education. According to Martine Brunet-Giry (2014), one of Buisson's first writings advocates "the abolition of war through education," asserting that, by means of education, "we can reform the nation in the citizen, and the citizen in the child; and we must go back to this point if we want to reach the very root of evil" (Buisson 2003, 54). At the same time, during a public lecture, Buisson caused a scandal in the Catholic religious milieu by sharply criticizing sacred history as it was then taught in schools in France. In particular, he faulted this sacred history for the harm it could do to the moral sense of children, and he concluded that it did not prepare young people for learning about democracy: "Abolish sacred history and in its place uphold the history of humanity." This statement would cause a sensation and would be taken up by James Guillaume (1905) in his book *L'Internationale: documents et souvenirs* (quoted in Brunet-Giry 2012).

From that time on, Buisson led an uninterrupted public life that lasted for some sixty years until the end of the 1920s. For lack of space, we will stick to the main points here. Buisson returned to France as soon as the Third Republic was proclaimed in September 1870. With Paris under siege, he became actively involved in the commune. In particular, he took care of orphaned children, an activity that led to the creation of an orphanage in Cempuis. In 1879, Jules Ferry, minister of public instruction, appointed Buisson director of primary education (he would remain in this position until 1896). Buisson held many positions in the administration of education and was notably one of the important actors in the implementation of the Ferry laws on public, secular, and compulsory schooling (the laws of 1881 and 1882), named after the French statesman and republican philosopher Jules Ferry (1832–93).[3] Buisson appointed his own successor, the anarchist Paul Robin (1837–1912), who would go on to make the directorate of primary education an important laboratory for fulfilling the libertarian ideal of integral education (Baillargeon 2016, 40–44, 209–52).

An important episode for our subject takes place during these years, when Buisson led an immense project that concerned both education and secularism: his publication of the famous and very influential *Dictionnaire de pédagogie et d'instruction primaire* (*Dictionary of Pedagogy and Primary Instruction*). The first edition appeared in 1887, and a second one (*Nouveau Dictionnaire de pédagogie et d'instruction primaire*) was published in 1911 (Buisson 2017). This work would require years of work and the contributions of more than 350 authors: it would have extraordinary influence in France on the educational field, in general, and on the training of teachers, in particular. The historian Pierre Nora would call this work "the cathedral of the primary school" (quoted in Buisson 2017, vii). Among those involved in this enormous task, Buisson's first and most important contributor was James Guillaume, whom he brought back to France from Switzerland. Guillaume wrote many articles, without signing them. According to Martine Brunet-Giry (2014), the anarchists Paul Robin and the Reclus brothers also wrote articles, without signing them either. Guillaume might even have invented the French neologism *laïcité* (laicity). As we can readily see from this historical overview, the objective of secularizing society and especially education was firmly rooted in the political Left and even the extreme Left.

Let us briefly recall several other important moments and achievements in Buisson's life. In 1891, he defended a doctoral thesis on Sébastien Castellion (1515–63), a Protestant theologian and precursor of the idea of freedom of conscience. In 1896, after leaving his job as a civil servant, he became a professor of pedagogy (later called educational sciences) at the Sorbonne. In 1898, Buisson threw himself heart and soul into the defence of Alfred Dreyfus, a French artillery officer unjustly convicted of treason, and helped found the League of Human Rights. Over the next few years, he continued his defence of secular education and free thought in various associations. From 1902 to 1924, Buisson was a member of the French National Assembly (first as a Radical, then as a Radical-Socialist). In the lead-up to the 1905 Law on the Separation of the Church and State, he presided over a commission for which Aristide Briand was rapporteur: this commission paved the way for the law and disseminated the idea of secularism among the public. In 1910, he came out in favour of women's right to vote.

For his efforts to bring people together, Buisson shared the Nobel Peace Prize in 1927 with the German pacifist Ludwig Quidde (1858–1941). According to a statement on Wikipedia, Buisson "dedicated the prize to public-school teachers." He died on February 16, 1932. Without being able to exhaust the subject here, I would like to provide more detail about what this idea and ideal of secularism are – values that Buisson never ceased to defend – and then underline their relevance to our recent debates and discussions and especially to what I have called the peculiar and unexpected ideological reversals we have been witnessing.

The Pathway of Secularism in Quebec in the Light of Buisson's Example

I maintain that the contrasting visions of secularism in Quebec are rooted in two different metaphysics, and I find this hypothesis both valid and enlightening; on the one hand, we have the classical, republican vision of secularism, as formulated by Buisson, and, on the other, we have open secularism. I also suggest (but I will come back to this) that conceptualizing the rift between the two metaphysics along these lines helps partly to explain the virulence of public debates on the subject. By metaphysics, for want of a better term, I mean a complex set of positions, both descriptive and normative, concerning in particular the nature of human beings and especially their freedom; the origin, nature, value, and functions of the knowledge that they can acquire; the nature of the social and political bond that unites human beings; the ends that we should expect from these human associations; and what we can hope for in terms of the future of the human species.

I will now contrast these two metaphysics as honestly and fairly as possible. I am an ardent defender of a republican vision of secularism.

I have never hidden my disagreement with other positions, but I will nonetheless take pains to avoid caricaturing them. Let us start with the idea of the individual and the correlative idea of freedom.

Individuals and Their Freedom(s)

I do not think I am distorting the position of opponents of republican secularism by saying that it has been all important for them to recall and defend the freedom to believe and to express one's faith, including through one's external appearance and, in particular, one's clothing and the symbols worn, everywhere and without prior conditions. The limitation of this individual freedom is required by republican secularism, notably for teachers. But it seems to the followers of open secularism an intolerable infringement of the rights of individuals that nothing can justify (see, for example, Bosset 2013). An important philosophical argument along these lines has been developed by the theorists of communitarianism. Charles Taylor (1989), Alasdair MacIntyre (1984), and Michael Walzer (1983) are among the most influential theorists of this school of thought: in the increasingly pluralistic framework of contemporary societies, they have contributed to developing greater sensitivity to the differentiated effects on the various communities of public policies that are intended to be neutral, and they have introduced the idea of the need for reasonable accommodation.

Thus, there are important arguments supporting this view. But there are also, of course, counter-arguments. Many people argue, for example, that it is commonly accepted as justified by custom, common sense, and the law to restrict the individual freedom to dress as one pleases, for example, for reasons of safety or image and that this, moreover, is seen and practised in many professions. And it is also true that, in countries where secularism exists, many laws restricting the expression by civil servants of all kinds of beliefs, including religious ones, have not been, and are not considered, illegal. Along these lines, we may note that in January 2020 the Parliamentary Assembly of the Council of Europe rejected a system of reasonable accommodation in the workplace that could have led to changes in the legislation of several member countries.[4]

This vision of secularism, which deems such restrictions inadmissible, is thus opposed by another vision, and another metaphysical one, in which the emphasis is no longer so much on the adult as on the child. The child must be helped to grow up and to assume their freedom – the child has the right to an open future. As for the adult, they must be at the service of the child's freedom and, therefore, of their freedom of conscience. This shift of focus toward the child and the school is very important and, moreover, is fraught with consequences.

The School, the Teacher, Knowledge, and the Child

The metaphysics of the proponents of Buisson-style secularism – of republican secularism – grants to the school a particular legal, ethical, political status because the school is the primary place for the transmission of knowledge. By means of this knowledge transmitted to the pupil, they have access, or at least can have access, to a complex set of facts and values (to simplify the content of instruction) that are held to have emancipatory virtues and that have accordingly been instituted as the object of teaching. For this reason, public education is compulsory. Some of these facts and values may of course conflict with others, typically derived from the child's own family environment.

But secularism defends its right to an open future – to a future that is not limited by each person's origins. In promoting freedom of conscience, secularism seeks a balance between freedom of religion and freedom from religion. It also forcefully promotes the idea that in any possible conflict between facts and values of all origins and facts and values promoted by the social and political organization through the secular nature of the school, the latter should prevail – not always or anywhere but in the type of sphere of which the school is an exemplary instance. Within the usual legal limits, people are by no means deprived of the opportunity to adhere to these other values elsewhere and by other means. And if the freedom of conscience of the adult proponents of these values is respected by the neutrality promoted by secularism, in the political and especially in the school setting, then the child can discover this possible distance, this tension, and what it means in a secular society.

The school is therefore the place where a legitimate and even necessary dual movement takes place. First, the school enables the child to leave the universe of the family and its values and beliefs by means of thought and knowledge; then, it begins to enrol the child in the social and political system as a citizen, once again by means of knowledge and values. Schoolteachers are adults and must put themselves entirely at the service of this ideal: the teacher's freedom therefore consists in adhering completely to this ideal or in refusing it. But, in the latter case, it is the teacher who chooses between isolation from society and the right to teach, and, in the first case, "he or she will exclude himself or herself" (Buisson 1911). We can measure the distance that separates these words from the arguments deployed in Quebec by opponents of Bill 21, which they consider a serious infringement on the rights and freedoms of people who are denied the right to teach simply because they refuse to remove symbols or clothing expressing their religious beliefs. Buisson's argument is worth considering:

> What, in any case, dominates the debate, is that the freedom of teaching should be treated just the same as the freedom of medicine or pharmacy, and the freedom to seek public employment should be treated just the same as the freedom of work and commerce. These are all rights limited by the rights of others, especially the rights of those for whom the State is the guardian. This is what authorizes the State to impose a certain number of preconditions on the exercise of each of these freedoms, such as guarantees of knowledge, competence, experience, morality, security, etc. Which means we are far from "inalienable freedom." (Buisson 1902b)

In short, Buisson (1911) writes, "The teacher in the school, the priest in the church, the mayor in the town hall. No one can claim to be banned from the domain where he or she is denied entry: the selection [of teachers] is made based on the distinction of attributions, which is neither hurtful for anyone nor prejudicial for any service." Another remarkable difference between the two metaphysics underlying republican and open secularism lies in the status, the place, and the value accorded by each of them to knowledge and, in particular, to knowledge within the school setting. It would be profoundly wrong and unfair to claim that proponents of open secularism do not place great importance and value on knowledge or that they do not wish the school to impart knowledge and enable critical and autonomous thinking.

But I submit that they maintain what I will call, as neutrally and objectively as possible, an acritical relationship toward beliefs, which cannot fail to have serious and sometimes deplorable repercussions on the policies they promote, especially in schools, which are after all institutions dedicated to the transmission of knowledge. A kind of relativism is emerging that forbids judging, condemning, and revising certain beliefs that deserve respect and recognition because they are believed and are important in the eyes of those who adhere to them. I see an indication of this relativism in Quebec's ethics and religious culture (ERC) course, which presents religious beliefs in an acritical manner, with little regard for atheism and anti-clericalism. And I note, not without deep amazement, that in Quebec's school curriculum, critical thinking is taught in the very course – ERC – that has as its premise not to criticize – and especially not with all the rigour that critical and free thought requires – those elements of religious beliefs that are, without a shadow of a doubt from my point of view, liberticidal, misogynistic, indoctrinatory, and obscurantist.

In this respect, Buisson's metaphysics are explicitly derived from the Enlightenment defence of the freedom to criticize all beliefs, including religious ones, and to blaspheme. The current threats to the freedom of expression and criticism of all doctrines seem to me to be extremely deplorable and dangerous. They are not unrelated to the penetration of metaphysics into minds and practices, which Buisson and his successors have opposed. On this question of knowledge, I suggest that we stand to benefit by conceptualizing Buissonian metaphysics as unfolding in two directions. The first direction is the particular form of relativism found in Buissonian metaphysics, which is very close to the rationalist ideal animating science. Knowledge is considered to be something that is provisional and perfectible. Buisson expresses this idea well in addressing his fellow deputies in the French National Assembly on January 19, 1910:

> Republican education does not believe in absolute, immutable, intangible truths. It accepts neither State doctrine nor Church doctrine as the perfect expression of the perfect truth. It believes that truth itself evolves and grows with the human spirit. It believes that in the transmission of our knowledge, we must be satisfied with indefinitely perfectible approximations, and this applies even in the case of morality. (Buisson 1902a)

The second direction is the search for an ethos corresponding to republican secularism. This ethos needs to be developed while resolutely avoiding religious or doctrinaire dogmatism:

> The child of the people needs something other than the technical learning of the alphabet and the Pythagorean table; the child needs a liberal education (the expression is a happy one), and it is the dignity of the teacher and the nobility of the school to give this education without leaving the modest setting of public education. Now who can claim education can be transmitted without a set of moral influences, without a certain general culture of the soul, without some notions about the human being, about human duties and about human destiny? We therefore need the teacher to be a master of ethics as well as a master of language or arithmetic, to complete the task of instruction. The teacher must continue to be in charge of souls, and to be deeply penetrated by them. The teacher must have the right and the duty to speak to the heart as well as to the mind, to supervise in each child the education of the conscience at least as well as any other part of the curriculum. (Buisson 1911)

Buisson's ideal of secularism strikes us as an ideal that we know has not been achieved but to which we aspire, and this aspiration extends to all students in the education system. I suspect many of the debates around secularism arise from the rejection of, or at least from the now widespread suspicion (and sometimes not without reason) about, what must be described as the optimistic vision – and some would surely say the naivety – that inspires the metaphysics I have just described, notably in its approach toward knowledge and the ability of knowledge to contribute to building a better world.

To take the measure of what this means, I now turn to a final contrast between the two metaphysics I am examining. This time I am concerned with what I propose to call the articulation of the individual and the collective, the particular and the universal.

The Individual and the Collective, the Particular and the Universal

We can, I think, state that the ideal embodied in the educational project of republican secularism is to shape a free, autonomous individual: we hope that these individuals will be able, through the universal aspects of the knowledge and republican ethics transmitted in the school setting, to join in a political project that not only encompasses but also moves beyond the confines of their immediate affiliations, including those more distant from the nation, to the point of meeting with humanity. Undeniably, this high hope exists in Buisson's thought and his particular vision of secularism. Indeed, republican secularism is inspired by the revolutionary motto that takes the two pillars of the democratic ideal – liberty and equality – and adds to them fraternity, the meeting place for all. Buisson deserved his share in the Nobel Peace Prize by taking important concrete actions (for example, in helping to create the League of the Rights of Man) and through his many writings.

This ideal has become suspect. No doubt, there are many reasons for this suspicion. I will not go into detail here, but I can mention at least two kinds of suspicions: the distrust of nationalism and the concern to respect and treat with justice (according to a particular conception of justice) oppressed minorities – in particular, religious minorities. Nevertheless, the universalist ideal can be emancipatory. Taking part in the universal requires us to respect human rights, even if they are seriously to be doubted, as I think I have shown above by citing relevant judgments on this question – that respect for these rights favours open secularism. In any case, the result for schools and education seems to be this convergence of multiculturalism, of a certain sensitivity to certain sources and forms of oppression, and of the metaphysics of open secularism: the individual is then adapted to the existing society – the child to the world from which he or she comes – rather than to a world to come, albeit (and by definition) a world imperfectly defined.

I hope I am not being unfair, but I would suggest that open secularism adapts the school to the existing society rather than trying to transform it by means of what the school promotes. I suggest, therefore, that it is in considering republican secularism and open secularism as two distinct mindsets, two metaphysics, and two complex sets of values, hopes, and facts considered particularly important that we can best appreciate how these visions of secularism have been, and are, contrasted one with the other. But it goes without saying, as I have already said, that in our debates on this subject we have not always been up to the task of understanding what is at stake, we have seriously not considered the contrasting points of view.

In closing, I would like to say a word about all this.

Malaise in the Democratic Conversation: A Diagnosis

I began this text by recalling the extraordinary virulence of some of the comments heard during our discussions in Quebec society on secularism and the themes and issues that it inevitably brings up. It is unfortunately not only on this subject alone that we are confronted by such brutality. I would also like to draw attention to some very singular aspects of these exchanges: often, we were not speaking to each other, we were not listening to what the person holding a different view had to say, and we did not try to find out whether there was any truth in what was being said. That other person holding a different view was not our adversary in terms of ideas or even of policies that possibly could be adopted: that other person was an enemy to be destroyed. My dear intellectual self-defence was not at the service of the search for truth and any distrust of what was being proposed for our approval: no, my self-defence was directed toward the sole and all-consuming search for weaknesses in that other proposal that was counter to my own views being offered. And this mental attitude had the dual purpose of freeing us of any need seriously and honestly to examine the proposal, enabling us to dismiss whoever put it forward and, if possible, to vilify that other person. The temper of our times reminds me far too much of the Chinese Cultural Revolution: some people spend a considerable amount of time looking for reasons to justify vilifying X or Y. This is how clans come into being and clash one with the other, how society becomes polarized into factions of people who are convinced they hold the truth and are virtuous, whereas people who hold opposing views are monsters.

I am convinced that this sorry situation can be attributed to many distinct causes beyond the usual suspects – namely, social networks, confirmation bias, and a certain neo-conformism. Honestly, I cannot identify them all. But I will identify one cause that, as a philosopher, I simply cannot ignore. My hypothesis, which needs to be refined but which I present to you anyway, is that we are living in a moment of social penetration of the most recent form of postmodernism concocted in the universities and that it is convenient to call "identity theories." These theories were taught about forty years ago by Jean-François Lyotard (1979) and combine a strong suspicion about, or even a rejection of, any normative ideal with a universalist claim, with the concept of blind powers as taught by Michel Foucault (1977): blind powers imposing themselves externally on individuals, who have no real power to escape them; Foucault defines these powers as having an ontological, conceptual, and normative primacy of identity. This explosive set of ideas is, in my opinion, neither true nor coherent, but it does lead to seeing the world in an essentially moral, even religious and dogmatic, way, as a place of cleavage and opposition between dominated and dominant, between executioners and victims. The slightest challenge to what stems from this view – namely, from the obligation to take the side of the oppressed – is held up as a moral fault that calls for a condemnation in much the same way as religion used to condemn sinners or unbelievers.

Researchers have sought to verify what looks very much like my hypothesis and the results they have arrived at are astounding. This episode, which is not well known, is called the "grievance studies affair." The authors (James A. Lindsay, Peter Boghossian, and Helen Pluckrose) proposed and sometimes succeeded in publishing, in supposedly serious peer-reviewed academic journals, absolutely nonsensical articles: one studied rape culture among dogs in dog parks; another advocated for various ways to make bodybuilding non-oppressive for the obese; another encouraged men to use anal sex toys in order to combat homophobia and transphobia; and yet another called for white male students to attend college classes chained to the floor (Lagerspetz 2020). What was targeted here was the whole area of academic study and research inspired in part by postmodernism and identity theories, for which the pranksters thought the conclusion alone counted as long as it conformed to the received dogma and was accepted no matter how vacuous or even stupid the argument presented to support it. This conclusion comes to the defence of a group defined by an identity conferred upon it by an oppression or an (intersectional) system of oppressions. This defence is almost religious in nature: whoever does not take part in the defence commits a grievous fault of an almost unbelieving nature, a sin. And this partly explains the virulence of the remarks reserved for that person by people one is tempted to call the members of the sect.

I think – but let everyone judge for themselves – that this scenario sheds light on certain aspects of our recent debates and on a certain retreat from the ideals of the Enlightenment. I think it likely that all of this leads to serious conceptual flaws in the analysis of social issues and problems; that these flaws in turn lead to seriously inaccurate diagnoses; and that, ultimately, the public policies proposed and adopted end up harming the populations they were intended to help. In any case, we can always dream, as I do, of a healthier and more serene democratic conversation and one that touches on highly controversial subjects, and we can hope that the academic world will contribute to this conservation in a generous and significant way.

Notes

1 Act Respecting the Laicity of the State, SQ 2019, c. 12.

2 Law on the Separation of the Church and State, December 9, 1905, https://www.legifrance.gouv.fr/loda/id/legitext000006070169.

3 Loi établissant la gratuité absolue de l'enseignement primaire dans les écoles publiques, Law no. 164, June 17, 1881; Loi sur l'enseignement primaire obligatoire, Law no. 87, March 29, 1882.

4 Parliamentary Assembly of the Council of Europe, Resolution 2318 on Protection of Freedom of Religion or Belief in the Workplace, 2020, http://assembly.coe.int/nw/xml/XRef/Xref-XML2HTML-en.asp?fileid=28556&lang=en.

References

Baillargeon, Normand. 2015. "Deux concepts de laïcité et leurs enjeux." In *Laïcité et humanisme*, edited by Charles Le Blanc, 109–21. Ottawa: University of Ottawa Press.

–, ed. 2016. *Anarchisme et Éducation. Anthologie*. Vol. 1: *1793–1918*. Montreal: M. Editor.

Baillargeon, Normand, and Jean-Marc Piotte, eds. 2012. *Le Québec en quête de laïcité*. Montreal: Écosociété.

Baubérot, Jean. 2017. *Histoire de la laïcité en France*. Paris: Presses universitaires de France.

Bosset, Pierre. 2013. "Réflexions d'un juriste sur l'idée d'interdire le port de signes religieux aux agents de l'État." *Vivre ensemble* 20 (70): 1–9. https://cjf.qc.ca/wp-content/uploads/upload/ve_bulletins/3236_a_VE_Art_P.Bosset_No70_Port-signes-religieux-agents-etat.pdf.

Brunet-Giry, Martine. 2012. "Ferdinand Buisson et James Guillaume, une histoire d'amitié." *La Révolution prolétarienne* 777: 1–9. http://www.antimythes.fr/individus/guillaume_james/rp_777_12_06.pdf.

–. 2014. *Ferdinand Buisson et les socialistes libertaires*. Lichères-sur-Yonne: M. Brunet-Giry.

Buisson, Ferdinand. 1902a. *La foi laïque. Extraits de discours et écrits 1878–1944*. Edited by Mireille Gueissaz, 1–12. Latresne: Éditions Le Bord de l'eau.

–. 1902b. "Liberté de l'enseignement." In *La foi laïque. Extraits de discours et écrits 1878–1944*, edited by Mireille Gueissaz, 122–23. Latresne: Éditions Le Bord de l'eau. http://www.inrp.fr/edition-electronique/lodel/dictionnaire-ferdinand-buisson/document.php?id=3059.

1911. "Laïcité." In *Nouveau dictionnaire de pédagogie et d'instruction primaire*. Paris: Hachette. http://www.inrp.fr/edition-electronique/lodel/dictionnaire-ferdinand-buisson/document.php?id=3003.

–. 2003. *Éducation et République*. Introduction by Pierre Hayat. Paris: Kimé.

–. 2017. *Dictionnaire de pédagogie et d'instruction primaire*, edited by Patrick Dubois and Philippe Meirieu, preface by Pierre Nora. Paris: Robert Laffont.

Cabanel, Patrick. 2016. *Ferdinand Buisson: père de l'école laïque*. Geneva: Labor et Fides.

Cadier-Rey, Gabrielle. 2015. "Review of Martine Brunet-Giry, *Ferdinand Buisson et les socialistes libertaires*." *Bulletin de la Société d'Histoire du Protestantisme Français* 161: 305.

Foucault, Michel. 1977. *Surveiller et punir*, Paris: Gallimard. Translated as *Discipline and Punish*, trans. Alan Sheridan. New York: Pantheon.

Guillaume, James. 1905. *L'Internationale: documents et souvenirs (1864–1878)*. Paris: Stock.

Lagerspetz, Mikko. 2020. "'The Grievance Studies Affair' Project: Reconstructing and Assessing the Experimental Design." *Science, Technology and Human Values* 46 (3): 402–24.

Lyotard, Jean-François. 1979. *La condition postmoderne: Rapport sur le savoir*. Paris: Minuit.
MacIntyre, Alasdair. 1984. *After Virtue*. 2nd ed. Notre-Dame, IN: University of Notre Dame Press.
Taylor, Charles. 1989. *Sources of the Self: The Making of the Modern Identity*. Cambridge: Cambridge University Press.
Walzer, Michael. 1983. *Spheres of Justice*. Oxford: Blackwell.

Secularism and the Symbolic

The Quebec School as a Place of Immanent Knowledge

12

PAUL SABOURIN

Most people involved in the Quebec debate on secularism agree on the need for a separation between the state and religions, although there are differences between their respective positions. The disagreements between the proponents of unqualified secularism and those favouring open secularism lie in the way in which secularism is brought about and the implications of this separation. This chapter will consider one of these disagreements – namely, the wearing of religious signs by teachers and school directors. In a pluralistic society, wearing religious signs can offend the freedom of conscience and religion of children and parents. As a sociologist of knowledge, I cannot reduce the question of the meaning given to religious objects to a personal, subjective, or psychological dimension alone. Meaning is always developed within social entities. Meaning brings into play languages and social objects that form a part of social relations and situations and are themselves inserted into social spaces constituting societies. Discourses and objects participate in the construction of these social entities. For several reasons that I will outline below, experiential and religious knowledge cannot and should not be transmitted through the school.

Instead, the school is the place for immanent knowledge, which, by virtue of its properties as a form of knowledge, can be considered a common good. I am in favour of unqualified secularism. I maintain that the separation of the state and religion implies that representatives of the state do not intervene in spiritual or religious affairs by any means whatever, whether in symbolic practices or in practices with material implications. In actual practice, the state therefore upholds its neutrality with respect to all kinds of spiritual or religious commitments. Neutrality does not mean arbitrating between spiritual beliefs with impartiality but, rather, that the spiritual dimension of human life and organizations is placed outside the domain of action of the state. Unqualified secularism endorses the pluralism that characterizes Quebec society. This pluralism can not only be observed at the individual level but also in the constitution of social spaces (private, public, and collective state) that are differentiated by their own rules. Pluralism is manifested in the organization of social life. In such a pluralist social configuration, it is vital that the state space be free of religious references so that the state can properly fulfill its role of instituting the collective.

As Guy Rocher (2011, 10–14) points out, during Quebec's socio-historical development, it can be seen that a series of political measures aimed at ensuring the secular character of the state has already been adopted and implemented. The fact remains that the separation of church and state is far from complete, and this fact is borne out by the state's subsidies to private denominational schools, just to consider an example from the educational domain. Nonetheless, secularism is of a more assertive character in Quebec than in the rest of Canada. Indeed, since the Quiet Revolution, Quebeckers have valued the state as a place for collective action more than other Canadians have (Côté, Lévesque, and Morneau 2015). At the cognitive level, social issues are articulated based on the kind of secularism advocated: in the case of unqualified secularism, by favouring political semantics (democracy, citizenship, and so on), or, in the case of open secularism, by favouring the economic semantics of liberal ideology (economic integration, individual rights, and so on).

According to this latter conception of open secularism, Quebec has already achieved the separation of church and state by secularizing society. But this secularization, which is an ongoing process, is also due to the action of the Quebec state, and this is a blind spot in the analyses of the proponents of open secularism, who rarely mention this subject. For them, religions today have only very limited functions of social regulation. Moreover, proponents of open secularism do not see how the wearing of religious symbols by state employees, or the financial assistance provided by the state to religious organizations or their activities (through subsidies or tax exemptions), undermines the separation between the state and religion. Nevertheless, the proponents of open secularism – for example, those who agree with the arguments of the Bouchard-Taylor Commission's report – recognize that the neutrality of the state, in its sovereign functions, is less evident when employees in a position of coercive authority are the ones wearing religious symbols, and this is why they agree to prohibit them (Bouchard and Taylor 2008).

The drafting and adoption of the Act Respecting the Laicity of the State (Bill 21) and subsequent legal challenges have focused debates on laicity in schools.[1] These debates have in turn highlighted the socio-symbolic presuppositions on which the various visions of secularism are based. The back-and-forth media exchanges between Gérard Bouchard and Guy Rocher in the spring of 2019 illustrate this point.

Secularism and the Symbolic

In support of open secularism, Gérard Bouchard (2019) argues that there is no research demonstrating the influence on students of religious symbols worn by teachers. For his part, Rocher (2019) explains that it is impossible to carry out conclusive research in this area and calls for invoking the precautionary principle to justify the ban on religious symbols in schools, along the lines of the already existing ban on political symbols. Rocher sees this as a matter of respecting the freedom of conscience and religious freedom of children and their parents, which we know are diverse in today's pluralistic society.

The symbolic is not only a social construction: it participates in the very construction of what we call social activities, social places, and social spaces (Livet and Nef 2009). As a researcher in the sociology of knowledge, I believe that the lack of persuasive research on this neuralgic question of the symbolic constitution of the state can be explained on political, more than on scientific, grounds. Not only are ethics committees reluctant to approve research that involves experimentation with children, but the right of withdrawal of parents upholding various religious and spiritual conceptions (such as agnosticism and atheism) would make the validity of the results problematic. Even on a scientific level, such research would be complicated. At the very least, it would be necessary to conduct a comparative study, without and with various religious signs, among parents and children of various religions and spiritual practices, in a series of social environments representative of Quebec over a long enough period to grasp the social implications in the children's learning and in the relations between parents, teachers, and school administrators. To these methodological constraints, we should add, as several sociologists have noted (Berthelot 2003; Becker 2020), that most of the time research in the social sciences and sociology reproduces ideological cleavages rather than resolving them, especially when they involve controversial political issues. Indeed, in the social sciences, we have not managed to get researchers supporting different theses to agree on a common empirical test to determine the value of each explanation of a phenomenon.

Even if we need to rely on the precautionary principle more than on the results of empirical research in order to ban the wearing of religious symbols by teachers and other school personnel in positions of authority, it remains that we can infer, from the current state of knowledge on socio-symbolic activities, that the regulation of knowledge in the school space would suffer from cognitive dissonance if it were to be constituted otherwise. In fact, it is possible to apply general findings in the sociology of knowledge and the sociology of Quebec to better understand how the social regulation of knowledge is transformed. This would also enable us to understand how these transformations, rather than being totally arbitrary, refer to specific social necessities resulting from collective social learning and leading Quebec democracy to adopt Bill 21, which prohibits the wearing of religious symbols in the school setting in the same way as the wearing of political symbols is also prohibited.[2]

Social Symbols and Their Uses with Respect to Secularism

For proponents of open secularism, the teacher wearing a religious sign does not hinder the secularism of the state because children and parents will perceive in it an individual manifestation, a symbolic reality parallel to the teacher's professional discourse. Does this view not reduce the school to a mere delivery point of educational services? Does the person representing the state not become a mere service provider, like in the private sector? We sometimes hear that a distinction should be drawn between the state and the people. It would seem to be delving into metaphysics to argue that the state, as an institution, exists separately from the concrete social arrangements and living reality of state representatives. In fact, these representatives constantly renew the state by means of their presence, actions, and words.

For the proponents of unqualified secularism, people who manifest their religious beliefs and a religious practice (such as the wearing of a religious sign) in the educational setting can create dissonance with the beliefs of children and parents. These beliefs are transmitted not only through what teachers say but also, perhaps even more importantly, through the teachers' attitudes and behaviours since teachers can be taken as role models by learners. Beyond arguments like this, the polemics over laicity reveal that taking a stand on the effects or lack of effects in using religious (or political, or commercial) symbols in schools presupposes a conception of human symbolic activity and of the way in which this activity intervenes in the make-up of human practices. Research in the sociology of knowledge has made it possible to bring to light the way in which social semantics constructing social representations are constituted and generalized.

In this respect, some proponents of open secularism argue that, in a pluralist society, the meaning of symbolic objects is very fluid. According to this view, each person has the creative freedom to invest a religious object with another meaning or to give it no meaning at all – in short, to "divert" its original meaning. In fact, the meaning of a social object is always updated as much by those sending it as by those receiving it. But can this be done in a stand-alone fashion, without reference to social groups or to society taken as a whole, that still recognizes the original meaning of the object and has succeeded in establishing its dominant meaning? Much research work in the sociology of knowledge shows that, empirically, human beings acquire the language and the meaning of social objects in relation to others, starting with their parents (Sabourin 1997). A person's mental activity reproduces dialogues between socially constituted points of view resulting from their social relations. This is done in an environment that, moreover, has developed concretely over time and shared a still generally common meaning about important objects such as religious signs.[3] The metaphysical vision, according to which the individual mind creates meaning on its own, does not stand up to critical analysis.

Convictions and Beliefs, Social Objectivity, and Scientific Objectivity

This link between secularism and symbolism is central when we talk about the secular school in a democratic society. Through its programs and teaching methods, the school institution has the role of transmitting what is considered necessary for the acquisition of common, communicable, and shared knowledge. Experiential knowledge or beliefs of all kinds are, of course, brought up at school. For example, teachers mention that some people believe in natural forces, in a state of nature of the human being (for example, *homo economicus*)[4] or in political "dogmas" that reduce human experience to a single and universal value, the way propaganda does. But it is not the school's role to transmit such beliefs. Indeed, starting in the 1960s, the Quebec Ministry of Education has expected teachers to help young people think critically about beliefs or experiential knowledge.

Teachers are therefore called on to distinguish between, on the one hand, experiential beliefs and, on the other hand, knowledge acquired through critical thinking, which includes scientific knowledge. The secular school must promote a critique of the foundations and limits of different kinds of social knowledge, including its own experiential knowledge, and this in turn ensures the school's coherence and credibility. Churches, political parties and movements, democratic states, and, nowadays, multinational Internet companies with their algorithms all operate a form of social regulation of knowledge. The questions of democratic control and determining the content of school education become all the more important so that we may preserve and consolidate the central role of the school in socialization and in the regulation of knowledge of the immanent world. Proponents of open secularism claim that secularized societies offer, by their very secularization, the best guarantee that our schools are henceforth fully secular. But this view has not really been thought through. Indeed, in societies nowadays, new forms of religious social regulation are at work: we can see that ideologists are trying to use certain totalizing religious rationales to shape public perceptions of the immanent world.[5]

From the Metaphysics of Meaning to the Discovery of Its Materiality

Many of the arguments supporting open secularism stem from a metaphysical and, by the same token, a meta-social approach to the production of meaning. To speak of the deep conviction of individuals or of an individual "will" to give a different meaning to an object identified with religion supposes that the "individual mind" creates that meaning. This confronts us with a particular representation of society, which is supposedly made up of a multitude of actions taken by individual nomads who think on their own and then act collectively. This approach does not stand the empirical test. Ever since the first works appeared on the sociology of memory (Halbwachs 1925), it has been shown that one can only think in social interaction with others. This observation does not deny the psychological dimension of thought, and it makes clear that thought is also irreducibly social, which is why theorists of unqualified secularism are justified in saying that the person using an object of appearance wants to impose it in the place where the memory reference of a group is located and in the social places with which they are associated. According to the state of social knowledge and the characteristics of the sign itself, everyone can identify the social group to which a particular sign is linked.

Human beings think through language and by using language. This observation applies to all symbolic forms including symbolic objects. From the point of view of open secularism, the religious sign is only an expression of an intention that is conveyed without this use of language and symbolic objects. But language and symbolic objects are more than a mere expression: they are the immanent place where thought takes place. The intention does not exist outside the activity of thought unless one considers thought as a purely metaphysical phenomenon. The semiologist Jean Molino (1985) highlights this discovery of secular interpretation in his history of interpretation: meaning has a physical materiality (sounds, traces on paper, monuments, arrangements). When we seek to interpret a text, we need to reconstitute its production by human beings, we need to describe the properties of the constructed socio-symbolic objects, and we need to understand how they are received socially.

However, as its name indicates, religious hermeneutics (at least in the case of revealed religions) supposes instead that meaning is divinely revealed to the faithful: meaning is conveyed through contact with discourses and objects, notably during religious rituals. As Molino (1985) mentions, the activity of scholarly religious interpretation of texts is certainly a rational activity, yet it employs this rationality to solidify the coherence of religious symbols, and, in so doing, it brings us back to the revelation of divine reality. If we consider how religious knowledge has evolved, we see a multiplication of interpretations throughout history rather than the setting down of common knowledge on the meaning of texts and divine objects. When intellectuals or religious leaders seek to impose their own interpretations, they must rely on their authority or their ability to arouse admiration and adherence. This way of transmitting interpretations takes us very far from argumentative thought.

Secular hermeneutics is based on the immanence of the production of meaning. In the history of interpretation, we are therefore witnessing a transition from a mythical mode of knowledge (where human facts are determined by superior forces) to an ideological mode of knowledge where human reality is posited as immanent: the human world is explained by the history of human actions (Houle 1979). Any interpretation can be questioned even in its foundations by studying the concrete conditions of its development over time – and this includes religious knowledge. Meaning becomes debatable as much for its content as for its organization and the way in which it has been established. This is where the democratic debate is grounded on the socio-symbolic level. Any political statement can be questioned in the shaping of the human experience which has produced it. Interpretation is both founded and relative, it gives an account of a certain point of view of human reality, and it must be confronted with the other interpretations to produce collective intelligence of a shared immanent experience. In the sciences, we see explicitly laid out all the elements and operations that come together in the construction of scientific facts. But the diverse forms of ideological knowledge imply a reference to an empirical test, whose rules are implicit or at least not very explicit.[6] In other words, ideological knowledge is transmitted through controversies between interpretations that become common referents: the debate between unqualified secularism and open secularism and the forms it takes is a common referent to this ideological debate.

Unlike political ideologies, the scientific process involves bringing together evidence by reducing it to a single limited dimension, explicitly defined, of one aspect of reality: the physical, the biological, the social, and so on. We can also situate knowledge from the point of view of the transmission of meaning. The accumulation of scientific knowledge can be communicated to all social beings, whatever their "natural" language and their social origins, provided they are educated and master the rules of verification.[7] On the other hand, one cannot live one's life scientifically because science can only make sense of what can be structured, which constitutes only a very limited part of the totality of reality (Granger 1982). Ideological knowledge takes forms that are not explicitly constructed: these forms depend on common sense and professional rules that ensure a certain constancy. Forms of ideological knowledge are not developed by reducing the real to a single dimension: instead, they consider immanent reality from the point of view of its totality. For example, politics addresses what exists only from the point of view of what ought to exist in all human activities. Philosophy is a borderline case. The epistemologist and philosopher Gilles-Gaston Granger (1991) posits that philosophy addresses the existential meanings of the shaping of experience by different kinds of knowledge because experience in its entirety eludes them: whether we are concerned with ordinary knowledge or different kinds of scientific knowledge, we make different types of abstractions that distinguish by means of contrast the presence of this character of totality of the real. Experiential and religious knowledge, which mystics define based on what they experience, cannot be directly expressed since no language and no object produced by the human being is up to the task. We are here in the realm of that which cannot be communicated. This kind of knowledge can therefore not form the basis of common knowledge in a pluralist society.

These brief statements of the properties of the forms of knowledge are taken from scholarly works in the field of comparative analytical epistemology and the theory of socio-symbolic interpretation.[8] The social rules assigning properties and status to social forms of knowledge and social discourse do not spring up during workshops between intellectuals. Implicit epistemological rules are formed over the course of the history of societies, and these epistemological rules concern an accepted social objectivity that aims at agreeing on referents concerning the determination of what reality is, of the ways of knowing it, and of what the various forms of knowledge enable us to know (Houle 1979). The debate on "fake news" provides one example, among others, showing that we need to update these rules.

The argument we put forward here is that the school in Quebec has gained its autonomy from the churches as well as from political parties. The school has done this in order to transmit a mode of ideological knowledge through various forms of knowledge in the sciences and the humanities: this mode is the relationship to discourses and symbolic objects defined by critical thinking. This mode of ideological knowledge is not to be confused with the particular discourse of political propaganda: instead, this mode considers human activities from an immanent point of view, including the activities that enable us to know them. Since the Quiet Revolution, the school has become one of the pillars in the edification of liberal political democracy in Quebec. The secularization of the school has taken place in stages. The deconfessionalization of Quebec's school boards in 1997 structured this secularization. But, before that, from the early 1960s, priests and nuns in Quebec took part in the process of secularization, in terms of discourse and the wearing of signs, by continuing to teach while removing traditional religious garments (cassocks, habits, and so on). In so doing, these priests and nuns avoided creating any cognitive dissonance between a secular discourse and the manifestation of religious signs that refer to places where a mythical relationship to the world is lived such as places of worship. In other words, the socio-historical development of knowledge in Quebec has led to the relativization not only of religious knowledge but also of all social knowledge and even of scientific knowledge.[9] The precise meaning that I give to the word "relativization" is different from the meaning of arbitrary cultural words. Relativizing knowledge means grasping its foundations as well as its limits, determining its relevant field of application (and therefore identifying what exceeds the relevance of such knowledge), and evaluating the means by which it is transmitted.

Bill 21 has been enacted by the Quebec government. This legislation avoids imposing a paradoxical injunction on children in elementary school children, teenagers in secondary school, and their parents, an injunction that would have undermined their commitment to public school. At the same time, the act avoids exposing them to the demands of state representatives to distance themselves from their own experiential or religious knowledge so that their children can learn critical thinking in the school setting, based on immanent human knowledge. It also avoids requiring them to accept that these same teacher representatives could, for their part, display their beliefs and conceptions of religious practice or, by means of these same signs, convictions that could be political in nature. The Quebec secular school clearly establishes that it is responsible for immanent human knowledge and the way to transmit such knowledge as well as critical thinking. And, in so doing, the Quebec secular school assumes realistically and with coherence some of the social requirements for the transmission of immanent knowledge, which can thus appear as a common good of all citizens.

Notes

1 Act Respecting the Laicity of the State, SQ 2019, c. 12.

2 In this chapter, we present a pragmatic conception of reason that is neither transcendent, nor universal, nor contextual; it is developed in collective social learning and forms social rationalities that can be more or less general (see De Munck 1999; Houle 1999). We could also make the connection between the criticism of political patronage in Quebec and the ban on political signs in the public service.

3 Commonality can be observed in social representations by the presence of a central core of notions despite individual variations and the diversity of social groups in a social whole (Vergès 2003).

4 It should be noted that for a long time the theorists of the economic "sciences" were identified along the lines of the religious distinction between orthodox thinkers

and heterodox thinkers, and, nowadays, even neo-liberal theorists try to base their observations on human nature not on universal dogmas but, rather, on research on psychology and neuroscience.

5 On this subject, see the positions taken by Alexis Cossette-Trudel, a very popular YouTuber and anti-masker in Quebec, on wearing a mask for COVID-19, who, we learn, has a background in religious semiology (Bélair-Cirino 2020).

6 Let us take a simple example of ordinary knowledge. We all say: "the sun rises in the morning," a statement that is false in astronomical terms but has the operative value of providing us with a reference giving a rhythm to our everyday life. The social frameworks of "everyday life" give shape to what is perceived from a socially localized point of view "with both feet on the ground," which constitutes the implicit rules of the knowledge/experience relation here.

7 In science, the meaning of the contents of a statement is determined by the morphosyntactic relation that defines this meaning. For example, we can cite in this respect the symbolic basis of the impressive capacity for international cooperation of researchers who have demonstrated that global warming is really occurring.

8 On this subject, we may consult Gilles-Gaston Granger's (1982, 1991) prolific work of analytical philosophy, which not only presents an epistemology of the sciences in their unity and diversity but also addresses the humanities and the social sciences.

9 As science communicator and astrophysicist Neil de Grasse Tyson points out in the conclusion of his audio series entitled *The Inexplicable Universe*, the state of a science has both internal and external limitations (see Sprenkel 2012–16). Contemporary physics explains only a very limited part of the universe because science captures only a very small dimension of reality.

References

Becker, Howard S. 2020. *Faire preuve: Des faits aux théories*. Paris: La Découverte.

Bélair-Cirino, Mario. 2020. "Portrait d'un homme 'en révolte.'" *Le Devoir*, September 19.

Berthelot, Jean-Michel. 2003. "Plaidoyer pour un pluralisme sous contrainte." *Revue européenne de sociologie* 41 (126): 35–49.

Bouchard, Gérard. 2019. "Un projet de loi 'radical' sur la laïcité, dit Gérard Bouchard." Interview conducted by Anne-Marie Dussault. *Radio-Canada*, April 9. https://ici.radio-canada.ca/nouvelle/1163447/laicite-projet-loi-gerard-bouchard-entrevue.

Bouchard, Gérard, and Charles Taylor. 2008. *Building the Future. A Time for Reconciliation*. Quebec City: Commission de consultation sur les pratiques d'accommodement reliées aux différences culturelles. https://numerique.banq.qc.ca/patrimoine/details/52327/1565995.

Coté, Louis, Benoît Lévesque, and Guy Morneau. 2015. "La gouvernance au Québec: rôle de l'État et participation citoyenne." *L'Observatoire de l'administration publique-ENAP,* October. https://cerberus.enap.ca/Observatoire/docs/Etude_gouvernance/Texte_gouvernance.pdf.

De Munck, Jean. 1999. *L'Institution sociale de l'esprit. Nouvelles approches de la raison*. Paris: Presses universitaires de France.

Granger, Gilles-Gaston. 1982. "Modèles qualitatifs, modèles quantitatifs dans la connaissance scientifique." *Sociologie et sociétés* 14 (1): 7–13.

–. 1991. "Science, idéologie et philosophie." *Raison présente* 97: 91–95.

Halbwachs, Maurice. 1925. *Les cadres sociaux de la mémoire*. Paris: Presses universitaires de France.

Houle, Gilles. 1979. "L'idéologie: un mode de connaissance." *Sociologie et sociétés* 11 (1): 123–45.

–. 1999. "La sociologie comme science du vivant: l'approche biographique." In *La recherche qualitative: Enjeux épistémologiques et méthodologiques,* edited by Jean Poupart, Jean-Pierre Deslauriers, Lionel-H. Groulx, Anne Laperrière, Robert Mayer, and Alavaro Pirès, 273–89. Montreal: Gaëtan Morin.

Livet, Pierre, and Frédéric Nef. 2009. *Les êtres sociaux. Processus et virtualité*. Paris: Éditions Hermann.

Molino, Jean. 1985. "Pour une histoire de l'interprétation: les étapes de l'herméneutique." *Philosophiques* 12 (1): 73–103.

Rocher, Guy. 2011. "Laïcité de l'État et des institutions publiques." In *Le Québec en quête de laïcité,* edited by Normand Baillargeon and Jean-Marc Piotte, 10–14. Montreal: Écosociété.

–. 2019. "L'enjeu de la laïcité." Interview conducted by Anne-Marie Dussault. *Radio-Canada,* May 14. https://www.youtube.com/watch?v=TxmqzW52jEE.

Sabourin, Paul, ed. 1997. "La mémoire sociale" (thematic issue). *Sociologie et sociétés* 29 (2): 139–61. http://classiques.uqac.ca/contemporains/sabourin_paul/memoire_soc_Halbwachs/memoire_soc.html.

Sprenkel, Hans. 2012–16. *The Inexplicable Universe with Neil deGrasse Tyson*. Documentary. IMDbPro Productions.

Vergès, Pierre. 2003. "18. Représentations sociales de l'économie: une forme de connaissances." In *Les représentations sociales,* edited by Denise Jodelet, 407–28. Paris: Presses Universitaires de France.

Conclusion
The Fate of Bill 21 in the Courts and in Public Opinion in English Canada

LUCIA FERRETTI AND FRANÇOIS ROCHER

This book was first published in French in November 2020. Since then, the Act Respecting the Laicity of the State (Bill 21) has been challenged in the Quebec Superior Court.[1] The judgment was pronounced on April 20, 2021.[2] We will first discuss these developments, including the arguments raised before the court, the judge's decision, as well as the reactions that this process has raised. This judicial process took place in Quebec, although it had important ramifications in the rest of Canada. Moreover, we can only note that the Quebec legislation was, to say the least, decried in the strongest terms by the political elite outside Quebec and received very negative media coverage. Second, we propose to report, albeit briefly, on the reception of Bill 21 in a few major newspapers in English Canada. For a fruitful and respectful discussion to take place, it seems to us that the essential prerequisite is to demonstrate a willingness to understand the reasons that led the Quebec government to intervene in order to better regulate the relationship between the state and religion, thereby imposing a framework on some of its employees who intervene on its behalf. However, this requirement has rarely been met. This book attempts to restore a certain balance.

Bill 21 in the Courts

Bill 21 was passed on June 16, 2019. Inspired by a strategy successfully deployed a year and a half earlier against the Act to Promote Respect for the Religious Neutrality of the State (Bill 62), the National Council of Canadian Muslims, the Canadian Civil Liberties Association, and Ichrak Nourel Hak (then a hijab-wearing education student) jointly and immediately challenged the law in the Quebec Superior Court.[3] They also requested that, pending the judgment on the merits, certain provisions of the law are suspended. In July 2019, the Quebec Superior Court refused to grant this last request.[4] Disappointed, the plaintiffs turned to the Quebec Court of Appeal. But, on December 12, 2019, the validity of the judgment was confirmed by Justice Robert M. Mainville, despite the dissent of Chief Justice Nicole Duval Hesler.[5]

These two courts therefore ruled that the law could remain in force pending a judgment on the merits. As for the Supreme Court of Canada, it refused in April 2020 to hear the opponents' appeal (*Journal de Montréal* 2019; Pineda and Riopel 2019; Labbé 2020). With the chief justice of the Quebec Court of Appeal to have publicly made comments that were very unfavourable to Bill 21 and having gone so far as to suggest a defence to opponents, the public began to seriously doubt her impartiality. In *Le Devoir*, renowned columnist Michel David (2019), who is also a political analyst for Radio-Canada television, did not hesitate to title one of his articles "La juge militante" ("The Activist Judge"). The judge was the subject of two formal complaints to the Conseil de la magistrature for failing to respect her duty of reserve. Her choice to take early retirement allowed the council to dismiss them. The vice-chair of the council's Judicial Conduct Committee, Glenn Joyal, said he did not think it would be in the public interest to pursue this complaint. Yet precedents exist for ethics decisions involving retired judges (*Radio-Canada* 2019; Canadian Press 2020; Court of Appeal of Quebec 2020).

The Trial on the Merits before the Superior Court: 2019–20

During the preparation of the trial on the merits before the Superior Court, the public had the opportunity to question the impartiality of two other judges – namely, the Honourable Eva Petras and the Honourable Marc-André Blanchard. It was initially agreed that the trial would take place before Judge Johanne Mainville. However, Associate Chief Justice Eva Petras of the Quebec Superior Court decided otherwise. She dismissed Justice Mainville on the grounds that her husband, Court of Appeal Justice Robert Mainville, had issued a favourable opinion on Bill 21 in his December 2019 ruling. Without lending thoughts to Justice Petras, one can surmise that either she doubted the professionalism of Justice Robert Mainville or that of Justice Johanne Mainville, whom she must have believed was susceptible to her husband's influence. As a result, the public became aware that she was a member of the Board of Directors of the Lord Reading Law Association. This group was appearing before the court to ask that Bill 21 be struck down. Not surprisingly, some wondered whether she was living up to her oath of impartiality (Robitaille 2021). Moreover, among all those who could have judged the case, Justice Petras chose Justice Marc-André Blanchard. In 2017, he was the one who suspended several provisions of Bill 62 before it even came into force. This appeared "disturbing" to many Quebeckers.

Finally, on November 2, 2020, the trial began at the Montreal courthouse. In addition to Ichrak Nourel Hak and her co-plaintiffs, other groups had asked that the law be struck down, in whole or in part, including the Fédération autonome de l'enseignement, which is a federation of nine teaching unions, and the English Montreal School Board. These separate challenges were merged into one. The Government of Quebec, the Mouvement laïque québécois, and the organization Pour les droits des femmes du Québec were among the supporters of Bill 21. Educaloi is a neutral and independent organization whose mission, in its own words, is legal education and clear communication of the law. It has published on its website a summary of the arguments for and against Bill 21 argued before the Quebec Superior Court (Educaloi 2020). We summarize them here.

Arguments against Bill 21

- Quebec violates the rule of law.
- Quebec has no jurisdiction to rule on religious symbols.

- Bill 21 violates section 23 of the Canadian Charter of Rights and Freedoms (Canadian Charter), which protects the right of the English-speaking minority to have their children educated in English.[6]
- Bill 21 contravenes section 28 of the Canadian Charter, which states that rights are guaranteed equally to male and female persons.

As can be seen, these arguments were aimed either at disqualifying once and for all Quebec's claim to legislate on the relationship between the state and religious organizations or at circumventing the notwithstanding clause in the Canadian Charter.

Arguments for Bill 21

- Seven parents and the Mouvement laïque québécois argued that the religious neutrality of teachers is a guarantee of respect for their children's freedom of conscience and their own freedom of religion. They argued that secularism gives precedence to the freedom of conscience of students over the desire of some teachers to display their religious beliefs ostentatiously and permanently in the classroom. Muslim parents have said that wearing the hijab in the classroom expresses a rigorous view of Islam that they disapprove of (Baril 2021).
- The Quebec government, on the other hand, reaffirmed that the law respects religious freedom and protects the equality of women and men. It argued that the purpose of the law is to ensure the equality of all before the state.

During the trial, pro-secularity observers noted that Justice Blanchard several times expressly indicated his closure to the arguments of the law's defendants and, on the contrary, his enthusiasm for the arguments of the opponents (Codsi, El-Mabrouk, and Girard 2020). Thus, the former awaited his judgment with apprehension, while the latter were filled with great confidence.

The Blanchard Decision

The judgment was released on April 20, 2021. Justice Blanchard did not accept arguments that the Quebec state had violated the rule of law or lacked jurisdiction over religious symbols, nor did he accept arguments that the law violated section 28 of the Canadian Charter.[7] His judgment upholds the validity of most of the law. But the judge admitted that he was bound by the government's decision to use the notwithstanding clause in the charters as a preventive measure to protect the law. Nevertheless, he refers to the Canadian Charter whenever possible. For example, he uses section 3 of the charter against section 8 of the Act Respecting the Laicity of the State to invalidate the prohibition on elected officials wearing religious symbols in the National Assembly. He uses section 23 (which declares the right of the English-speaking minority of education in English and to the management and control of its schools) to exempt English-language school boards from the obligation to respect the sections of Bill 21 relating to the wearing of religious symbols by persons in authority during their working hours.

The notwithstanding clause is an integral part of the Constitution Act, 1982, and was inserted at the request of the English-speaking provinces and the British Parliament. In the 1988 decision *Ford v Quebec (Attorney General)* on the language of commercial signage, the Supreme Court of Canada made it clear that a government does not even have to explain why it feels it is necessary to use it.[8] Justice Blanchard invited the courts, and, in particular, the Supreme Court, to better supervise the use of this clause by specifying the criteria that could justify its use. This has been interpreted as an indication that the judge believed that the Constitution leaves too much discretion to parliaments and elected members in this country (Jourmet 2021). Such an idea finds an audience among some legal scholars in English Canada (Leckey 2019). But constitutional scholar Benoît Pelletier (2021), a former minister in Jean Charest's Liberal governments and former assistant dean of the University of Ottawa's Faculty of Law, is concerned. In an expert opinion submitted to Justice Blanchard, he argued that Quebec, like all national minorities in the world, is under threat from the uniformizing effect of judicial decisions. For Pelletier, the notwithstanding clause allows the Quebec legislator to assert its own conception of the content and scope of fundamental rights, which is legitimate even if it differs from that of English Canada (Trudel 2021).

Quebec Liberal Party leader Dominique Anglade has said that if her party were to take power, it would not use the notwithstanding clause again to protect the law. *Le Devoir* political columnist Michel David (2021) notes that such a government would leave the law to the Canadian courts rather than risk the political cost of repeal, which would at least preserve the powers of the National Assembly. As for the left-wing Québec solidaire party, it broke with its tradition of support for secularism in 2019 to come out against any ban on religious symbols; however, its position became less clear at its November 2021 convention (Carabin 2021).

The Aftermath of the Blanchard Decision

The National Council of Canadian Muslims and the Canadian Civil Liberties Association, unhappy with the ruling, said that their fight against Bill 21 would continue because they believe it turns Quebeckers who wear religious symbols into "second-class citizens." The Fédération autonome de l'enseignement, also dissatisfied, maintained that the law infringes on its members' right to work. As for the Quebec government, it was of the opinion that Justice Blanchard erred in law when he ruled that the ban on the wearing of religious symbols by persons in authority in the school violates the right of anglophones to instruction in their language. For Minister Simon Jolin-Barrette, this is an overly broad interpretation of section 23 of the Canadian Charter, which has the effect of creating "two Quebecs," where one can escape the authority of the state. The government also challenged the decision to declare unconstitutional the requirement to uncover one's face to sit in the National Assembly (Bellerose 2021; Canadian Press 2021). As a result, all parties have appealed.

During the federal election campaign, the party leaders participated in a televised debate on September 9, 2021. Speaking to the leader of the Bloc Québécois, host Shachi Kurl asked a question that implied that Bills 21 and 96 (the latter amending the Charter of the French Language) were "discriminatory" and that Quebec "has a racism problem."[9] The case caused an uproar in Quebec. Expressing the widespread view, jurist and former Quebec government minister Benoît Pelletier (2021) called the issue "twisted, insipid, full of dubious amalgams, inaccuracies and imprecisions." The Quebec National Assembly called for an apology from the host and the debate broadcasting group, which never came (Lévesque 2021).

Wishing to override the presumption of constitutionality that applies to any law enacted pending the Quebec Court of Appeal's decision, the English Montreal School Board asked the court of appeal in October 2021 that the portion of the Blanchard decision concerning it be applied immediately. The Attorney General of Quebec and the Mouvement laïque québécois objected. In court, they argued that section 23 of the Canadian Charter grants constitutional rights to minority language instruction, not rights for English-speaking teachers to evade the law. Since no students would be deprived of their right to English-language instruction during and after the appeal, there would be no justification for the exemption request. The appeal was denied in a ruling issued on November 9, 2021 (Morasse 2021).

In the fall of 2021, the Western Quebec School Board hired a teacher for an elementary school in Chelsea and allowed her to remain veiled in class, even though both parties knew it was against the law. The Department of Education intervened, and the teacher retained her employment relationship but was reassigned to other duties. For lawyer Julius Grey, the case is proof that the law infringes on individual rights, but, for the Mouvement laïque québécois, it is more a political act of defiance (Roy-Charbonneau 2021). Daniel Baril (2021), president of this organization, points to the words of two leading figures in the opposition to the law as proof:

> In her testimony before the Superior Court, Ichrak Nourel Hak, the main plaintiff against Bill 21, repeatedly stated that removing her hijab to teach was a denial of "practicing one's religion." There is no international declaration that gives a believer the right to practice his religion at work ... Chelsea teacher Fatemeh Anvari said that wearing her veil was a sign of ideological and religious struggle: "For me, [the hijab] carries meaning. It's important for me to continue to wear it, because I know there are ideologies that don't want me to wear it. That's my resistance."

At the same time, we are witnessing a mobilization of the federal government and civil society groups against Bill 21. Ottawa is actively participating in the legal challenge to Bill 21 in several ways:

- The Canadian Human Rights Commission's complaint against Bill 21 is funded 100 percent by federal public funds (Baril 2021).
- The Trudeau government appointed lawyer Azim Hussain as a judge of the Quebec Superior Court. Hussain was involved in the legal challenge to Bill 21; in an exchange with Justice Blanchard, he did not directly or indirectly compare Bill 21 with the Nuremberg laws, but he did find a way to evoke them. This probably says something about both him and about the direction of the federal government (Leblanc 2021).
- Ottawa funds the Court Challenges Program, which is managed by the University of Ottawa. The main opponents of Bill 21 have already obtained one hundred thousand dollars from this program to pay the lawyer Julius Grey, who was awarded the contract without competition (Leblanc 2022a).
- The federal government has already announced that it will go to the Supreme Court of Canada when the challenge to Bill 21 is taken to that level. Minister David Lametti, a colleague of McGill University lawyer Robert Leckey, has hinted that the federal government will have its say on the Quebec government's use of the notwithstanding clause.

In Quebec, the new battle is over public opinion. Anti-legislation organizations are commissioning polls, the methodology of which may have been questioned, and they are disseminating and commenting widely on the results if they show some decline in support for the law, in the hope of triggering a movement of disaffection (*COR Communication* 2022; Lowrie 2022). Several experts and stakeholders have argued that these hearings could have been held in the spring or summer of 2022, but the court may have preferred to avoid the inevitable stirrings of these hearings spilling over into the political arena in Quebec during an election year (Leblanc 2022b).

Bill 21 as Seen through the Lens of English Canada's Newspapers: No Debate, Just Condemnation

It is, of course, possible and even legitimate to express disagreement with Bill 21. Prohibiting certain categories of government employees from wearing religious symbols can be criticized from the perspective of a certain understanding of the principle of freedom of conscience and religion that gives precedence to individual rights. Another approach, as discussed in this book, holds that this prohibition is not incompatible with the principles of secularism. Indeed, several European countries have adopted similar or even more restrictive measures as they affect students attending public schools at the local or national level (Germany, Belgium, Netherlands, France, Switzerland, and Denmark). These laws may affect not only government employees but also citizens in their public activities or even conditions of employment in the private sector. The European Court of Human Rights recognizes the right of member states to impose limits on freedom of conscience and religion in order to guarantee the secular organization of public institutions. In this respect, Quebec is not an aberration or an anomaly in pluralistic liberal democracies. Yet, to read the English-language newspapers in Canada, one would think that Quebec is on the fringe of liberal societies and that the worst abuses against ethnocultural or religious minorities are taking place there. In other words, the analyses and opinions expressed in the newspapers have been largely one-dimensional since Bill 21 was introduced.

This conclusion is not unreasonable. We conducted an analysis of opinion or analysis pieces (columns, editorials, commentaries, and letters to the editor) expressed in four major newspapers based on their readership across Canada or in selected regions from the end of March 2019 to the end of September 2022. The search excluded factual articles. For the purposes of this study, we selected the *Globe and Mail* (the most widely read newspaper), the *Toronto Star* (the second-largest newspaper in Canada) and, to ensure we did not have an Ontario-centric bias, the *Calgary Herald* and the *Chronicle Herald* (Halifax). We used the Eureka and Factiva databases and a keyword search (secular*, Bill 21, laici*). In the end, 237 articles were identified for the period. Figure C.1 shows that the first two newspapers gave more prominence to this debate, while it

Figure C.1 Occurrences: March 2019–September 2022

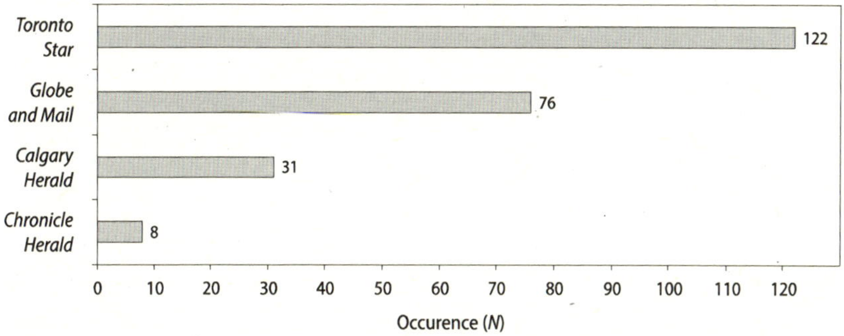

was clearly less present in the pages of the *Calgary Herald* (31) and the *Chronicle Herald* (8).

In the end, 87.7 percent of the articles were negative about Bill 21. As Figure C.2 shows, it was proportionately less well received in the Prairies and Atlantic provinces, although almost 19 percent of views were favourable in the *Globe and Mail*. However, this is a far cry from a "debate" in that those who support the legislation were significantly under-represented. In other words, there was a strong imbalance in the points of view put forward so that readers were literally bombarded with comments denouncing, sometimes virulently, both the approach put forward by the Quebec government and Quebec society as a whole.

Figure C.2 Negative, neutral, and positive opinions (%)

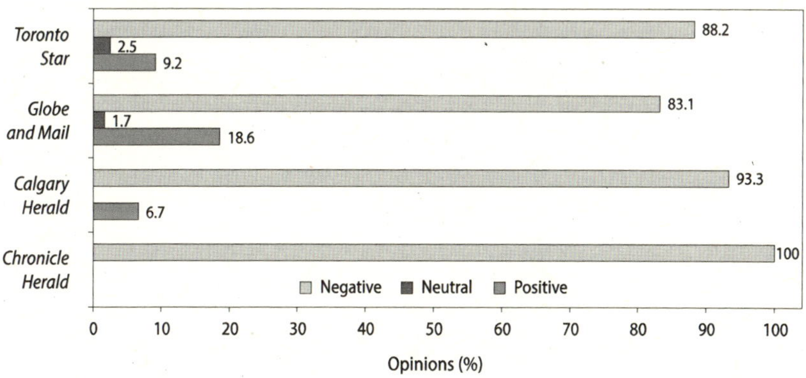

While there was no real debate, and Bill 21 has been widely criticized, a closer analysis reveals the main arguments put forward. The recurring arguments relate to the discriminatory nature of the provisions concerning the prohibition of the wearing of religious symbols by certain government employees. It should be noted that the requirement to obtain services with an "uncovered face" raised a few comments, and, while Bill 21 was directly criticized following its introduction, several articles published over the past two years linked it to other events and used it as a foil to denounce what they considered to be abject values in Canada. In total, 66.7 percent of the arguments referred to some form of discrimination or social exclusion, sometimes in its most ignominious expressions. Within this broad category, discrimination based on limitations on religious freedom was most often denounced (55.1 percent), followed by accusations of Islamophobia or measures that specifically targeted Muslim women (27.6 percent), and even a sizeable proportion of racism (17.3 percent) or xenophobia (5.4 percent).

Some articles used more than one argument. For example, in the wake of the removal of a teacher from her classroom in December 2021, a *Toronto Star* (2021, IN6) editorial argued that "Quebec's Bill 21, the law that bars people who wear 'religious symbols' like kippas or hijabs from a range of jobs in public institutions, is an abomination. It's the clearest example in recent years of a law that is frankly, unapologetically discriminatory against religious and, in some cases, racial minorities." In the *Chronicle Herald,* following the attack on a Pakistani family in London, Ontario, the author, a professor of sociology and Muslim studies option, could not refrain from making a connection with Bill 21: "Bill 21, the Quebec law that bans civil servants from wearing religious symbols, follows decades of policies mandating the coerced unveiling of Muslim women who wear Islamic attire that effectively institutionalizes gendered Islamophobia ... Through these policies and practices, liberal Islamophobia normalizes anti-Muslim racism and constructs Muslims as suspect and inferior citizens" (Zine 2021, A12). Academic researchers write that "our research shows that laws like Bill 21 can have much worse consequences for religious minorities than the specific provisions they entail. Such laws also embolden those who harbor deep-seated xenophobia – specifically, Islamophobia – and they therefore intensify minorities' encounters of hostility and mistreatment" (Doering and Peker 2019, A11). In sum, the prevailing view is that Bill 21 is not only discriminatory, but also fuels and legitimizes Islamophobic sentiment and actions across Canada.

While more than half of the arguments relate to discrimination, others condemn it as inconsistent with the "Canadian values" enshrined in the Canadian Charter and the Canadian Multiculturalism Act.[10] For example, 15.7 percent of the arguments refer to the un-Canadian character of Bill 21. The use of the notwithstanding clause is often cited as evidence of this criticism. Not only are the Quebec political elites who support this legislation in violation of the Canadian Charter and multiculturalism, but the debate over secularism in Quebec also masks an aversion to diversity on the part of many Quebeckers. While such sentiments may be present in the rest of Canada, political actors are far-sighted and generous enough not to go so far as to trample on fundamental rights. In this regard, the editorial in the *Toronto Star* (2019, A16) a few days after the bill was introduced speaks volumes:

> If this was happening in any other province, under a conservative government in, say, Alberta or Ontario, liberal-minded people would not hesitate to call it out for what it is – bigotry, even racism given that the minorities most obviously targeted are Muslims and Sikhs. But because it's happening in Quebec, many of the same kind of people counsel us not to go down that path ... The reality, though, is that many Quebeckers are less concerned with debating the fine points of secularism than with something more visceral. They don't think they and their society should be required to adapt to the minorities among them. The burden, they believe, should be the other way around. Quite a few English-Canadians have felt the same way over the years. But political leaders outside Quebec, from all major parties, have generally resisted the temptation to pander to the fear of newcomers. They have upheld the rights of minorities and the importance of the Charter. Beyond all that, it's important that Canadians hold fast to the principle that the majority should not ride roughshod over the rights of the minority, that mutual accommodation is the only way to make a multicultural society work for everyone.

Many comments are along the same lines, contrasting Quebec's obscurantism with a rather jovial rereading of Canadian history. Are we supposed to believe Canada never supported the oppression and dispossession of its original inhabitants, had no openly racist immigration policy until the mid-1960s, did not abolish the rights of French-Speaking Canadians in Ontario and the Prairie provinces, and never opposed the recognition of Quebec's distinctiveness as a constituent reality of Canada? For example, a letter from a Calgary reader to the *Toronto Star* argues that "Quebec's secularism bill (Bill 21) is an attack on Canadian values of multiculturalism and religious freedom. This is a stain on Canada's wonderful history of inclusivity and celebration of cultural differences. Simply put, this bill is extremely un-Canadian and must be condemned in the strongest possible terms ... Thus, this bill seeks to discriminate based on religious values and is a violation of basic human rights. The foundations of Canada were not laid to be dismantled like this" (Malik 2019, A12). This means that there is only one way to organize the relationship between the state and religions, and any other form of arrangement must be denounced.

Finally, the use of the notwithstanding clause was debated and criticized (3 percent of the arguments), and some individuals invited the political authorities to take measures to counter the Quebec legislation, including the use of the power of disallowance or the threat to stop transfers to Quebec (3 percent). As we can see, and we can only regret this, the conditions are not ripe for a calm and open-minded discussion between the advocates of secularism "à la québécoise" and those of secularism "à la canadienne." In such a context, which will undoubtedly be marked by the decisions made by the courts, the dialogue of the deaf is likely to continue.

Conclusion

At the time of writing, we are all awaiting the Quebec Court of Appeal's decision. Whatever it is, everyone expects the case to go to the Supreme Court of Canada. And judges are not impervious to the jolts of public opinion and debate to which they are necessarily exposed. By reading the newspapers in English Canada and making the reasonable assumption that the judges of the final court of appeal do not frequent the French-language media, it is easy to determine which way the wind is blowing in Canada. If the Supreme Court takes the opportunity of this case to limit the legitimacy of parliamentary use of the notwithstanding clause, then the Act Respecting the Laicity of the State will have had an immense impact, far beyond its modest ambitions to regulate the wearing of religious symbols by Quebeckers during working hours. It may well be that the Supreme Court will subject all democratically elected parliaments to the will of the "government of the judges" with greater force than ever.

In the end, we hope that this book will contribute to a more nuanced and respectful discussion and that the legitimacy of the principles at the heart of the Loi sur laïcité de l'*État* will not be dismissed out of hand as seems to have been the case since it was first discussed in Quebec.

Notes

1 Act Respecting the Laicity of the State, SQ 2019, c. 12.

2 *Hak v Attorney General of Quebec*, 2021 QCCS 1466.

3 Act to Promote Respect for the Religious Neutrality of the State and Aimed in Particular at Regulating Requests for Accommodation for Religious Reasons in Certain Organizations, SQ 2017, c. 19.

4 *Hak v Attorney General of Quebec*, 2019 QCCS 2989.

5 *Hak v Attorney General of Quebec*, 2019 QQCA 2145.

6 Canadian Charter of Rights and Freedoms, Part 1 of the Constitution Act, 1982, being Schedule B to the Canada Act 1982 (UK), 1982, c. 11.

7 The section reads as follow: "Notwithstanding anything else in the Charter, the rights and freedoms in it are guaranteed equally to male and female persons." Canadian Charter of Rights and Freedoms, Part 1 of the Constitution Act, 1982, being Schedule B to the Canada Act 1982 (UK), 1982, c. 11.

8 *Ford v Quebec (Attorney General)*, [1988] 2 SCR 712.

9 The question was phrased as follows: "You deny that Quebec has problems with racism yet you defend legislation such as Bills 96 and 21 which marginalize religious minorities, anglophones and allophones. Quebec is recognized as a distinct society, but for those outside the province, please help them understand why your party also supports these discriminatory laws?" Bill 96 refers to the Act Respecting French, the Official and Common Language of Québec, SQ 2022, c. 14. For the wording of Ms. Kurl's question, see Tunney 2021.

10 Canadian Multiculturalism Act, SCR 1985, c. 24 (4th Supp.).

References

Baril, Daniel. 2021. "Hijab à l'école. Un cas qui illustre la nécessité de la loi 21." *La Presse,* December 16.

Bastien, Frédéric. 2021. "Invalidation partielle de loi 21: l'importance du choix du juge." *TVA Nouvelles,* April 20. https://www.tvanouvelles.ca/2021/04/20/invalidation-partielle-de-loi-21-limportance-du-choix-du-juge.

Bellerose, Patrick. 2021. "Québec dépose son appel sur la loi 21." *Le Journal de Québec,* June 4. https://www.journaldequebec.com/2021/06/04/quebec-depose-son-appel-sur-la-loi-21.

Canadian Press. 2020. "Pas de décision contre l'ex-juge en chef de la cour d'appel du Québec." *Le Devoir,* April 26. https://www.ledevoir.com/societe/577744/pas-de-decision-contre-l-ex-juge-en-chef-de-la-cour-d-appel-du-quebec.

–. 2021. "Deux troupes ayant contesté la *Loi sur la laïcité* font appel de la décision." *Le Devoir,* May 6. https://www.ledevoir.com/societe/600223/deux-groupes-ayant-conteste-la-loi-sur-la-laicite-en-appellent-de-la-decision.

Carabin, François. 2021. "La position de Québec solidaire sur la loi 21 s'embrume." *Le Devoir,* November 21. https://www.ledevoir.com/societe/648894/la-position-de-quebec-solidaire-sur-la-loi-21-s-embrume.

Codsi, Claude, Nadia El-Mabrouk, and Marie-Claude Girard. 2020. "Laïcité. Et si on revenait à l'esprit de la loi 21?" *La Presse,* December 21. https://www.lapresse.ca/debats/opinions/2020-12-21/laicite/et-si-on-revenait-a-l-esprit-de-la-loi-21.php.

COR Communication. 2022. "Un sondage révèle les répercussions de la Loi 21." August 10. https://www.newswire.ca/fr/news-releases/un-sondage-revele-les-repercussions-de-la-loi-21-805738945.html.

Court of Appeal of Quebec. 2020. "Retirement of Chief Justice Daval Hesler Hesler." April 7. https://courdappelduquebec.ca/en/news/details/retirement-of-chief-justice-duval-hesler/.

David, Michel. 2019. "La juge militante." *Le Devoir,* December 3. https://www.ledevoir.com/opinion/chroniques/568275/la-juge-activiste.

–. 2021. "Les termes du débat." *Le Devoir,* April 22. https://www.ledevoir.com/opinion/chroniques/599299/les-termes-du-debat.

Doering, Jan, and Efe Peker. 2019. "Laws That Limit Religious Rights Fuel Racism." *Toronto Star,* May 14.

Educaloi. 2020. "Contestation de la *Loi sur la laïcité de l'État:* des éléments pour bien comprendre." November 4. https://educaloi.qc.ca/actualites-juridiques/contestation-de-la-loi-sur-la-laicite-de-letat-des-elements-pour-bien-comprendre/.

Jourmet, Paul. 2021. "Ce n'est pas réglé." *La Presse,* April 21. https://plus.lapresse.ca/screens/c7a96645-5ec7-4e81-a40b-ab744f92f013%7C_0.html.

Journal de Montréal. 2019. "La loi sur la laïcité ne sera pas suspendue." April 9. https://www.journaldequebec.com/2020/04/09/la-loi-sur-la-laicite-de-letat-du-quebec-ne-sera-pas-suspendue.

Labbé, Jérôme. 2020. "La Cour suprême rejette la demande de suspension des opposants à la loi 21." *Radio-Canada,* April 9. https://ici.radio-canada.ca/nouvelle/1692441/cour-supreme-canada-rejet-demande-loi-quebecoise-laicite-etat.

Leblanc, Daniel. 2021. "Magistrature: Ottawa nomme un opposant à la loi 21." *Radio-Canada,* December 21. https://ici.radio-canada.ca/nouvelle/1849007/ottawa-nomination-juge-azim-hussain-loi-21.

–. 2022a. "Ottawa finance-t-il la contestation de la loi 21? Oui et non." *Radio-Canada,* March 28. https://ici.radio-canada.ca/nouvelle/1871706/programme-contestation-judiciaire-loi-quebecoise-laicite-etat.

–. 2022b. "Loi 21: la Cour d'appel du Québec laissera passer les élections." *Radio-Canada,* June 6. https://ici.radio-canada.ca/nouvelle/1888818/loi-laicite-quebec-contestation-judiciaire-appel.

Leckey, Robert. 2019. "Advocacy Notwithstanding the Notwithstanding Clause." *Constitutional Forum constitutionnel* 28 (4): 1–7. https://doi.org/10.21991/cf29389.

Lévesque, Caroline. 2021. "Question de la modératrice du débat: le consortium refuse de se rétracter." *Le Soleil,* September 23. https://www.lesoleil.com/2021/09/11/question-de-la-moderatrice-du-debat-le-consortium-refuse-de-se-retracter-fed36f5f0b13dcb996bb4920734339d6.

Lowrie, Morgan. 2022. "L'appui à la loi sur la laïcité baisserait au Québec, selon un sondage." *La Tribune,* January 16. https://www.latribune.ca/2022/01/16/lappui-a-la-loi-sur-la-laicite-baisserait-au-quebec-selon-un-sondage-64efa6888f69498418404243c8d82f8b.

Malik, Fasih. 2019. "Quebec's Secularism Law Attacks Canadian Values." *Toronto Star,* June 21.

Morasse, Marie-Eve. 2021. "La commission scolaire *English Montreal* déboutée en Cour d'appel." *La Presse,* November 9. https://www.lapresse.ca/actualites/education/2021-11-09/loi-21/la-commission-scolaire-english-montreal-deboutee-en-cour-d-appel.php.

Pelletier, Benoît. 2021. "La question bancale et saugrenue de Shachi Kurl." *La Presse,* September 16. https://www.lapresse.ca/debats/opinions/2021-09-16/debat-des-chefs-en-anglais/la-question-bancale-et-saugrenue-de-shachi-kurl.php.

Pineda, Améli, and Alexis Riopel. 2019. "La loi 21 s'applique, tranche la Cour d'appel." *Le Devoir,* December 13. https://www.ledevoir.com/politique/quebec/568954/la-loi-quebecoise-sur-la-laicite-de-l-etat-est-maintenue.

Radio-Canada. 2019. "Loi 21: la juge en chef de la Cour d'appel du Québec visée par une plainte." December 1. https://ici.radio-canada.ca/nouvelle/1412915/bastien-duval-hesler-laicite-plainte.

Robitaille, Antoine. 2021. "Il faut parler de l'impartialité des juges." *TVA Nouvelles,* March 20. https://www.tvanouvelles.ca/2021/03/20/il-faut-parler-de-limpartialite-des-juges.

Roy-Charbonneau, Marie-Pierre. 2021. "Hijab en classe à Chelsea: loi mal conçue ou geste politique." *Le Droit*, December 11. https://www.ledroit.com/2021/12/11/hijab-en-classe-a-chelsea-loi-mal-concue-ou-geste-politique-d8cad565839531ce76aa03b00c44cf3e.

Toronto Star. 2019. "Nuance Aside, Ban Is Wrong." *Toronto Star*, March 31.

–. 2021. "Speak Out on This Law." *Toronto Star*, December 12.

Trudel, Pierre. 2021. "L'abus de dérogation." *Le Devoir*, September 28. https://www.ledevoir.com/opinion/chroniques/635823/chronique-l-abus-de-derogation.

Tunney, Catharine. 2021. "Trudeau, O'Toole Call Debate Question on Quebec's secularism offensive, unfair." *CBC News*, September 11. https://www.cbc.ca/news/politics/trudeau-debate-blanchet-bill21-1.6171124.

Zine, Jasmin. 2021. "Islamophobic Violence Resurfaces in Canada." *Chronicle Herald*, June 14.

Contributors

NORMAND BAILLARGEON is a professor of education at the Université du Québec à Montréal, an essayist, a sceptic, a libertarian activist, a columnist for the newspaper *Le Devoir,* and a contributor to various alternative magazines. Among his many works, we can mention *Légendes pédagogiques. L'autodéfense intellectuelle en éducation* (Poètes de brousse, 2013) and *Propos sur l'éducation* (M éditeur, 2016).

MARC CHEVRIER is a professor of political science at the Université du Québec à Montréal. His work focuses on Canadian and Quebec politics, federalism and integration, and political ideas in Quebec. He is the author of *L'empire en marche. Des peuples sans qualités, de Vienne à Ottawa* (Presses de l'Université Laval, 2019).

YASMINA CHOUAKRI is a senior consultant. She is responsible for the women's component of the Table de concertation des organismes au service des personnes réfugiées et immigrantes. She is a former president of the Canadian Institute for the Advancement of Women. Her contributions and research in the community and feminist fields have focused on the inclusion and exclusion of immigrant women in civic participation, the underfunding of ethnocultural women's organizations, the practices of immigrant community organizations and feminist groups with respect to immigrant and racialized women, the linkage of immigrant and racialized women's demands to feminist struggles, the development of projects promoting the empowerment of these women, and the fight against discrimination and racism.

LUCIA FERRETTI is a historian and a professor in the Department of Humanities at the Université du Québec à Trois-Rivières. She is mainly a specialist in the socio-religious history of Quebec. But she has also published works on the history of Trois-Rivières and on intellectual history. She is the author of several monographs, including *L'Action nationale. Le long combat pour le Québec* (Del Busso, 2019).

CHARLES-ÉTIENNE GILL is a professor of communication at the Cégep de Saint-Jérôme.

MICHELINE LABELLE is professor emeritus of sociology at the Université du Québec à Montréal (UQAM). She held the Concordia-UQAM Chair in Ethnic Studies (1993–96; 2006–8) and the Research Chair in Immigration, Ethnicity and Citizenship at UQAM (2008–14). She also founded the Centre de recherche en immigration, ethnicité et citoyenneté in 2014. At the request of the United Nations Educational, Scientific and Cultural Organization, she participated as an expert in the elaboration of the Plan of Action of the International Coalition of Cities against Racism and wrote two reports on the same subject that are still used by various municipalities across the country. Her most recent books include *Racisme et antiracisme au Québec. Discours et déclinaisons* (Presses de l'Université du Québec, 2011); *La communauté politique en question. Regards croisés sur l'immigration, la diversité et la citoyenneté* (Presses de l'Université du Québec, 2012); *Les nationalismes québécois face à la diversité ethnoculturelle* (Éditions de l'Institut d'études internationales de Montréal, 2014). She was awarded the Prix Hommage – 40 ans de la Charte des droits et libertés de la personne by the Commission des droits de la personne et des droits de la jeunesse du Québec in 2015 for her work on racism.

JULIE LATOUR is an attorney-at-law admitted to both the Quebec Bar and the New York State Bar. She holds degrees in civil law and common law from McGill University. She is a former President (*bâtonnière*) of the Bar of Montreal (2006–7) and of the Canadian Bar Association – Quebec Division (2004). Latour was notably appointed in 2009–10 to the Content Advisory Committee of the Canadian Museum for Human Rights, which led hearings throughout Canada to determine the content of this new national museum, inaugurated in Winnipeg in 2014. For the last fifteen years, Latour has been at the forefront of legislative developments regarding the secular nature of the state and is the author of several legal publications on this subject. As the founder of Les Juristes pour la neutralité religieuse et laïcité de l'État, she has written and presented briefs on all the public bills that led to the Act Respecting the Laicity of the State.

ROBERTO PERIN is a professor emeritus at York University. He has taught at the Universities of Edinburgh and York and was director of the Canadian Academic Centre in Rome, Italy. A specialist of immigration, he was vice-president of the Italian committee of the Community Historical Recognition Programme, established by the federal government, and historical consultant for the exhibitions at the Canadian Museum of Immigration at Pier 21. An expert as well in Canadian religious history, he has often been a commentator for Radio Canada on questions involving immigration, cultural and religious diversity, as well as reasonable accommodation.

FRANÇOIS ROCHER is a professor in the School of Political Studies at the University of Ottawa. He is a founding member of the Research Group on Plurinational Societies. His research focuses on Canadian federalism, nationalism, citizenship and immigration policy issues, and the management of ethnocultural diversity. His most recent publications include *Essential Readings in Canadian Politics and Government,* with coauthors Peter Russell, Debra Thompson, and Amanda Bittner (2nd ed., Emond Montgomery, 2015), and *Trust, Distrust, and Mistrust in Multinational Democracies: Comparative Perspectives,* with coauthor Dimitrios Karmis (McGill-University University Press, 2018).

GUILLAUME ROUSSEAU is a professor in the Faculty of Law at the Université de Sherbrooke. In recent years, he has also been an advisor to the Quebec National Assembly, notably during the consultations on the draft bill for the new Code of Civil Procedure. He is a regular researcher at the Centre de recherche sur la régulation et le droit de la gouvernance. He is the author of *Loi sur laïcité de l'État commentée et annotée: philosophie, genèse, interprétation et application* (Éditions RDUS, 2020) and *Restaurer le français langue officielle. Fondements théoriques, politiques et juridiques pour une primauté du français langue du droit,* with coauthor François Côté (Institut de recherche sur le Québec, 2020).

PAUL SABOURIN is an associate professor in the Department of Sociology at the Université de Montréal. His research focuses on the sociology of economic practices and forms of knowledge. Another part of his research is on fundamental sociology dealing with qualitative methodology and sociological epistemology with the aim of examining the possibilities of the cumulativity of sociological knowledge. He will soon publish "Poverty Is Not a Concept. De la connaissance de ceux qui sont désignés comme 'pauvres'" in the journal *Recherches sociographiques*.

PATRICK TAILLON is a professor in the Faculty of Law at Laval University and teaches constitutional law and administrative law. He is the author of *La révision constitutionnelle dans tous ses états,* with coauthors Dave Guénette and Marc Verdussen (Éditions Yvon Blais et Anthemis, 2021) and *La démocratie référendaire dans les ensembles plurinationaux,* with coauthor Amélie Binette (Presses de l'Université Laval, 2018).

DANIEL TURP is a professor in the Faculty of Law at the Université de Montréal. He teaches advanced constitutional law, public international law, and international and constitutional law of fundamental rights. He is president of the Quebec Association of Constitutional Law and president of the Council of the Quebec Society of International Law. He is also a member of the Board of Directors of the Réseau francophone de droit international and founder of the Charles-Rousseau International Law Moot Court Competition. He has published several books and articles on international law and constitutional law. His publications include *La Constitution québécoise: Essais sur le droit du Québec de se doter de sa propre loi fondamentale* (Éditions JFD, 2013) and an article in *Dix ans plus tard, la commission Bouchard-Taylor: succès ou échec?* (Québec-Amérique, 2018).

Index

Note: "(f)" after a page number indicates a figure; "(t)" after a page number indicates a table.

Printed and bound in Canada by Friesens
Set in Myriad and Sabon by Artegraphica Design Co.
Copy editor: Stacy Belden
Proofreader: Sophie Pouyanne
Indexer: Margaret de Boer